ADVANCED FINANCIAL ACCOUNTING

By
Abimbola Olowe MSc, FCNA

DISCLAIMER

'' All dates used in the book are for illustration purposes only.''

'' All dates used in the book are for illustration purposes only.''

The book is a property of Molowe Limited, All rights reserved.

ACKNOWLEDGEMENT

This book is dedicated to my students far and near. My children, especially Vicky, Enny, Debbie, and Segun. You all have been a source of strength when I needed one.

I acknowledge Prof. Joseph Femi Adebisi, Prof.Suleiman A.S Aruwa, Prof. Tijjani Shehu Bello, Dr Farouk Edieza Musa and Dr Amina Sani my beloved Head of Department for their immense impart, guidance, and contributions.

Table Of Content

CHAPTER ONE
THE NATURE AND PURPOSE OF ACCOUNTING

Accounting has various definitions depending on how it is viewed, either as an activity or as a system. As a technique or as a discipline of study, Mr F.O Agboroh (ACA) defined accounting as the application of book keeping principles and techniques in recording, classifying and summarizing financial transactions and interpreting the results thereof to various users of such information.

The American Association of Accounting defined accounting as the identifying, measuring and communicating of economic information to print informed judgments and decisions by users of the information (AAA 1966)

The American Institute of Certified Accountants (AICPA) defines accounting as the art of recording, classifying and summarizing in a significant manner and terms of money. Transaction and events which are, in part at least, of a financial character, and interpretation of the result thereof.

Accounting can be defined as a branch of knowledge that applies the scientific method of observation experiment and measurement. Hence science may be defined as any body of knowledge organized systematically.

Accounting as an art. As it employs a great deal of human skill and judgment in the creation of aesthetic subjects. Or in the imitation of an existing form.

The history of accounting cannot be complete without the mention of Franciscan monk Lucca Piccolo who published his work in 1494 titled "Summa de Arithmetical, geometrical, proportionate, Proportionality". This book expounded the principle of the double-entry system of accounting.

Accounting is deferent from book keeping as a book keeper does the actual record-making phase of accounting while extending to the use to which these records are put. Their analysis and interpretation.

The major need for accounting is to communicate economic measurement of and information about the resources and performance of the reporting entity useful to those having reasonable right to such information.

Accounting confirms what we call the control function in I management of organizations, it is also useful because of absentee ownership and the emergence of transit shareholders.

Accounting is also useful in cost control and taxation functions. Another is arithmetical accounting. Management accounting concentrates on the internal organizational requirement for planning and control while financial accounting concerns itself more top external use and users of the information.

Financial accounting has different faces i.e. Financial Accounting, Management Accounting, Public sector Accounting, Auditing, etc. Accounts are either real or nominal accounts or personal.

ONE
THE NATURE AND PURPOSE OF ACCOUNTING

Accounting has various definitions depending on how it is viewed, either as an activity, as a system, as a technique or as a discipline of study. According to Mr. F.O. Agboroh (ACA), "Accounting is the application of Book-keeping Principles and Techniques in recording. Classifying and summarizing financial transactions and interpreting the results thereof to various users of such information.

The American Institute of Certified Public Accountants (AICPA) defined Accounting as the art of recording, classifying and summarizing in a significant manner and in terms of money transactions and events which are, in part at least, of a financial character, and interpreting the result there of" (AICPA) 1966).

The American Accounting Association defined accounting as "The process of identifying measuring and communicating economic information to permit informed judgments and decisions by users of the information" (AAA 1966).

Accounting may be regarded as a science if science is viewed as any branch of knowledge that applies the scientific method of observation experiment and measurement. Hence science may be defined as anybody of knowledge organized systematically.

Accounting as an art employs a great deal of human skill and judgment in the creation of aesthetic subjects or the imitation of existing forms.

The history of accounting cannot be complete without the mention of Franciscan Mouk Luca Pacioli who published his work in 1494 tilted "Summa de Arithmetic, Geometrical, Proportionate, Proportionality. This book expounded the principles of the double-entry system of accounting.

Accounting is different from bookkeeping as a bookkeeper does the actual record-making phase of accounting while accounting extends to the use to which these records are put, their analysis and interpretation.

The major need for accounts is to communicate economic measurement of and information about the resources and performance of the reporting entity useful to those having reasonable rights to such information.

In fact, accounting conforms to what we call 'The Control' Function in the management of organizations. It is also useful because of absentee ownership and the emergence of transit shareholders.

Accounting is also useful in Cost Control and Taxation Functions. Others are arithmetical and authorization controls and the use for internal checks.

Accounting has two broad branches, these are: Management Accounting and Financial Accounting. Management Accounting concentrates on the internal organizational requirement for planning and control while financial accounting concerns itself more with external use and users of the information.

Financial Accounting has different faces. Accounts are either Real Nominal Accounts or Personal.

REAL ACCOUNTS

Accounting being the language of Business has many users. These users of accounting information are:

1. Managers of the company- for effective control and planning decisions.
2. Shareholders of the company – for Stewardship function, profits and dividends.
3. Trade contacts like suppliers – payment of debts.
4. Providers of finance to the company e.g. Banks – interest payments and repayments of loans.
5. The inland revenue authorities – profits and taxes
6. Employees of the company – size of their salaries and job securities.
7. Financial analysts and advisers e.g. stock brokers advise investors and journalists to read the public.

1. Characteristics of useful accounting information

a) Relevance – Satisfy the needs of the information users.
b) Comprehensibility
c) Reliability
d) Completeness
e) Objectivity
f) Timeliness
g) Comparability.

DEFINITION OF TERMS IN MAIN FINANCIAL STATEMENTS.

The two principal financial statements are the Balance Sheet and the Profit and Loss Account.

A Balance Sheet is a financial statement that provides a summary of all the assets owned and all the liabilities owed by a business as of a specific date. It serves as a snapshot of the business's financial position at a particular point in time, showing what the business owns and owes.

It can also be defined as a summary of the assets held by an accounting entity showing how these have been financed either through owner's funds or debts. It is also called the statement showing the amounts invested in or entrusted to an accounting entity by various parties and the various classes of assets on which the amounts have been expended. A Balance Sheet must always Balance, hence there are three basic elements in a Balance Sheet. They are the "Assets", "Liabilities" and "owner's fund" or ("equity")

This leads to the Accounting Equation:

Capital = Assets or

Capital + Liabilities = Assets.

ASSETS AND CLASSIFICATION

Assets are valuable things owned by a company. They are either tangible assets like Buildings, Motor vehicles, fixtures and fittings or intangible assets like Goodwill, patents and trademarks. Tangible assets are classified as fixed and current assets. Fixed assets have a durable life of more than one year. These assets are held not for conversion or resale but for purposes of assisting in the conduct of business e.g. land and building s, plant and machinery etc.

Current Assets are assets which change form in the course of the business or during the conduct of the organization's operations e.g. stocks, debtors, pre-payments, bank and cash.

LIABILITIES

Liabilities represent financial obligations to external parties, arising from borrowings or credit purchases. They can be classified as long-term or short-term, with short-term liabilities also known as current liabilities. Examples include trade creditors, bank overdrafts, and accruals. Current liabilities are typically settled within one year.

Long-term liabilities are principally loans and other debts that can be repaid in more than one year e.g. Debentures.

EQUITY

This is a source of funds available to the owner. Owners' funds are made up of amounts or items introduced into the business at commencement or a later date. This equity is also called Capital.

PROFIT AND LOSS ACCOUNT

A profit and loss account is a record of income generated and expenditure incurred over a given period. It is made up of a year.

Examples:

1. Distinguish from the lists of items below whether Assets or Liabilities:

(i) Office Machinery,

(ii) Loan from C. Shop,

(iii) Furniture and Fittings,

(iv) Motor Vehicles,

(v) Bank Balance and

(vi) Amount owed as a rent to a Landlord.

2. Complete this table:

	ASSETS	LIABILITIES	CAPITAL
(a)	12500	1800	-
(b)	28000	4900	-
(c)	16800	-	12500
(d)	19600	-	16450
(e)	-	6300	19200
(f)	-	11650	39750

Solution to Illustration One

Assets	Liabilities
Office Machinery	Loan from C. Shop
Furniture and fittings	rent owing to the Landlord
Motor vehicles	
Bank Balance	

Solution to Illistraion Two

	ASSETS	LIABILITIES	CAPITAL
(a)	12500	1800	10700
(b)	28000	4800	23100
(c)	16800	4300	12500
(d)	19600	3150	16450
(e)	25500	6300	19200
(f)	51400	11650	39750

Example 3

Draw up Mr. Tunda's Balance sheet as at 30th October 2022 from the following:

Capital	10000
Office Machinery	9000
Creditors	900
Stock of goods	1550
Debtors	1275
Cash at Bank	5075
Loan from C. Small	2000
Drawing	500
Profit and loss account	1000

Solution (3)

MR. TUNDA'S BALANCE SHEET AS AT 30TH OCTOBER 2022

	$		$	$
Capital	18000	Fixed Assets		
Add Profit and Loss Account	1000	Office Machinery		9000
	19000	Current Assets		
Less Drawing	5000	Debtors	1275	
Current Liabilities		Stock	1550	
Loan from C. Small	2000	Bank	5075	7900
Creditors 900	2900		-	
	16900		-	16900

ASSIGNMENT AND REVISIONAL QUESTIONS

1. What is Accounting? Distinguish it from book-keeping

2. State some users of Accounts information and why they need such information.

3. Write short note on:

(a) Assets

(b) Liabilities

(c)   Capital

(d)   Profit and Loss Account

4. Draw up Mr. Davis Balance sheet as at 31st Dec. 2022 from the following:

Motor van	36,000
Premises	5,000
Loan from D. Daudu	1,000
Cash at Bank	1,650
Drawings	2,000
Capital	20,650
Stock of goods	4,800
Creditors	2,560
Cash in hand	1,250
Profit and loss account	1,000

Debtors   6,910

5. Classify the following items into liabilities and assets. Motor vehicles, premises, creditors for good, stock of goods debtors, Bank overdrafts, cash at hand, Loan from A.Bally and Machinery.

6. Complete this table

	ASSETS ₦	LIABILITIES ₦	CAPITAL ₦
(a)	55000	16900	-
(b)	-	17200	34400
(c)	36100	-	28500
(d)	119500	15400	-
(e)	88000	-	62000
(f)	-	49000	110000

7. Draw up Mr Johnson's Balance Sheet as at 31 Dec. 2022 after deducting Capital

    Office Machinery   14,500

    Creditors   2,450

    Stock of goods   5,770

    Debtors   7,250

    Cash at Bank   15,000

    Loan from E. James   4,000

    Drawings   1,750

    Profit and loss account   3,250

    <u>Note:</u> See solutions at the back of the book

CHAPTER TWO
ACCOUNTING CONCEPTS AND CONVENTIONS

Accounting Concepts are the basic assumptions that underline the preparation of financial statements of business enterprises. These are according to IAS , IAS ,IFRS.

1. **The Entity Concepts**: A Business is a separate entity distinct from its owner(s)

2. **The Measurement Concepts**: Accounts only deals with items to which monetary values can be attributed.

3. **The Going Concern Concepts**: Unless there is evidence to the contrary, it is assumed that a business will continue to trade normally for the foreseeable future.

4. **Periodicity**: The business community and financial statement users required that the business be divided into accounting periods (usually one year) and that changes in position be measured over these periods.

5. **Realization**: The concepts establish the rule for the periodic recognition of revenues as soon as it can objectively measure.

6. **Matching**: The concept holds that for any accounting period, the earned revenue and all the incurred costs generated, that revenue must be matched and reported for the period.

7. **Consistency**: The concepts of consistency hold that when a company selects a method, it should continue to use it in subsequent periods so that a comparison of accounting figures over time is meaningful.

8. **Historical Costs**: This concept holds that cost is the appropriate basis for initial accounting recognition of all asset acquisitions and services rendered.

ACCOUNTING METHOD

This is the medium through which the forgoing fundamental accounting concepts are applied to financial transactions.

ACCOUNTING BASES

These are the totality of method adopted by an enterprise for applying for fundamental accounting concepts either in through the cash or Accrual basis.

ACCRUAL BASES

Revenue and expenses recognized in the period to which they relate.

CASH BASES

Revenue actually received and expenses actually paid are recognized in that period. The approaches to all these accounting concepts are known as conventions. These include materialism, consistency and prudence.

APPLICATION OF THE ACCOUNTING CONCEPTS

The going concern concepts

Example:

Bolle commences business on 1st January and buys stock of 20 washing machines, each costing $100,000.00. During the year, he sells 1 machines at $150,000.00 each. How should his profit be calculated and how should the remaining machines be valued at 31 December, if:

1. He is forced to close down his business at the end of the year and the remaining machine will realize only $60,000.00 each in a forced sale or

2. He intends to continue his business into the next year.

Solution

1. If the business is to be closed down, the remaining three machines must be valued at the amount they will realize in a force sale i.e. 3 x 60 = $180,000.00 Profit would be calculated as:

Sale of 17 machines at $150,000.00	2,250,000.00
Forced realizations of 5 machines	300,000.00
	2,550,000.00
Less cost of 20 machines at $100,000.00	2,000,000.00
Profit for the year	550,000.00

2. If the company is regarded as a going concern, the stock unsold at 31 December will be carried forward into the following year. The five machines in the Balance sheet at 31 December at cost 5 x $100,000 = $500,000.00

Sales of 15 machines at $150,000.00	=	2,250,000.00
Less cost of 15 machines at $150,000.00	=	1,500,000.00
Profit for the year	=	850

Illustration 2

On Prudence Concept

The company begins trading on 1 January 2015 and sells goods worth $100,000 during the year to 31 December. On 31 December, the debts were outstanding at $15,000. The company is now doubtful whether $6,000 will ever be paid. Apply the prudence concept when treating profit and loss items.

Solution

The company should make a provision for doubtful debts of $6000. Sales for 2015 in the P &L is $100,000. The prudence concept dictates that $ 6,000 should not be included in the profit for the year but as a reduction.

Illustartion 3

Prudence

Given that prudence is the main consideration, discuss under what circumstances, if any, revenue might be recognized when:

1. Goods have been acquired by the business, which is confidently expected to resell very quickly.

2. A customer places a firm order for goods

3. Goods are delivered to the customers

4. The customer is invoiced for goods

5. The customer pays for the goods.

6. The bank has cleared the customer's cheque in payments for the goods.

Solution

1. Sale must never be recognized before the goods have been ordered.

2. A sale must never be recognized when a customer places an order

3. A sale will be recognized when delivery of the goods is only when

a) The sale is for cash

b) The sale is on credit, and the customer accepts delivery.

4. A legally enforceable debt occurred in a credit sale when an invoice was dispatched to the customer.

5. Sale takes place in cash sale when cash is received.

6. It would again be over-cautious to wait for clearance of the customer's cheques.

Materialism

Example:

A balance sheet shows fixed assets of $20 million and stocks of $30,000 an error of $20,000 in the depreciation calculations and error of $20,000 in the stock valuation probably would be.

Solution

The depreciation calculations of $20,000 is not material but an error of $20,000 in the stock valuation is material.

Example

Adahu set up a business in January 2020 selling Humble Tutors Books. He buys 100 books for $5 each, and by 31 Dec. 2020, he will have managed to sell his entire stock all for cash for $8 each. On 1st January 2021, he replaced his stock by purchasing another 100 books; by this time, the cost of the books had risen to $6 each. Calculate the profit earned by Adahu in 2020.

Solution

Using the conventional Historical Cost Accounting, Adahu's profit would be computed as follows:

Sale of 100 books at$8 each	800
Cost of 100 books at$5 each	500
Profit for the year	300

Using an alternative accounting convention, Adam's profit will be:

Sale of 100 books	800
Cost of replacing 100 books sold	(600)
Profit for the year	200

CHAPTER THREE
ACCOUNTING PROCESSES

What is Business?

A business is a commercial or industrial concern that deals with the manufacture, re-sale or supply of goods and services.

It is also defined as an organization that uses economic resources to create goods and services that customers buy.

What is profit?

Profit is the excess of income over expenditure

What is the business equation?

The business equation gives a definition of profits earned. This can be represented as: $P = I + D - C$

Where:

P = Profit

I = Increase in net assets = after the proprietor has taken out drawings.

D = Drawing

C = Extra Capital Introduced.

Example:

	1Jan. 2010	Dec. 2010
Net Assets	20000	26500
Drawings	4500 for the year	-
Additional capital		
Introduced	5000 for the year	-

Solution

$P = I + D - C$
N6500 +4500 - 5000 = N6000

The Cash Cycle

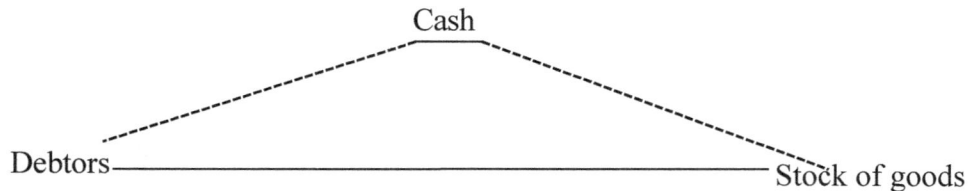

Cash

Debtors ——————————————————————— Stock of goods

BOOKS OF ACCOUNTS

Illustration 1

(a) List four advantages of double entry Book-keeping system.

(b) What is meant by the accounting cycle?

(c) Enumerate the Books of prime entry and explain the function(s) of each of them.

Solution

The accounting function comprises of two broad processes:

The generation of information and the interpretation of the information thus generated.

The accounting cycle entails collecting data from the source documents, recording it, and processing it until information is generated in the financial reports.

THE LEDGER

The ledger is the principal Book of Accounts, while subsidiary Books are books of prime entries. They are called so because they exist to provide periodic totals for posting into the ledger.

These Books of prime entry are:

a) Purchases Day Book- For credit purchases

b) Sales Day Book – for credit sales

c) Returns Inward Day Book- Sales returns

d) Returns Outward Day Book- purchases returns

e) The General Journal- other events apart from those above.

Ledger on the other hand, can be divided into different ways according to:

a) The nature or class of Accounts

b) To geographical zones of operations

c) To product lines or divisions.

The class of Accounts can be grouped into these ledgers

1. Debtors (or sales) ledger

2. Creditors (or purchases) ledger

3. General ledger – for Assets, income and expenses.

THE CASHBOOK

This is a book of account which combines the features of both the Day book and the ledger and performs a dual role. They involve transactions in cash.

ILLUSTRATIONS

The Accounting Cycle

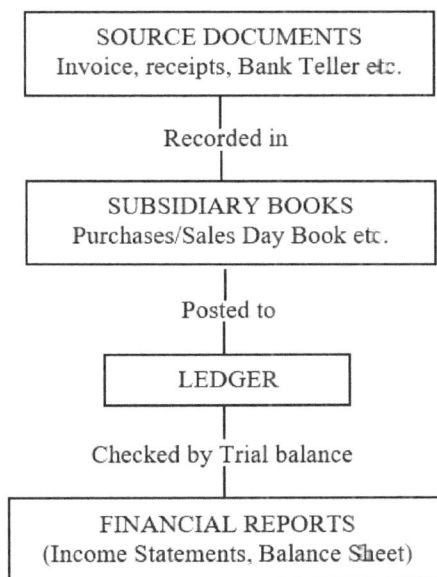

```
┌─────────────────────────────────────┐
│ SOURCE DOCUMENTS                     │
│ Invoice, receipts, Bank Teller etc.  │
└─────────────────────────────────────┘
              Recorded in
┌─────────────────────────────────────┐
│ SUBSIDIARY BOOKS                     │
│ Purchases/Sales Day Book etc.        │
└─────────────────────────────────────┘
              Posted to
        ┌──────────────────┐
        │ LEDGER           │
        └──────────────────┘
      Checked by Trial balance
┌─────────────────────────────────────┐
│ FINANCIAL REPORTS                    │
│ (Income Statements, Balance Sheet)   │
└─────────────────────────────────────┘
```

CLASSIFICATION OF ACCOUNTS

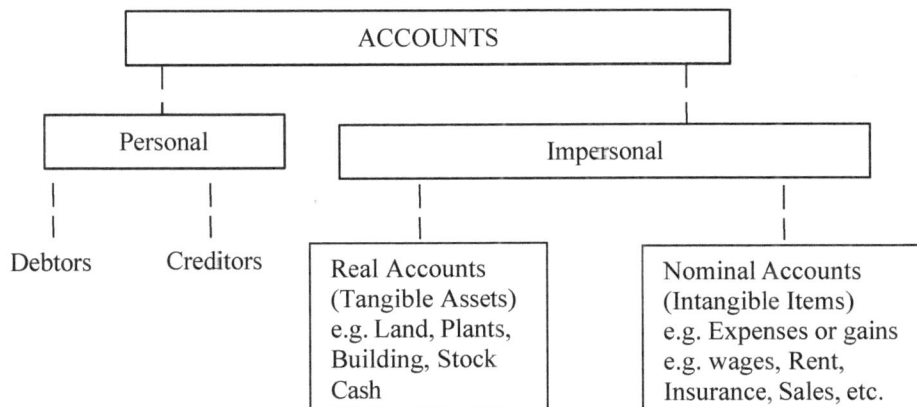

```
                    ACCOUNTS
           ┌───────────┴────────────┐
        Personal                 Impersonal
      ┌─────┴─────┐          ┌────────┴─────────┐
   Debtors    Creditors   Real Accounts    Nominal Accounts
```

Real Accounts (Tangible Assets) e.g. Land, Plants, Building, Stock Cash

Nominal Accounts (Intangible Items) e.g. Expenses or gains e.g. wages, Rent, Insurance, Sales, etc.

DOUBLE ENTRY SYSTEM

Every transaction involves the exchange of value on two sides. First in giving out and secondly in receiving, this double-entry system employs the concept of 'Debit' (Dr) and 'Credit' (Cr). Thus, every transaction triggers off two entries, one a debit, the other a credit, both of equal amounts. Accounts that are giving out are credited, while accounts that are receiving are debited. So, this technique of recording, which recognizes these two sides to transactions, is termed the 'Double Entry System'.

ADVANTAGES OF DOUBLE ENTRY

i. It aids Arithmetical accuracy

ii. It helps in recognizing the simultaneous gain or loss resulting from each transaction.

iii. It serves as a self-checking device of transactions.

iv. It ensures complete recording of transactions.

v. It aids an unqualified Accounting officer who is just a Boo-keeper.

vi. It facilitates the interpretation of Accounts from the financial statements.

GENERAL RULES OF POSTING

Assets and expenses are debited while liabilities, income and capital are credited in accounts as shown below:

Debit items which	Credit items which
(i) Increase Assets	(i) Increase Liabilities
(ii) Increase expenses	(ii) Increase Income
(iii) Decrease Liabilities	(iii) Decrease Assets
(iv) Decrease Income	(iv) Decrease Expenses

ACCOUNTING INCOME

Income means "Profit" to the accountant in order to compare economic and accounting theories. In accounting, income may be measured as a change in the capital value of a business entity between the beginning and end of a period.

Illustration:

A company is established on 1 April with $20,000 in cash financed by ordinary shares (16,000 of $1.00 each) and $4,000 of 12% loan stock. During the year:

(a) The company buys fixed assets for cash at a cost of $14,000;

(b) On 1 April stocks are bought at a cost of $4,000 also for cash;

(c) During April, all of these stocks are sold for $9,000 of these sales $6000 was unpaid at 30th April;

(d) Depreciation for April amount to $200

(e) Other expenses for June accounted to $2,000 of which $300 were unpaid at the end of the month.

(f) Extra stocks were bought for cash on 30April, at a cost of $3,000.

Required

Calculate the profit and prepare the Balance Sheet.

Solution:

	$	$
Sales		9,000
Cost of stock sold	4,000	
Depreciation	2,00	
Other expenses	2,000	
Loan stock interest (1/2 x 12% of 4,000)	40	6,240
		2,760
The Balance Sheet		
	$	$
Fixed assets, Net		13,800
Depreciation		
Stocks	3,000	
Debtors	600	
Cash	5,700	
	9300	
Less current liabilities		
Loan interests 40		
Unpaid expenses 300		
Long-term liability 4000	4340	4960
		18760
		16000
Ordinary share capital		2760
Profit and loss account		18760

Summary

Formulae

i. A1 + P = A2

ii. A1 + P – D = A2

iii. P = D + (A2-A1)

Meaning:

A1= are assets at the beginning of the period

P = is the profit

A2 = are assets at the end of period

D = dividend payment

ECONOMIC INCOME

According to economist theorist Sir. John Hicks, the economic concept of income means the sum of:

(a) Cash flows realised by the individual during a period of time and

(b) Changes in the value of the individual's capital between the period's beginning and end.

As a formula:

$1 = C + CK2 - K1)$

C = is the cash flows realised by the individual in the period

$K2$ = is the value of his capital at the start and the end of a period

$K1$ = is the value of his capital at the start of a period.

$K2 = K1$ is therefore the value of the individual's saving.

From the above analysis, the accounting definition of profit and the economic concept of personal income are similar.

The economic value of capital

The difference between accounting and economics relates to the methods of valuing capital.

(a) To the accountant, capital is valued in terms of net assets

(b) To the economist, capital is a store of wealth that will be used up in future receipts and, therefore future consumption.

INCOME AND CAPITALMAINTENANCE

According to Hicks, capital could be defined as 'Stoch of productivity' and this could be valued as the capitalised money value of prospective future receipts.

The value of capital can be valued in a number of ways:

(a) Economist value capital as the present value of future receipts from an asset, discounted at the individual's cost of capital

(b) Accountants value assets at historical cost, including net depreciation, market values, replacement costs, net realizable value, and deprive value.

Income according to Hicks, is the maximum value which an individual can consume during a week and still expect to be as well off at the end of the week as he was at the beginning. But the Sandilands Committee (in Report of the Inflation Accounting Committee) described accounting profit in terms of Hicks' definition that A company's profit for the year is the maximum value which the company can distribute during the year and still expect to be as well off at the end of the year as it was at the beginning.

Using the concept of capital maintenance, profit is the sum that may be distributed or withdrawn from a business while maintaining intact the capital that existed at the beginning of the period.

That is the business's capital at the start of a period is used as a benchmark to determine the business's profit for a period.

Some revision questions

1. Define Capital in accounting
2. Compare the Accounting definition of capital to that of Economics
3. Define Income in Accounting
4. Compare the Accounting concept income with that of Economics
5. Identify and explain income's proprietary and equity concepts and their implications for capital maintenance.

INCOME AND VALUE MEASUREMENT

The concept of capital maintenance is a vital part of income determination because of the need to incorporate a measure of the change in capital during the relevant period in income computation. Value is necessary in the computation of capital, and the capital maintenance concept is then applied to determine income.

The concept of valuation and capital maintenance ignore the problem of inflation. Since the purchasing power of the currency changes and it is a correct accounting practice that all assets and liabilities should be measured in money terms, it is therefore necessary for the value of a limit of money to be stable, hence the inflation problem.

The entity and Proprietary concept of capital

The entity concept of capital is that a business consists of assets and liabilities. The asset are owned and the liabilities are owed by the person or people who finance the business fact the sources of finance are of secondary importance.

$A - L = C$, (where A = Assets L = Liabilities while C = the capital of people financing the business).

The entity concept of capital suggests that before a profit can be made, the value of the asset minus liabilities must be maintained, regardless of the sources of finance of the business, because the entity should be seen primarily as a set of assets and liabilities which combine to make the business operate.

Entity concept concentrates on the business as an operating unit. On the other hand, proprietary concept of capital focuses on the equity ownership of the business, thus:

$E = A - L - D$, Where E = Value of Equity, A = the value of Assets L = is the value of liabilities (excluding debt capital) and D = Debt capital. Proprietary concept concentrates on the purposes of a business to make profits for its owners.

Example

Fountain Professional Ventures Ltd is financed by equity and 50% by debt capital, it's balance sheet as at 8th January 2016.

	$
Cash	16,000
Less debt capital	8,000
	8,000
Equity	8,000

The company buys an assets for $16,000 and pays in cash. It then sells the assets for $22,000 by which time the replacement cost of the assets has risen to $20,000.

Required:

Calculate the profit and show the balance sheet of the company arising:-

i. Replacement cost of the Entity concept

ii. Proprietary concept of capital

iii. State Six reasons why profit is important in accounting statement measurement.

Solution

Using Entity Concept

	$
Sales revenue	22,000
Less replacement cost of sale	20,000
Profit	2,000
Balance sheet after the sale cash	22,000
Less debt capital	8,000
	14,000
Original equity	8,000
Profit	2,000
Revaluation reserves (20,000=16,000)	4,000
	14,000
Using the proprietary concept of capital	
	$
Profit would then be:	
Sales revenue	22,000
Less cost of sale(50% of 20,000 + 50% of 16,000)	18,000
	4,000
The balance sheet after the sale cash	22,000
Less debt capital	8,000
Original equity	8,000
Profit (including debt interest)	4,000
Revaluation reserve (50% of 20 = 16)	2,000
	14,000

Profit is an important measure in accounting statement, because:

(a) It indicates to shareholders the nature of the company's dividends and profit retention policies.

(b) It measures the efficiency of the company's management

(c) It helps creditors and investors to decide whether they can safely lend money to the company.

(d) Past profit may guide predictions of future profit and the likely return from the company's investments.

(e) This means of imposing direct taxation on the company.

(f) Helps managers make decisions about pricing, etc.

ECONOMIC THEORY OF INCOME AND VALUE

Living Fisher's concept of income

Income is the psychological enjoyment an individual gets from spending the money on the consumption of goods and services. "Income = Consumption".

Fisher defines cost of capital as the prevailing market rate of interest. While Hicks defined the cost of capital as the rate of return which an individual would obtain by investing his capital in the best alternative.

Sir John Hicks's concept of income

Hicks (in value and Capital 1946) suggested that Economics income should be measured as the sum of:

  (a) Realised cash flows, plus or minus

  (b) Changes in the value of capital during the period.

$I = C + (K2 = K1)$. He said that the purpose of income calculations in practical affairs is to give people an indication of the amount they can consumed without improvising themselves.

INCOME EXANTE AND EXPOST

Income Exante:

If the individual's expectations change as time goes on, or if he finds that his actual receipt deferred from his expected receipts, he can adjust his values for income and capital. This is referred to as income exante model, whereby values and income are estimated in advance from future expectations.

The disadvantage of the income exante model is that it is based on the subjective guesswork of the individual.

On the other hand, Hicks export economic income model occurs whereby income for a period is calculated as the end of the period. The formula is:

$1 = c + kt = 1$

c = is the actual revenue

kt = the revised estimate of capital

$kt -1$ = the revised estimate of capital value at the beginning of period.

The limitations of economic income model

1. Fishers and Hicks writes about individual's income, whereas accountants are concerned with income/profit of a business entity.

2. There are large element of subjective judgment which may result in windfall game as losses.

3. Hicks assumption that c – (1 = w) can be invested to earn a single predictable rate of interest is also questionable.

4. If a company plans to achieve capital growth by re-investing some of its income, Hicks model does not decide how much should be re-invested.

COMPANY ACCOUNTS AND INFLATION

Traditional accounting works on the assumption that profit should be measured in money terms, and money is an objective measurement of profit, the issue of inflation becomes imperative because the major effect of inflation is to reduce the real value of money over time.

Another relevance of inflation is the historical cost convention, which means that items are recorded in the account at their actual historical cost regardless of purchase date.

There are five consequences of historical cost accounting.

(a) Fixed assets values and depreciation.

Depreciation is based on historical cost rather than the current operational cost of the wear and that if asset. Because of inflation depreciation charges based on historical cost could never provide enough funds to replace worn-out fixed assets.

(b) The cost of sales and inflation

In a period of inflation, the cost of sales will be understood, in the sense that historical cost fails to replace items sold.

(c) The need for working capital

In a period of inflation, company's need more working capital to finance their stocks and debtors. This, therefore means that more often be funded out of profits. This fact is completely omitted by historical cost accounting convention.

(d) Borrowing benefits in a period of inflation

The real value of loans decreases over time, and so a company that borrows balance sheet liabilities.

(e) The comparability of figures over time

In a period of inflation, an accurate and reliable comparison of a company's results from one year to another is not easy.

 How could accounts be made to allow for inflation?

 The two systems that serve as an alternative to historical cost accounting are:

(a) Current purchasing power Accounting

(b) Current cost Accounting

CHAPTER FOUR
CURRENT PURCHASING POWER
ACCOUNTING (CPP) IAS 29

This was based on the idea that the effects of inflation should be measured in terms of the general purchasing power of money, and so changes in the retail price index. Under this system, assets and liabilities are valued in the balance sheet, not at current value, but in terms of a stable monetary unit, called current purchasing power or CPP. CPP profit and loss account and balance sheet would, therefore value income, expenditure, assets and liabilities in terms of common (stable) monetary unit.

Advantage of CPP Accounting

1. The restatement of assets values in terms of a stable money value provides a more meaningful basis for comparison with other companies.

2. Profit is measured in "real" terms and excludes inflationary value increments. This enables better forecast of future prospects to be made.

3. CPP avoids the subjective valuations of current value accounting, because a single price index is applied to all non-monetary assets.

4. CPP provides a stable monetary unit with which to value profit and capital

The disadvantages of CPP accounting

1. The generalized purchasing power as measured by the retail price index has no relevance to any person or entity because no such thing exists in reality, except as a statistician's computation.

2. The use of indices inevitable involves approximations in the measurement of value.

3. The value of assets in a CPP balance sheet has less meaning than a current value balance sheet.

CURRENT COST ACCOUNTING IAS 15

Under this system, assets are stated in the balance sheet at their value to the business with the value to the business is defined as the value that would be lost if the company were to be deprived of using the asset. Deprival value means the value to the business.

For fixed assets, deprival value means the net replacement cost, i.e., the current replacement cost minus the accumulated depreciation based on this cost.

In historical cost accounting, capital maintenance means keeping the net book value of the company's net assets unchanged. Under CCA, capital maintenance is regarded as keeping the business substance or operating capital unchanged.

Advantages of CCA

i. By excluding holding gains from profit, CCA can be used to indicate whether the dividends paid to shareholders reduce the operating capability of the business.

ii. CCA is a useful guide for management in deciding whether to hold or sell assets

iii. A current cost balance sheet can also be prepared with reasonable simplicity

iv. CCA helps users in assessing the stability of the business entity.

Disadvantages of CCA

i. It is impossible to make valuations, expected, or net realizable value without subjective judgment.

ii. The mixed value is at replacement cost while some at net realizable or economic value.

iii. The argument for deprive value is an unrealistic concept.

ACCOUNTING STANDARDS
PART 1

STATEMENTS OF ACCOUNTING STANDARDS (IAS)

An Accenting Standard is a rule or set of rules which prescribed the method (or methods) by which accounts should be prepared and presented. A national or international body of the accountancy profession issues these working regulations. In Nigeria, such standards are called IAS (Statements of Accounting Standards) and are formulated by the NASB (Nigerian Accounting Standards Board).

INTERNATIONAL ACCOUNTING STANDARDS (IAS)

The International Accounting Standards Committee (IASC) was set up in June 1973 in an attempt to coordinate the development of international accounting standards. It includes representatives from many countries worldwide, including the USA, the UK and Nigeria.

International standards are not intended to override local regulations. In Nigeria, however, the NASB has supported international standards by incorporating them within the Nigerian standards. Not every IAS has so far been incorporated in this way.

THE DEVELOPMENT OF NIGERIA ACCOUNTING STANDARD

The Nigerian Accounting Standards Board (NASB) was formally inaugurated on September 9, 1982 after consultations initiated by the Institute of Chartered Accountants of Nigeria (ICAN). The board of NASB consists of 15 members, drawn from not only accountants in practice, but also from the public sector, commerce, users of accountants, bankers stock exchange and academic. The composition of the membership is as follows:

i.	Central Bank of Nigeria (CBN)	2
ii.	Federal Ministry of Finance (FMF)	2
iii.	Nigerian Accounting Teachers Association (NATA)	1
iv.	Nigerian Association of Chambers of Commerce	
v.	Industry, Mine and Agriculture (NACCIMA)	1
vi.	Nigerian Bankers Association (NBA)	1
vii.	Nigerian Stock Exchange (NSE)	1
viii.	Security and Exchange Commission (SEC)	1

ix. Both ICAN and the Association of National Accountants of Nigeria (ANAN) each nominate two members to the board. The board comprises 15 members, representing various stakeholders in the accounting and financial reporting landscape.

Under the constitution, the business of the NASB is conducted by a council whose membership of Fifteen is representatives from the above establishments/organizations which make up the NASB.

OBJECTIVES OF NASB

The objectives of NASB, as set out in its constitution, are:

(a) To formulate and publish in the interest of accounting standards to be observed in the preparation of financial statements and to promote the general acceptance and adoption of such standards by prepares and users of financial statements.

(b) To promote and sponsor legislation, when necessary, in order to ensure that standards developed and published by the Board receive nationwide acceptance, adoption and compliance.

(c) To review from time to time the standards developed by the Board in the light of changes in the social, economic and political environment.

The council of NASB is responsible for issuing Statements of Accounting Standards (IAS) after going through the processes stipulated in the NASB constitution.

THE SCOPE OF IAS

Each Statement of Accounting Standards will apply to all financial accounts of material or significant items. However, A standard may specify its application's' scope'.

Standards issued by the NASB do not override the laws of the Federal Republic of Nigeria or regulations and orders issued under such laws. IAS do not apply to accounts prepared for the use of management.

Although there are some areas where the contents of IAS overlap with provisions of company Laws, standards are detailed working regulations within the framework of Government Legislation, and they cover areas where the law is silent. They have no direct full effect, and they are not intended to override exemptions from disclosure requirements enjoyed by certain companies under the Company Laws. However, they are rules of professional conduct that ICAN and ANAN regards as binding on its members.

To enforce IAS, these Bodies of Accountants in Nigeria requires its members:

(a) To disclose and explain in the accounts any significant departure from the provisions of IAS: and to disclose in the accounts the financial effects of any such departures

The standard-setting process is illustrated in the diagram below for the case of a IAS where no discussion paper is issued before the Exposure Draft (ED) is published.

1. The Council of the NASB selects an accounting practice for standardization.

2. The steering Committee of six members drawn from all sectors of the Nigerian economy

3. Steering Committee develops and presents to NASB for consideration and approval of the technical point outline.

4. Steering Committee carried out detailed development of the exposure draft.

5. NASB discuss the draft and may require amendments to be made before publication and is satisfied, approves the draft by at least two-third majority of the council. A pre-exposure draft may be issued for limited circulation and comments.

6. Normally at three months, the NASB receives letters of comment and further consultation takes place.

7. Steering Committee presents its final draft to NASB. NASB discusses it and may require amendments to be made before approving it, if satisfied the council approves by at least seventy five percent of members.

Identification of a Topic

Steering Committee set up for detailed study

Initial feedback to NASB

Technical Drafting

Consideration and approval of draft by the NASB The publication of the Exposure Draft

Summary of Comments and Decision of future progress

Redrafting by Steering Committee to accommodate Suggestions and Comments

Consideration of Draft Standard by NASB

Standard Issued by the Council of NASB

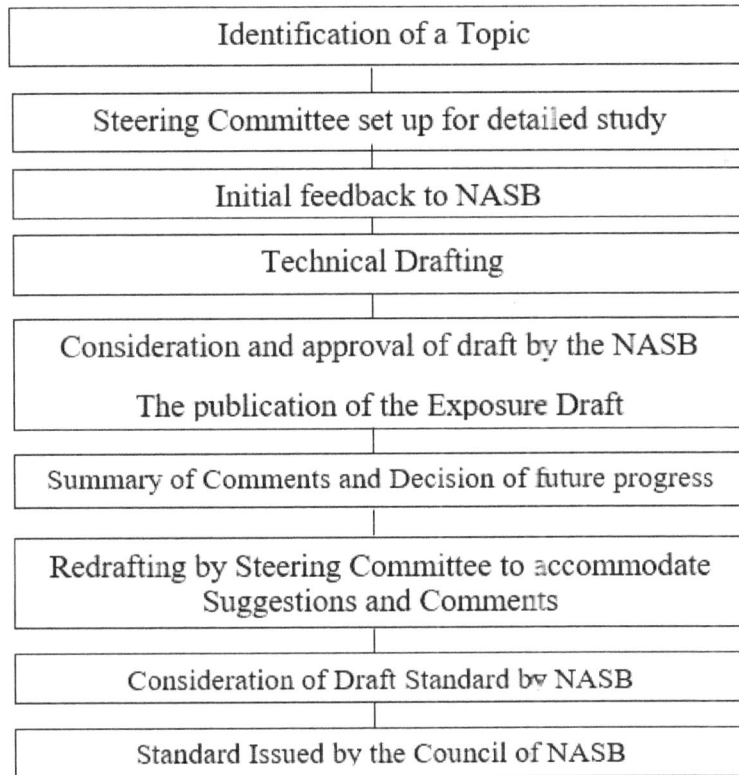

DISCUSSION PAPER

Where the Draft has been adequately exposed and even a public hearing has been held, the Council may decide to issue a Discussion paper in a place of Standard in Order. For example, to promote further discussion and give the general public the time to be familiar with the implications of the proposed standard. A simple majority of the council is required to issue a 'discussion Paper'

THE ADVANTAGES AND DISADVANTAGES OF IAS

Advantages

a) They reduce or eliminate confusing variations in the methods used to prepare accounts.

b) They provide a local point for debate and discussions about accounting practice

c) They oblige companies to disclose the accounting bases used in preparation of account.

d) They are a less rigid alternative or enforcing by means of legislation.

e) They oblige companies to disclose more accounting information than they otherwise have done if IAS did not exist.

Disadvantages

(a) A set of rules backing up one method of preparing accounts might be inappropriate in some circumstances. For example, IAS 4 on Depreciation was inappropriate for investment properties.

(b) Standards may be subject to lobbying or government pressure.

(c) They are not based on conceptual framework of accounting.

(d) Although the NASB invites comments and discussions, users group are not directly evolved in the creation of IAS.

(e) There may be a trend towards rigidity and away from flexibility in applying the rules.

DISCLOSURE OF ACCOUNTING POLICIES IAS 1

1. The end product of financial process is the preparation and publication of financial statements. A substantial number of alternative postulates, assumptions, principles and methods adopted by a reporting entity in the preparation of its accounts can significantly affect its results of operations, financial position and changes thereof. It is therefore essential to the understanding, interpretation and use of financial statements, whenever there are several acceptable accounting methods which they are based. The Companies Act, 1968 requires in the Eighth Schedule the disclosure of the method or basis used to deal with or calculate the amount of an item or information, where the accounts could be misleading because of failure to explain such methods or basis.

2. The purpose of the relevant provisions of the Companies Act 1968 and this Statement is to assist any reader in the understanding and interpretation of financial statements and the information disclosed therein.

3. This statement does not seek to establish accounting standards for individual items as these will be dealt with in separate Statement of Accounting Standards to be issued from time to time.

PART 2
EXPLANATORY NOTES

Financial Statements are based on conventions derived from experience. These conventions originate from such concept as: Entity, Going-Concern, Periodicity, Realization, Matching, Consistency and Historical Cost. The Purpose of this statement is not to evolve a basic theory of accounting but to identify some of these generally accepted concepts.

These fundamental accounting concepts are seldom disclosed because they are generally accepted as the underpinnings of preparing and presenting financial statements. Disclosure is however necessary, if these fundamental accounting concepts are not followed.

The fundamental accounting concepts referred to above are described below:

a) Entity

Entity economic unit, regardless of its legal form of existence, is treated as a separate entity (in accounting) from parties with proprietary or economic interest.

b) Going Concern

The assumption is that the business unit will operate in perpetuity; that is, the business is not expected to be liquidated in the foreseeable future. A business is considered a going concern if it is capable of earning a reasonable net income and there is no intention or heat from any source to curtail significantly its line of business in the foreseeable future.

c) Periodicity

Although the results of a business unit cannot be determined with precision until its final liquidation, the business community and users of final accounting statements require that the business be divided into accounting periods (usually one year) and that changes in position be measured over these periods.

d) Realization

The concept establishes the rules for the periodic recognition of revenues as soon as (a) it is capable of objective measurement and (b) The value of asset received or receivable in exchange is reasonably certain. It is possible to recognize revenue at various points, e.g., When goods are produced, when goods are delivered, or when the transaction is completed. Choice, in most cases, is an industrial norm; and depends on which of the points is the critical event. Only when event is passed can revenue be legitimately recognized.

e) Matching

The concept holds that for any accounting period; the earned revenue and all the incurred costs that generated that revenue must be matched and reported. Suppose revenue is carried over from a period and deterred to a future period. In that case, all elements of cost and expense relating to that revenue are usually carried over or deferred as the case may be.

f) Consistency

Usually, there is more than one way in which an item may be treated in the accounts, without violating accounting principles. The concept of consistency holds that when a company selects a method, it should continue (unless conditions warrant a change) to use that method in subsequent periods so that comparison of accounting figures over time is meaningful. The concept ensures that the accounting treatment of like items is consistency, taking one accounting period with another.

g) Historical Cost

The historical cost concept holds that cost is an appropriate basis for initial accounting recognition of all asset acquisitions, services rendered or received, expenses incurred, creditors' and owners' interests and it also holds that after acquisitions, cost values are retained throughout the accounting process.

ACCOUNTING METHOD

An accounting method is the medium through which the foregoing fundamental accounting concepts are applied to financial transactions and the preparation of financial statements. It is also the method adopted in recognizing, measuring and valuing an item of revenues, expenses, gains, loss or any asset or liability. Because accounting practice have evolved in response to the variety of more than one recognized accounting method can be rationalized.

Different methods exist for recording financial transactions, calculating profit, measuring depreciation, valuing stocks, etcetera. Therefore, the disclosure of the accounting methods adopted in preparing financial statements usually assists readers in their interpretation.

ACCOUNTING BASES

These are the totality of methods adopted by an enterprise for applying fundamental accounting concepts to its financial transactions. They include, for example, the determination of the accounting period for revenue and costs recognition and the method used to measure the values to place on items appearing in the balance sheet at the end of each accounting period. There are two distinctive accounting bases: the Accrual and the Cash.

Accrual Basis

Under this basis, only revenue and expenses are recognized in the accounting period to which they relate and in which they are earned and incurred; and not when they are received or paid.

Cash Basis

Under this basis, only revenue received and expenses paid during an accounting period are recognized during that period. However, a modified cash basis permits applying accrual basis to selected transactions.

ACCOUNTING POLICIES – CRITERIA FOR CHOICE

Accounting policies are those bases, rules, principles, conventions and procedures adopted in preparing and presenting financial statements. Judgment is required in choosing the accounting policies appropriate to an enterprise's circumstances and best suited to present the "true fair view" of its result and financial position.

There are alternative treatments for a number of items appearing in financial statements. The following non-exhaustive list, contains example of areas in which different accounting policies exist:

General

Consolidation Policy

Taxation

Long term Contracts

Events after the Balance Sheet date

Leases, hire purchase, or installment transactions and related interest

Conversion or translation of foreign currencies including the disposition of exchange gains and losses

Franchises

Overall Accounting Policy (e.g., Historical Cost, General Purchasing Power, Replacement Value).

Assets

Debtors or Receivables

Stock and Work-in-progress (inventories) and related cost of goods sold

Depreciable Assets and Depreciation:

Growing Crops

Land held for development and related development costs

Investments" subsidiary companies, associated companies, and other investments.

Research and development

Patents and Trademarks

Goodwill

Liabilities and Provisions:

Warrants

Commitments and Contingencies

Pension cost and retired plan

Severance and redundancy payment

Profits and Losses

Methods of Revenue Recognition

Maintenance, repairs and Improvement Expenditure

Gains and Loss on Disposal of Property

Reserves Accounting, Statutory or otherwise, including direct charges and credits to surplus accounts.

Establishment and Building costs.

Example of accounting policies are set out in the appendix.

In choosing and applying the appropriate accounting policies, some fundamental concepts contradict one another. It is not possible to develop general rules for the exercise of judgment, but some practical principles have been involved for use in particular circumstances. Some of these principles are explained below:

1. Substance Over Form

Although legal principles usually govern business transactions, they are nevertheless accounted for and presented by their substance and financial reality and merely with their legal form.

2. Objectivity

This principle connotes independence of judgment on the part of the accountant preparing the financial statements. Objectivity requires support by verifiable evidence, in contrast to subjectivity or dependence on the unverifiable opinion of the accountant preparing the financial statements.

3. Fairness

This is an extension of the objectivity principle. In view of the fact that there are many users of accounting information, all having differing needs, the fairness principle requires that accounting reports should be prepared not to favour any group or segment of society.

4. Materiality

The principle holds that only items of material value are accorded their strict accounting treatment.

5. Prudence

The principle demands great care in recognizing the profit when all known losses are adequately provided for. This is, however, not a justification for the creation of secret or hidden reserves

USERS OF FINANCIAL STATEMENTS

1. Financial statements interest various users, especially shareholders, banks, creditors, employees, revenue, and regulating authorities.

2. The users of financial statements are not likely to make a reliable valuation of a reporting enterprise unless its financial statements disclose the significant accounting policies adopted in their preparation.

DISCLOSURE OF ACCOUNTING POLICY

1. Many more enterprises have in recent years, disclosed in Notes to their financial statement the significant accounting policies they have adopted. However, the disclosure of accounting policies in financial statements varies from enterprise to enterprise. Some present them boldly and separately from the financial statements; some present them as an integral part of footnotes to items appearing in the financial statements. In some cases, accounting policies are not disclosed.

2. It is particularly useful in providing an overview of an enterprise's accounting policies, as these are disclosed together rather than as notes to individual items in the financial statements.

CHANGES IN ACCOUNTING POLICY

Although every enterprise endeavors to be consistent in the use of the accounting policies it has adopted, a change in an accounting policy is usually made to conform to:

a) A new Accounting Standard; and

b) Legislative regulation; or

c) When it is considered that the change would result in a more appropriate presentation of transactions in the financial statements of the enterprise.

A change in Accounting Policy is usually disclosed because it affects or have a potential effect on their net income or shareholders' equity and may also affect working capital or other items.

Changes in Accounting Policy would include, for example, a change in the basis of stock valuation or a change in the method of calculating depreciation.

The following are examples of circumstances that are usually not considered to amount to changes in Accounting Policies:

a) A change in the rate at which depreciation is calculated arising from a re-appraisal of the useful economic life of an asset;

b) The adoption of an accounting policy for a transaction either not previously dealt in or which was previously not a significant part of the business of an enterprise; and

c) The initial adoption of an Accounting Policy in recognition of events or transactions occurring for the first time.

PART 3
ACCOUNTING STANDARD

DISCLOSURE OF ACCOUNTING POLICIES

1. The Accounting Standard comprises paragraph 19-24 Statement. The Standard should be read in the concept of all the parts of this Statement and the preface to the Statement of Accounting Standard published by the NASB.

2. Where fundamental accounting concepts are followed in the preparation of financial statements, the disclosure of such concept is not required. That fact should be disclosed if a fundamental accounting concept is not followed.

3. Rational judgment aided by principles of economic substance over form, objectivity, fairness, materialism and prudence should govern the selection and application of accounting policies.

4. Whenever several acceptable bases may be adopted, a reporting enterprise should disclose, the basis used, especially where the knowledge of that accounting basis is significant in the understanding and interpretation of the financial statements.

5. Accounting policies should be prominently disclosed as an integral part of the financial statements under one caption rather than as notes to individual items in the financial statements.

6. An adopted accounting policies should be followed consistently, but a change may be made if it is decided that a different policy will better reflect the net profit or loss of the current or subsequent period. When such a change is made, the nature, justification, and effect of the current year's profit or loss should be disclosed. The cumulative effect of such a change on the (net of taxes) profit or loss of prior periods should be adjusted in the retained earnings or appropriate reserve account of the year immediately preceding the year of change. The fact should be indicated where such an amount is not ascertainable, wholly or in part.

7. Wrong or inappropriate treatment of items in financial statements is not rectified either by disclosure of the accounting policies adopted or by the notes or explanatory materials.

8. Effective Date: This Standard becomes operative for financial statements covering periods beginning on or after 1st January,1985.

PART 4
NOTES ON LEGAL REQUIREMENTS

The application of the foregoing Accounting Standard will provide the disclosure required by the 8th Schedule of the Companies Act, 1968, particularly paragraph 14 (6) which requires the following to be stated by the way of note if note otherwise shown: "Any material respects in which any item shown in the profit and loss account are affected … by the change in the basis of accounting".

PART 5
COMPLIANCE WITH INTERNATIONAL ACCOUNTING STANDARD NO. 1

"DISCLOSURE OF ACCOUNTING POLICIES"

The requirements of this Standard and national legal requirements stated above accord very closely with the requirements of International Accounting Standard No.1 – "Disclosure of Accounting Policies". Compliance with this Standard will ensure compliance with IAS 1 in all material respects.

EXAMPLE OF ACCOUNTING POLICIES

BASIS OF ACCOUNTING

The financial statements are prepared under the historical cost convention except for certain fixed assets which are included at their professional valuation, and comply with all Statements of Accounting Standards issued to date by the Nigerian Accounting Standard Board.

Consolidation

The group Profit and Loss Account and Balance Sheet include the accounts of the company and all its subsidiaries made up to 202

The company's share of the after tax less losses of the associated companies is consolidated where the company participates significantly in the financial and operating policy decisions of the associates and its holding in their equity is substantial and long-term.

Where a subsidiary or associated company is acquired or disposed off during the year, the group profit and Loss Account includes the result from the date of acquisition or to the date of disposal.

CHAPTER FIVE

Goodwill

Any excess of the cost of acquisition over the fair values of the underlying net assets is recognized as an asset in the group balance sheet as goodwill arising on acquisition.

Investments

Investment in subsidiary and associated companies is stated at the lower of cost or the company's share of their net tangible asset values at the year end.

Where the cost is higher than the company's share of net tangible assets value, the difference is written off to the Profit and Loss Account.

Any excess of attributable net tangible assets of associated companies over their cost is included in non-distributable reserves.

Fixed Assets

Land and Building are stated at their professional valuation at 19 Plus subsequent additions at costs. Other fixed assets are stated at cost.

Depreciation

Depreciation on fixed assets is calculated to write off their cost or valuation on the straight-line basis so as to write off each asset over its expected useful life. Periodic reviews are made to take into account greater or lower than normal usage and obsolence; any adjustment necessitated by these reviews is recognized in the Profit and Loss Account of the year in which the review is made.

The principal annual rate of depreciation which are applied consistently are:

1. Freehold land

2. Freehold Building

3. Leasehold land and building – more than 50 years unexpired less than 50years unexpired.

4. Plant and Machinery

5. Heavy Vehicles

6. Light Vehicles

7. Furniture, fixture and fittings

Stock and work-in-progress

Stocks are stated at the lower of cost and net realizable value after making adequate provision for obsolescence and damaged items. In the case of goods manufactured by the company cost includes a proportion of factory overhead.

Work-in-progress is stated at the Lower of cost and net realizable value. Cost in this case consist of Direct Labour and Materials plus appropriate proportion of factory overhead.

Turnover

Turnover represents the net value of goods and services invoiced to third parties.

Contracts-in-Progress

Contract in progress are stated at the values of independent engineers' certificates for work done but in respect of which payments were not received at the year end plus estimated values, made by officials of the company, of the realizable value of work done not yet certified or charged to clients. Full provision is made for anticipated future losses on unprofitable contracts. Claims receivable arising from contracts are accounted for when agreed upon or received.

Long Term Contracts

In respect of the uncompleted long-term contract, credit is taken only for the proportion of the total profit estimated to arise from the contract which the directors consider is prudently attributable to work done and alter after making full provision for all anticipated losses.

Foreign Currencies Conversion

Transactions in foreign currencies are translated into local currency Naira at the rate of exchange ruling at the date the relevant invoices are received. Differences arising at the date of settlement are charged to profit and loss account.

Foreign currency balances are converted to local currency Naira at the rate of exchange ruling at the balance sheet date. All differences arising on conversion are charged or credited to profit and loss account.

Deferred Taxation

Provision is made for deferred taxation by the liability method to take account of all timing differences between the accounting treatment of certain items and their corresponding treatment for income tax purposes. No provision is made where there is reasonable evidence that these timing differences will not reverse for some considerable period (at least three years). The significant timing differences involved are:

1. The excess of capital allowances claimable over the charge for depreciation on qualifying capital expenditure;

2. Retirement gratuity provision made in the accounts under the terms of an unapproved employee retirement gratuity scheme;

3. General provision for doubtful debts and other anticipated losses.

IAS 1 – DISCLOSURE OF ACCOUNTING POLICIES

This is similar to IAS 1 and SSAP 2

Illustration 1

1. Define these terms:

a) Accounting Bases

b) Accounting Policies

c) Accounting Concepts

d) Accounting Methods

2. Before the profit and loss account and balance sheet there is a page headed "Accounting Policies". Is there the same thing as Accounting Principles? Does every company have to show that, and how are they supposed to help? (ICAN, November, 2022).

Solution

An Accounting Method is the medium through which fundamental accounting concepts are applied to financial transactions and the preparation of financial statements. It is also the method adopted in recognizing, measuring and valuing an item of revenue, expense, gain, loss or any asset or liability.

Accounting bases are the methods used for expressing or applying these concepts to financial transactions and items. They are the methods developed for applying accounting concepts for the purpose of financial accounts, in particular for determining:

i. The Accounting periods in which revenue and costs are recognized; and

ii. The basis of Balance Sheet valuation.

There are different accounting bases for depreciation of fixed assets, stock and work in progress.

There are two distinctive accounting bases:

The accrual bases and cash bases

Accrual policies are the specific accounting bases followed for items judged to be material in determining profit and loss for the period and in stating the financial position. The management adopts them.

In fact, accounting policies are those bases, principles, conventions and procedures adopted in preparing and presenting financial statements.

Accounting concepts are the basic assumptions which underline the preparation of financial statements of business enterprises. These include: Entity, Going Concern, Periodicity, Realization, Matching, Consistency and Historical Cost.

Account policies should be disclosed as an integral part of the financial statements. These policies have to be followed consistently and justifiable change of policy has to be made.

Where fundamental accounting concepts are followed in preparing financial statements, disclosing such concepts is not required. That fact should be disclosed if a fundamental accounting concept is not followed.

The selection and application of accounting policies should be aided by principles of economic substance over form, objectivity, fairness, materiality and prudence.

Illustration 2

Incompliance with the pronouncements of professional accountancy bodies, most companies include a statement of accounting policies as part of their financial statements. Mention five items normally dealt with under such a statement of accounting policies and briefly discuss the nature of the information to be disclosed under them. ICAN, May 2023.

Solution

Five items which are normally dealt with under a statement of accounting policies are:

a) Basis of Accounting

b) Turnover or Gross Income

c) Depreciation

d) Stocks and Work in Progress

e) Investments

1. Basis of Accounting

Methods of Accounting convention adopted should be stated. This could be historical cost convention, etc.

2. Turnover or Gross Income

Indicates how turnover has been arrived at. It usually represents amount invoiced (net of returns).

3. Depreciation

The method and rate of depreciation should be stated

4. Stock and Work-in-Progress

The basis of valuation and method of determination of cost must be disclosed.

5. Investments

The basis of valuation must be disclosed. This could be at the lower of cost and net realised value, cost or market value depending on whether it is a current or fixed asset.

Illustration 3

Omoyo buys 200 items of a product at a cost of N5 each on 1st September, and sells 150 of them during September for N8 each. At 30th September, he therefore has 50 unsold items in stock. What is the gross profit he has in calculating will relate to only 150 units.

Solution

	$	$
Sales 150 units + 8		1,200
Purchases 200 units +5	1,000	
Less cost of closing stock 50 + 5	250	
Cost of units sold 150 units + 5		(750)
Gross Profit		450

From the above, you can see that, we have matched the value of sales with the cost of sales (150) units of sales values matched against 150 units of cost.

Illustration 4

Given that prudence is the main consideration, discuss under what circumstances, if any, revenue might be recognized when:

1. Goods acquired by a business for quick resell

2. A customer places a firm order for goods

3. Goods are delivered to the customer

4. The customer is invoiced for goods

5. The customer pays for the goods

6. The bank has cleared the customer's cheque in payment for the goods.

Solution

Using prudence or conservatism concepts in IAS 1

1. A sale must never be recognized before the goods have been ordered as there is no certainty about the value of the sale.

2. A sale must never be recognized when the customer places an order as there is no certainty that the sale transaction will go through.

3. A sale will be recognized when delivery of goods are made only when:

a) The sale is for cash and cash is received at the same time

b) The sale is on credit and the customer accepts delivery by signing a delivery note.

4. The critical event for credit sale is usually the dispatch of an invoice to the customer as there will be a legally enforceable debt, payable on specific terms. For a completed sale transaction.

5. The critical event for cash sale is both when delivery takes place at the same time.

6. It would again be over-cautious to wait for clearance of the customer's cheque before recognizing sales revenue.

INFORMATION TO BE DISCLOSED IN FINANCIAL STATEMENTS IAS 2

PART 1

INTRODUCTION

1. Accounting information about a business entity or enterprise is required by various users. This need dictates the fundamental objectives of accounting and the mode of reporting information.

2. Firms, organizations, enterprise carry on business activities in a given economic, social political environment and there is public interest in their operations; for instance:

a) Individuals, financial institutions or group of investors need accounting information to determine the liquidity, profitability and viability of the enterprise.

b) Managers in an enterprise need accounting information to measure performance, plan and control operations.

c) Employees and customers of an enterprise need accounting information in order to assess the ability of the enterprise to produce goods or to render services continuously.

d) Government and regulatory bodies need accounting information in order to be able to impose and collect taxes, to regulate certain business activities and plan, execute and evaluate government projects.

e) Quasi-Government establishments need accounting information in order to meet their statutory obligations.

Thus, the information expected to be provided in financial statements are quantitative and qualitative to aid their users in making informed economic decisions.

3. Financial statements are therefore expected to be simple, clear and easy to understand by all users.

4. Financial statements are the means of communicating information on the resources, obligations, and performance of the reporting entity of an enterprise to interest parties.

5. Meaningful information can be gathered, collated and presented in different forms. The format recommended in this IAS is expected to be the best practice in Nigeria.

PART 2

DEFINITION

In this IAS, following terms are used as described below:

1. Accounting information refers to data that are found in financial statements.

2. Accounting period refers to the time span, usually one year, financial statements cover that.

3. Financial statements consists of Balance Sheet, Profit and Loss Account of Income Statement, the Notes on the Accounts, Sources and Application of Funds Statements, Value Added Statement and Historical Financial Summary.

4. Long Term relates to a period in excess of 12 months.

PART 3

EXPLANATORY NOTES

Clear and understandable information about the nature and ownership of an enterprise or entity reported on, are usually disclosed in one of more of the contents of financial statements described in the following paragraph:

1. The Balance Sheet shows the assets, liabilities, and proprietors' interests at a point in time. Generally, enterprises present their balance sheet in the form of assets and claims against those assets by creditors and owners.

2. Profit and Loss Account or the Income Statement – reports revenue earnings or turnover and the expenses of an enterprise for a given accounting period.

3. Notes to the Accounts – Usually form an integral part of financial statements and provided detailed or supplementary information in respect of items disclosed in the Balance Sheet and the Profit and Loss Account.

4. Source and Application of Funds – Provides information on the derivation and utilization of funds during the period covered by the financial statements. When the statement of source and Application of Funds is taken together with the Balance Sheet and the Profit and Loss Account, a better insight is obtained as to how the activities of an enterprises have been financed.

5. Historical Financial Summary – enables instant comparisons over a period, usually five years, of vital financial information about an enterprise particularly with regard to its:

a) Turnover

b) Profit before and after taxation

c) Dividends assets employed

d) Issued and paid up capital

e) Reserves

f) Medium and long term liabilities

g) Earnings and dividends per share

6. At present, the information disclosed by some enterprise is limited to the minimum legal requirements. Whist other enterprise disclose additional information such as Application of Funds Statement and Value Added Statements, little information is provided in respect of related company transactions.

7. Disclosure of financial implications of inter-company transfers and technical/management agreements between subsidiaries/associated company and its immediate an/or ultimate parent/related company usually provides additional insight into the understanding of financial statements. This standard takes the view that disclosure which goes beyond minimum legal requirement is useful for more meaningful understanding of financial statements.

PART 4
ACCOUNTING STANDARD

INFORMATION TO BE DISCLOSED IN FINANCIAL STATEMENTS

The Accounting Standard comprises paragraphs 10-24 of this Statement, the standard should be read in the context of all the other parts of this statement and the preface to statement of Accounting Standards published by the NASB.

GENERAL DISCLOSURE

1. All Accounting information that will assist users to assess the financial liquidity, profitability and viability of a reporting entity should be disclosed and presented logically, clearly and easily.

2. The financial statements of an enterprise should state:

   (a) The name of the enterprise

   (b) The period of time covered

   (c) A brief description of its activities

   (d) Its legal form

   (e) Its relationship with significant local and overseas suppliers, including the immediate and ultimate parent, as well as the associated or affiliated company.

3. Financial Statements should include the following:

(a) State of Accounting Policies

(b) Balance Sheet

(c) Profit and Loss Account or Income Statement

(d) Notes to the Accounts

(e) Statement of Source and Application of Funds

(f) Value Added Statement

(g) Five-year Finical Summary

4. Financial implication of inter-company transfer and technical/management agreements between the enterprise and its significant local and overseas suppliers including its immediate and/or ultimate, associated affiliated company should be disclosed.

5. Financial Statements should show corresponding figures for the preceding period.

Specific Disclosure

Assets

Fixed Assets – property, plant and equipment

1. Land, Freehold and Leasehold

2. Buildings

3. Plant and Equipment

4. Other categories of assets, suitably identified

5. Accumulated Depreciation for each category

Separate disclosure in a note form should be made of assets on lease and assets acquired on installment purchase plans. Such a disclosure should include the types of assets, include their amounts, and the period covered.

1. Other long-term assets

a) Long-term investments (quoted or unquoted) distinguishing between:

(i)   Investment in subsidiaries

(ii) Investment in associated companies

(iii) Other investments

a) Long-term debts

(i)   All long-term debts including their nature

b) Intangible Assets

(i) Goodwill

(ii) Patents, trademarks and similar assets

(iii) Deferred charges such as: pre-incorporation and formation expenses.

Any write-offs during the period and the market value of investments should be disclosed.

2. Current Assets

a) Stock and spare parts

b) Current portion of long-term debts

c) Trade debts

d) Payment and sundry debtors

e) Directors debt balances

f) Subsidiary and associated companies debit balances

g) Short-term investments (including) Treasury Bills, certificate of Deposit and Commercial Notes

h) Deposit with Central Bank against import

i) Amount awaiting remittance to overseas creditors

j) Cash and bank balances.

3. Capital and Reserves

a) The variety of ownership interests such as ordinary shares, preference shares, cumulative, non-cumulative and participating preference shares:

(i) The number, nominal value and amount of shares authorized and issued.

(ii) The rights, preferences and restrictions concerning the distribution of dividends and the repayment of capital.

(iii) Cumulative preference dividends in arrears.

(iv) Shares are reserved for future issues under options, sales contracts and options for conversion of loans and debentures into shares including the term and amounts.

(v) Movement in the share capital accounts during the period.

b) Other shareholders' interest, indicating movement during any restriction on their capitalization by way of bonus shares.

(i) Share premium or discount

(ii) Revaluation surplus

(iii) Revenue and capital reserves

(iv) Retained earnings.

Liabilities

4. Long term liabilities

a) Secured loans

b) Unsecured loan; and

c) Loans from holding, subsidiary and associated companies

Details of the applicable interest rates, repayment terms, covenants, subordinations etc, should be disclosed.

5. Current Liabilities

a) Amount due to holding subsidiary and associated companies

b) Trade creditors

c) Other creditors and accrued expenses

d) Dividends payable

e) Current taxation

f) Current portion of long-term liabilities

g) Bank loans and overdrafts

6. General

a) Restrictions on the titles to assets

b) Restrictions on the distribution of dividends

c) Securities given in respect of liabilities

d) The method of providing for pension and retirement schemes together with a statement as to whether the scheme is funded or unfunded.

e) Contingent assets and contingent liabilities

f) Amount approved or committed for future capital expenditure

g) Events that have occurred after the balance sheet date but before the Board approves the financial statements.

Profit and Loss Account (Income Statement)

The following information should be disclosed:

1. Turnover/sales and other operating revenue

2. Other earnings: Distinguishing between interest income, income from investments and other sources

3. Interest charges

4. Taxes on income

5. Unusual charges.

6. Unusual credits

7. Depreciation

8. Auditors' remuneration

9. Directors' emoluments

10. Net income

Source and Application of Funds

The following disclosures should be made:

1. Source of funds:

a) Funds generated from operations

b) Funds from other sources

2. Application of funds

a) Loan repayment

b) Fixed assets acquisition

c) Payments of dividends

d) Payments of taxation, etc.

3. Increase or decrease in working capital in respect of:

a) Stocks

b) Debtors

c) Creditors, etc

4. Movement in net liquid funds

a) Value Added Statement

5. The statement should show separately the following:

a) Sales to outsiders

b) Purchases (goods and services): Distinguishing between imported and local items

c) Benefits to various groups such as:

(i) Employees

(ii) Owners and other supplier of capital

(iii) Government

d) Money retained for maintenance and expansion of the enterprise

6. Effect Date

a) This standard becomes operative for financial statements covering periods beginning on or after 1st January 1985.

PART 5

NOTE ON LEGAL REQUIREMENTS

The requirements of this standard are complimentary to any disclosure requirements of the companies Act 1968 and related Regulations

PART 6
COMPLIANCE WITHINTERNATIONAL ACCOUNTING STANDARD NO 5

The requirements of this standard are substantially in line with the requirements of the International Accounting Standard No. 5 – information to be disclosed in financial statements.

	$	$
Loss cost of closing stock 50 x 5	250	
Cost of units sold 150 units x 5		750
		450

From the above we can see that we have matched the value of sales with the cost of sales (150 of sales value matched against 150 units of cost)

Illustration 4

Given that prudence is the main consideration, discuss under what circumstances, if any, revenue might be recognized when:

1. Goods acquired by a business for quick resell

2. A customer places a firm order for goods

3. Goods are delivered to the customer

4. The customer is invoiced for goods

5. The customer pays for the goods.

6. The bank has cleared the customer's cheque in payment for the goods.

Solution

Using prudence or conservation concepts in IAS 1

1. A sale must never be recognized before the goods have been ordered as there is no certainty about the value of the sale.

2. A sale must never be recognized when the customer places an order as there is no certainty that the sale transaction will go through.

3. A sale will be recognized when delivery of the goods is made only when:

a) The sale is for cash and cash is received at the same time.

b) The sale is on credit and the customer accepts delivery by signing a delivery note.

4. The critical event for credit sale is usually the dispatch of an invoiced to the customer, as there will then be a legally enforceable debt, payable on specific terms, for a completed sale transaction.

5. The critical event for cash sale is both when delivery takes place at the same time

6. It would again be over-cautious to wait for clearance of the customer's cheque before recognizing sales revenue.

ACCOUNTINGFOR PROPERTIES, PLANTS AND EQUIPMENT

IAS 16

PART 1

INTRODUCTION

Property, Plant and Equipment, generally referred to as fixed assets, are those tangible resources of an enterprise that are employed in its operations. In many enterprises, these assets are grouped into various categories such as land and buildings, plant and machinery, equipment, furniture, fixtures, and fittings vehicles etc.

This statement deals with accounting for property, plant and equipment under the historical cost concept and the revaluation of specific property plant and equipment items. It does not deal with the effect of changing prices accounting for these assets.

This statement does not deal with accounting for expenditure on:

1. Regenerative natural resources such as forest, standing timber cattle, etc.

2. Non-regenerative resources include mineral deposits, oil and gas deposits, etc.

3. Real estate development by property companies

This statement makes brief reference to the accounting treatment (under certain circumstances) of:

1. Lease hold property

2. Depreciation of property, plant and equipment; and

3. Depreciation of property, plant and equipment and

4. Capitalization of borrowing cost.

PART 2

DEFINITIONS

The following terms are used in Statements with the meanings specified.

PROPERTY, PLANT AND EQUIPMENT are tangible assets that:

1. Have been acquired or constructed and held for use in the production or supply of goods and services and may include those held for maintenance or repair of such assets; and

2. Are not intended for sale in the ordinary course of business. Leasehold rights over assets which met the above criteria may also be treated as property, plant and equipment in certain circumstances.

The foregoing definition is provided as a guide only.

Fair value is the amount for which an asset could be exchanged between a knowledgeable, willing buyer and a knowledgeable willing seller in an arm's length transaction.

Net Book Value is the amount (historical cost or valuation) at which an asset is carried in the books less the related accumulated depreciation.

Useful Life of an asset is the net book value of an item of property, plant and equipment that the enterprise can recover in the future through depreciation of the item including its net realizable value on disposal.

Recoverable Amount is that part of the net book value of an item of property, plant and equipment that the enterprise can recover in the future through depreciation of the item including its net realizable value on disposal.

PART 3

EXPLANATORY NOTES

1. In many enterprises, the major part of total assets is represented by property, plant and equipment. Proper classification of, and accounting for, of property, plant and equipment are essential for an understanding financial statements. The classification of assets as property, plant equipment is usually guided by their functions, physical attributing essential useful lives.

2. It may be appropriate to aggregate individually insignificant homogenous or diverse items such as molds, tools and dies, and the definition to the aggregate value. Specific industry norms, requirements, and the overriding factor of presenting relevant and useful information may indicate modifications in classification and presentation.

3. In some cases, initial spare parts supply are capitalised and servicing equipment are carried as stock.

4. In certain situations, it may be necessary to buy a group of items of property, plant and equipment in order to obtain some particular items of property, plant and equipment that are of interest. Where such a purchase is made the purchase price less any recoveries from the disposal of the unwanted items are usually allocated proportionately over the items retained. The basis for allocating the purchase prices to the items retained is fair value of each of such items.

COMPONENTS OF ACQUISITION COSTS

1. In general, the cost of an item of property, plant and equipment comprises its purchase price, including import and non-recurring levies (e.g. development levies, consent fees, etc.) and any directly attributable Of bringing the assets to its location and working condition for its intended use. Any trade discounts and rebates are deducted in arriving at purchase price.

2. The following are example of elements of cost of different types property, plant and equipment:

Land and Improvements

1. Original purchase price

2. Broker's or Estate Agent's commissions

3. Legal fees for examining, recording and securing title

4. Cost of survey

5. Cost of obtaining vacant possession.

Payment of non-recurring levies on the land at the date of purchase is payable by the purchaser.

The cost of demolishing any old structure (net of salvage) is sometimes added to the cost of land and the cost of the building on the site.

Some additional costs may be incurred subsequent to purchase in order to improve the land for the intended purpose. Such costs which are often capitalised include the following:

Plant and Equipment

1. Original purchase price or cost of construction

2. Foreign, import duties and handling charges

3. In-transit insurance charges

4. Taxes and levies

5. Cost of preparation of foundations, insulation, protective and other special devices.

6. Commissioning, including testing and running-in cost in preparation for use.

7. If the item is a second hand one, cost of refurbishing it for the intended use.

RECOGNITION OF INTEREST ON DEFERRED PAYMENT CONTRACTS

The acquisition of items of property, plant and equipment may involve the deferment of payment and such future payment usually includes an element of interest. However, interest accruing before the item of property, plant and equipment is put to use is added to the cost of the item. Other subsequent interests are expended.

COMPONENT OF COST OF SELF-CONSTRUCTED PROPERTY, PLANT AND EQUIPMENT

1. Enterprises sometimes self-construct, for their own use, buildings, plants and equipment, furniture, fixtures, and fittings, usually to save costs, meet unique specifications, or utilize idle capacity.

2. The cost elements of items of self-constructed property, plant, and equipment are the cost of materials, labor, and overhead directly attributable to the construction, less any trade discount, rebates, or internal profits. Interest costs, which are attributable to the period of constructing the item, are sometimes added to its cost. Other costs, including inefficiency in the production of self-constructed items of property, plant, and equipment, such as idle capacity, industrial disputes, and similar costs, are expended in the period in which they arise.

CONSIDERATION OTHER THAN CASH

1. When an item of property, plant and equipment is acquired in exchange for another item of property, plant and equipment, its cost is usually determined by reference to the fair value of the items of property, plant and equipment acquired. If this is more clearly evident. An alternative accounting treatment that is sometimes used for an exchange of items of property, plant, and equipment, particularly when the equipment at the net book value of the item given up. In each case, an adjustment is made for any balancing receipt or payment of cash or other consideration.

2. When an item of property, plant, and equipment is acquired in exchange for shares or other securities in the enterprise, it is usually recorded at its fair value, or the fair value of the securities issued, whichever is the more readily ascertainable.

EXPENDITURE SUBSEQUENT OF ACQUISITION

1. Expenditure incurred after the acquisition of an item of property, plant and equipment is either capitalised or expended. The expenditure is generally capitalised if it is deemed to:

a) Prolong the expected useful life of the item of property, plant and equipment

b) Improve significantly the performance of the item; or

c) Enhance the quality of the item's output.

d) The types of Expenditure that are usually capitalised because they meet any or all criteria 17 (a), (b) and (c) above are:

(i) Major additions to existing items of property, plant and equipment; and

(ii) Major improvements.

Any other expenditure is charged to Profit and Loss Accounts.

AMOUNT SUBSTITUTED FOR HISTORICAL COSTS

1. Sometimes, financial statements that are otherwise prepared on a historical cost basis include part or all property, plant, and equipment, and as a valuation for historical cost depreciation, they are calculated accordingly. Such financial statements are to be distinguished from financial statements prepared on a basis intended to reflect comprehensively the effects of changing prices.

2. A commonly accepted method of restating property, plant, and equipment is appraisal, which is normally undertaken by professionally qualified valuers. Other methods sometimes used are indexation and reference to current prices.

3. In practice, there are two methods of presenting revalued amounts of property, plant and equipment in financial statements in the first method, both the gross amount and the accumulated depreciation are restated in order to give a net book value equal to the amount revalued. Under the second method, the accumulated depreciation is eliminated while the gross book value is adjusted to equal the newly established value.

4. When the second method is used, the accumulated depreciation is often eliminated by a credit to either the Revaluation Surplus Account or Income Account. This later treatment is unacceptable because an upward revaluation does not provide a basis for crediting the accumulated depreciation to an Income Account at the revaluation date.

5. Different revaluation bases are sometimes used in the same financial statements to determine the net book value of the separate items within each of the property, plant and equipment categories. In these cases, it is useful to disclose the gross book value included in each basis.

6. Any surplus arising from a revaluation of an item or group of items of property, plant and equipment is usually credited to a revaluation surplus account. Revaluation defines are usually charged to income.

7. The depreciation charge base on the new value of an item of property, plant and equipment is sometimes allocated between the historical cost of the item and the surplus arising on the revaluation of the item and charged to income and the revaluation surplus accounts respectively. This practice is, however, not generally accepted.

RETIREMENT AND DISPOSAL

1. Items of property, plant and equipment that have been retired from active use or held for disposal are usually stated at the lower of their net book or net realizable values. Any anticipated loss is immediately charged to income for the period.

2. When an item of property, plant and equipment is disposed of or retired, it is eliminated from property, plant and equipment; and any gain or loss arising there from is transferred to income for the period.

3. Upon the disposal of a previously revalued item of property, plant and equipment, the difference between the net proceeds from disposal and the net book value is normally charged or credited to income. Any related evaluable surplus is transferred to income or retained profit.

4. Where the usefulness of an item or group of items of property, plant and equipment is permanently impaired, in which case, the recoverable amount is less than the net book value, the net book value is usually reduced to the recoverable amount and the difference is charged to income immediately.

PART 4
ACCOUNTING STANDARD

ACCOUNTING FOR PROPERTY, PLANT AND EQUIPMENT

The Accounting Standard comprises paragraphs 29-45 of this Statement. The standard should be read in the context of all other parts of this Statement and of the Preface to the Statement of Accounting Standards published by the NASB.

1. The items determined in accordance with the definitions in paragraph 5 of this Statement should be included under property, plant and equipment in financial statements and disclosed in accordance with IAS 2 information to be disclosed in Financial Statements.

2. The gross value of an item of property, plant and equipment should be either the historical cost or the revalued amount computed in accordance with this Standard. Property, plant and equipment carried at historical cost.

3. At the date of acquisition, items of property, plant and equipment should be recorded at their initial cost including directly attributable expenses incurred in order to bring them into operation for their intended use.

4. Cost of self-constructed item of property, plant and equipment should comprise those costs that relate direct and other Expenses attributable to the construction of the item. Costs of inefficiencies in the construction of the item should not form part of its cost.

5. When an item of property, plant and equipment is acquired in exchange or in part exchange for and other items, the cost of item acquired should be recorded either at its fair value or at an expert's valuation of the item exchanged, adjusted for any balancing payment or receipt of cash or other consideration.

6. Any property, plant and equipment acquired in exchange for shares or securities in an enterprise should be recorded at its fair value or the fair value of the shares or securities issued whichever is more readily ascertainable.

7. Expenses made after the acquisition of an item of property, plant and equipment, should be added to the net book value of the item if the expenditure significantly improves the item's performance, enhances the quality of the item's output or prolong its expected useful life.

8. Suppose a permanent improvement to an item of property, plant, or equipment causes the recoverable amount to fall below the net book value. In that case, the net book value should be immediately reduced to the recoverable amount and the difference charged to income.

9. An item of property, plant, and equipment should be eliminated from the property, plant, and equipment at its disposal or when a decision has been made to discontinue its use.

10. Gains or loss resulting from the retirement or disposal of an item of property, plant and equipment should be recognized in the income statement.

PROPERTY, PLANT AND EQUIPMENT CARRIED AT VALUATION

1. Where an item of property, plant and equipment are to be carried at revalued amounts, an entire class of property, plant and equipment should be revalued or the selection of the items for revaluation should be systematic and consistent.

2. When an item of property, plant and equipment, an increase in the net book value should be credited to a revaluation surplus account. A decrease in the net book value should be reduced by the amount of any existing revaluation surplus on the same item before it is charged to income.

3. The difference between the net proceeds and the net book value should be transferred to income upon sale or disposal of an item of property, plant and equipment. Any balance in the revaluation surplus account with respect to such an item should be transferred to income or retained profit.

4. Subsequent depreciation on revalued items of property, plant, and equipment should be calculated based on the new value and charged to income.

DISCLOSURE

1. In addition to the disclosures required by IAS 1 – Disclosure of Accounting Policies, and IAS 2- Information to be Disclosed in Financial Statements the following disclosures should be made:

a) The bases for determining the book value of property, plant and equipment

b) When more than one basis has been used, the book value is determined under each basis in each category of property, plant and equipment.

c) Where property, plant and equipment are stated at revalued amounts, the methods adopted to compute these amounts should be disclosed, including the policy with regard to the frequency of revaluations, the nature of indices used and whether external valuers are involved.

d) Movement in each category of property, plant and equipment (i.e. addition and disposal) during the year.

e) Contingent capital gains tax and deferred income tax liabilities attributable to any revaluation surplus incorporated in or referred to in financial statements.

EFFECTIVE DATE

This standard becomes operative for Financial Statements covering periods beginning on or after 1st January, 1985.

PART 5

NOTES ON LEGAL REQUIREMENTS

The requirements of this Standard are complementary to any disclosure requirements of the Companies Act 1968 and related regulations.

PART 6

COMPLIANCE WITH INTERNATIONAL ACCOUNTING STANDARD NO. 16

The requirements of this Standard accord substantially with the requirements of the International Accounting Standard No.16 –Accounting for Property, plant and Equipment.

ACCOUNTING FOR PROPERTY, PLANT AND EQUIPMENT

These Standard covers treatment of fixed assets and depreciation in historical cost accounts. This IAS 3 is similar to IAS 16 and SAP 19.

It has the following sub-headings:

1. Determination of cost

2. Components of Acquisition costs

3. Land and Improvements

4. Buildings

5. Plant and Equipment

6. Recognition of Interest on Deferred Payment Contracts

7. Components of cost of self-constructed property, plant and equipment.

8. Consideration other than cash

9. Improvements and repairs\revaluations and Disposal

10. Retirement and Disposal

11. Self-Constructed Property

The cost elements of items of self-constructed property include materials cost, labor cost, overhead that are directly attributable to the construction less any trade discount and internal profits, cost in efficiencies in the production of self-constructed assets, examples temporary idle capacity industrial disputes or other causes are normally not considered to be suitable for capitalization.

Recognition of Interest on deferred payments contract.

The acquisition of property, plant, and equipment may include an interest component. Any interest incurred before the asset is ready for use is capitalised as part of its cost.

Revaluation of property, plant and equipment

Two methods exist for presenting a revalued amount of property, plant and equipment in Financial Statements.

METHOD 1

Both the Gross amount and the accumulated depreciation and reinstated in order to give a net carrying amount equal to the net revalued amount

METHOD 2

Under this, accumulated depreciation is eliminated, and the net revalued amount is treated as the new gross carrying amount.

RETIREMENT AND DISPOSAL

When an item of PP & E is disposed of or retired it is eliminated from property, plant and equipment and any gain or loss arising there from is transferred to income for the period.

On disposal of a previously revalue item of property, plant and equipment, the difference between the net proceeds from disposal and the net book value id normally charged or credited to income. Any related revaluation surplus is transferred to income or retained profit.

INVESTMENT PROPERTIES

Investment properties as an interest in and/or buildings in respect of which construction work and development have been completed and which is held for its investment potential, rental income being negotiated at arm's length.

Investment properties should not be subject to periodic depreciation charges unless held or lease.

DISCLOSURE REQUIREMENT

1. Movements in each category of property, plant and equipment
2. The amount of payments accounts property, plant and equipment on the course of construction or acquisition.

3. The carrying amount of temporary idle property, plant and equipment.

4. The contingent capital gain tax and deferred income tax liabilities attributable to any revaluation surplus in the financial statements.

Illustraion:

The valuation basis normally adopted in accounting for physical fixed assets in the books of account is cost. However, there are certain difficulties in applying this basis where physical fixed assets are acquired with immediate legal title for consideration other than immediate cash payments.

You are required to outline instances where difficulties may be encountered in the application of cost as a basis of valuation and the solutions that are normally accepted (ICAN, 20xx).

Solution:

The areas of difficulties are:

1. If the fixed asset is acquired in exchange or in part exchange for another asset, the cost of the asst acquired should be recorded at its fair value or at an expert's valuation.

2. For assets acquired in exchange for shares or securities, the cost should be its fair value or the fair value of the shares or securities issued, whichever is the more readily ascertainable.

STOCK VALUATION
IAS 4

PART 1

INTRODUCTION

Stocks (otherwise referred to as Inventories) are items of value held for use or sale by an enterprise and usually comprise raw materials and supplies used in production, work-in-progress and finished goods.

Depending on the nature of an enterprise, the value of stocks may be substantial, surpassing or only second to that of property, plant and equipment.

Appropriate classification and accurate determination of the quantity and cost of stocks are necessary to properly determine the result of an enterprise's operations and present current assets in its Balance Sheet.

The use of several methods for valuing and reporting stocks gives rise to wide differences in the results of the operations of enterprises in the same line of business. This statement seeks to narrow such differences by setting a standard for the presentation of items of stock in the context of the historical cost concept.

This state deals with the valuation and presentation of items of stocks including livestock and agricultural produces.

This statement does not deal with:

1. Valuation under replacement cost account concept

2. Valuation under the inflation accounting concept

3. Valuation of work-in-progress under long-term contracts

4. Valuation of by-products

5. Valuation of forest products.

PART 2

DEFINITIONS

The following terms are used in this Statement with the meaning specified:

1. Stocks include those finished goods livestock awaiting sale, work-in-progress, raw materials and supplies to be consumed in producing goods or rendering services.

2. Historical cost comprises the cost of purchase and other incidental costs incurred in order to bring the items of stocks to their present condition and location. For manufacturing enterprise, such costs would include the cost of conversion.

3. Cost of purchase usually includes the initial cash or consideration given to acquire an item of stock and payments of duties, taxes freight inwards and other costs necessary to bring the item to its location. Trade discounts and rebates, if any, are usually deducted in arriving at the cost of purchase.

4. Cost of conversion comprises direct labor and attributable production overhead costs incurred in bringing an item of stock to its present condition and location.

5. Absorption costing is a method of costing in which all production costs such as variable and fixed cost are included as part of the cost of such items.

6. Variable or direct costing is a method of stock costing in which only variable production costs form a part of the cost of items produced. Variable or direct costs change in proportion to the level of production.

7. Net Realizable value is the estimated proceeds from sale less all additional costs incurred to the point of completion, marketing, settling and distribution of an item of stock.

8. Arable stocks are commercially grown farm produce. The value of such stock would include the cost of tillage, planting and nurturing plants to harvesting stage.

9. Livestock refers to farm animals such as poultry, sheep, cattle, etc. which are especially raised for commercial purposes.

10. Plantation products are cocoa, coffee, kola, oil palm, plantain, rubber, tea and tobacco, etc., cultivated on a large estate.

11. Consumable farm stocks include items such as seeds, fertilizers, sprays, feedstuff, small implements, spares, fuel silage, hay and straw, etc.

12. Replacement cost is the amount at which an identical stock could be bought or manufactured, with regard to normal purchasing or production quantities and conditions.

PART 3
EXPLANATORY NOTES

MANUFACTURED AND GENERAL PRODUCTS

1. Stock values sensitive to general fluctuation in economic activities. For example, in periods of high business activities, stock are sold or utilized very rapidly; but during a downturn in economic activities, stock on hand may build up quickly resulting in over-stocking. Business enterprises minimize the cost of carrying stocks by carefully planning and timing their acquisition and utilization.

2. Cost in the usual basis for recording and carrying stock in accounts because they are acquired and held either for use in producing goods and services or for direct sale to customers.

3. Where the utility or value of an item of stock is impaired through damage deterioration or obsolescence, the value assigned to such item of stock will not be cost-based. In such situations, net realizable value is used.

4. When the value of an item of stock is less than its original cost, the rule of cost or net realizable value whichever is lower is applied. The value of such stock is written down to the net realizable value by charging the loss in value to income. Similar treatment is usually accorded the aggregate value of homogeneous items of stock.

5. Two system of stock-taking are generally in use, namely:

a) Perpetual – Under this system, up-to-date records of quantity and type of items of stock received, issued, and on hand are kept. This system involves continuous physical count.

b) Periodic – under this system, record of quantity and type of items of stock are up-dated periodically after physical count.

6. In practice, problems may arise as to which items are to be included in closing stock. The following items are generally included:

a) Goods in transit – when legal title is assumed to have passed to the enterprise.

b) Consigned goods – goods on consignment legally remain the consignor's property and are accordingly included in the consignor's stock.

7. The amount reported for stocks by an enterprise at the end of the year results from determining the quantity of items on hand and the assignment of value to such items.

8. The following valuation methods facilitate the determination of both the quantity and the value to such items.

a) Specific identification – under this method, items of stock specifically identified by particular attributes are assigned their values.

b) Average – under this method, the closing stock is assigned a value determined by a weighted average of the cost of the opening stock and all acquisitions during the period. Calculations may be made on a continuous basis after each acquisition or at fixed interval.

c) First In, First Out (FIFO) – This is a method of computing the value of the closing stock based on the assumption that the first items in stock or acquired are the first ones used in production or consumed.

d) Last In, First Out (LIFO) – This is a method of computing the value of closing stock based on the assumption that the last items purchased are the first issued or consumed.

e) Standard Cost – This is a method of computing the value of closing stock based on a predetermined cost. For this method to reflect the actual cost, a system of allocation of variances as well as review of the standard cost must be in constant use.

f) Later Purchase Price – Under this method, a minimum level of stock, carried at the historical cost of acquisition, is held at all times. However, any additions to or excesses over the base stock are carried at different bases such as FIFO, LIFO, etc.

g) Latest Purchase Price – Under this method, a minimum level of stock is determined by applying the cost of the latest item purchased to the number of items on hand.

h) Adjusted Selling Price (Retail Inventory Method) – It is a method of determining the value of closing stock in which the historical cost of stock is estimated by applying the gross profit margin to the retail value of items or group of items in stock. The amount so determined is then deducted from the retail price to arrive at the value of the stock.

9. The principle of matching costs with revenue usually guides the selection of each method. The LIFO, Latest purchase price and the base stock methods of valuation do not always adequately match costs with revenue because the value of stocks reported in the balance sheet is either overstated or understated, and the profit for the period is similarly distorted.

10. In a manufacturing enterprise, the value of items of stock produced comprises the cost of direct material and conversion costs. These taken together are known as product costs and are carried as stock cost or work-in-progress until the items are sold or consumed. Where the intrinsic value of some products is appreciated by virtue of storage over time, e.g., timber, wines, and spirits, such storage costs are sometimes included as part of the product cost.

11. Other costs which are not attributable to the production of items of stock are expended in the period in which they are incurred. Thus, they do not form a part of the cost of the items of stock.

12. The value of work-in-progress is usually determined by aggregating actual direct material cost, direct labour cost and attributable overhead charges. The attribution of overhead costs is usually based on normal plant utilization so as to exclude production inefficiencies from the cost of stock

13. A departure from historical cost is usually prudent where there is a decline in the value of items of stock due to physical deterioration, obsolescence a fall in market price below cost or other causes. The loss is recognized by a write down of the stock value to its net realizable value, which is usually applied to individual items, a sub-group or group of items.

14. The cost of conversion of raw materials to finished or semi-finished items of stock is often separated into variable and fixed costs. Under the absorbing cost method, all production costs form a part of product cost whereas, under the variable or direct costing method, only direct or variable costs of production form part of the product cost. Both methods are widely used in practice.

15. In computing the value of raw materials used in production or the value work-in-progress, normal wastage or spoilage cost is included as part product cost. By contrast, the cost of abnormal wastage or spoilage expended.

ARABLE CROPS

1. First-time land clearing and stumping may involve substantial costs which are sometimes capitalised.

2. Tillage's, in-ground and harvested crops are three distinct operations stage requiring valuation. Each operational stage has its own peculiar valuation problem, and costs incurred are charged to each category.

3. The value of tillage usually includes the accumulated costs of labour and machinery usage for preparing the land for planting, ploughing a fertilizer spreading.

4. In-ground crops are usually valued by including the costs associated with tillage's, labour, seedlings, disease control and the attributable cost of machinery used.

5. The valuation of harvested crops involves the correct determination of actual input costs, labour, depreciation and storage costs at the time of harvest, and the proper allocation of in-ground costs to the portion harvested to ensure that the value of harvested crops includes all the cost incurred from tillage to harvesting.

6. Most farm products are perishable or deteriorate quickly, therefore, it is appropriate to make reasonable provisions for deterioration or normal spoilage based on industry norm or after consultation with experts.

7. Where there is adequate record keeping and an appropriate cost accounting system, costs form the basis for the valuation of arable products. In other situations, however, net realizable value is used.

8. Official prices for certain products such as maize, sorghum and millet are published seasonally by the appropriate Commodity Boards. For example, National Grains Board. The use of such official price for valuing stock is generally not preferred, except where they are below cost, as the prices are intended market values.

PLANTATION PRODUCTS

1. The major problem with the determination of the value of plantain product is that a plantation does not usually start to produce until after a long gestation period. Thus, all costs associated with land preparation, planting, pruning and development are accumulated until the trees mature or begin to bear fruits. The accumulated costs of maturity are amortised over the estimated productive life of the plantation.

2. It is normal practice to have planting done in lots or batches so as to have a continuous flow of plantation output. Where possible, costs of such lots or batches are accumulated separately so as to match their revenues with their costs when harvested and sold.

3. Each year, the cost of plantation output consists of the proportion of the cost accumulated for the quantities harvested plus the cost of extracting and transporting them to the point of sale.

4. Some enterprises prefer to use the average cost of production to assign value to the quantities harvested and those unharvested. This method is justifiable because most plantation products are homogeneous.

5. Some plantation crops, such as sugarcane and banana usually yield produce within the first year of planting. Stocks of such produce are valued in the same manner as arable produce. On the other hand, cashed and mangoes are often grown on a much smaller scale than would normally be regarded as plantations. However, stocks of their products are valued in the same manner as those in plantations.

LIVESTOCK

1. Two major problems are associated with the value of livestock, namely:

a) Determining the actual number and their existence especially animals that graze, and

b) Identifying the various stages of their development.

2. Animals may be segregated on the basis of their age, breed, sex, productivity. In some enterprises, appropriate and detailed record categories are kept. Such records help in the allocation costs to animals that are on hand. A proper accumulation and records of costs incurred for livestock are essential for determining the profitability of different categories of livestock.

3. The following three approaches to the valuation of livestock are generally use:

a) Cost Approach: The value is based on the actual cost incurred each category of livestock.

b) Net Realizable Value: The value is based on the expected return allowing for the cost of fattening, preparation for sale and selling

c) Appraisal Value: The value is determined by a professional value taking into consideration the current market value, the mortality factor and the relative marketability of the breed or class of stock.

4. Where livestock is raised primarily for its products rather than for consumption, for example, dairy cattle or egg-laying poultry, different considerations arise in the valuation of such live stock. It usually accumulates the cost of bringing such livestock to the point of maturity, when they begin to yield products and amortize such costs over the estimated productive lives.

5. The stores on livestock enterprises usually include feed-stock, drugs small implements and other essential materials. They are usually valued at cost after a physical count.

PRESENTATION ON FINANCIAL STATEMENTS

1. In practice, different enterprises present items of stocks in financial statements using different titles for similar items. In addition, enterprises indicate the classes of stocks in their possession without specifying the amount for each class.

PART 4

ACCOUNTING STANDARD ON STOCK

1. The Accounting Standard comprises paragraphs 42-59 of this Statement. The Standard should be read in the context of paragraphs 1-41 of this statement and of the Preface to Statements of Accounting Standards published by the NASB.

2. In order to provide proper understanding of the valuation, methods adopted in arriving at the values of stocks, a reporting enterprise should state its accounting policies with respect to these items.

3. For accurate determination of the results of operations and fair presentation of items of stocks in the Financial Statements, appropriate classification and determination of the quantity and cost of items of stocks should be undertaken.

4. Subject to certain exceptions stated herein, stocks should be valued at lower cost or net realizable value.

5. To apply the lower of cost or net realizable value rule, stock items may be treated individually or as a group.

6. In determining the cost of stocks under the historical cost concept, one or more of the following valuation methods should be used where appropriate.

a) First In, First Out,

b) Average Cost, where it consistently approximates historical cost

c) Specific Identification.

d) Standard Cost with the adjustment for cost variances described in paragraph 15 (v) which brings it close to actual cost.

e) The Adjustment Selling Price Method where bulk purchases are made in which costs of individual items are not readily ascertainable.

7. The following stock valuation methods should not be used:

a) Latest Purchase Price

b) Last In, Fist Out

c) Base Stock

8. Goods in transit should be included in closing stock as long as their legal titles are deemed to have passed to the enterprise. Goods on consignment are the stock of consignor but not of the consignee.

9. In a manufacturing enterprise, the cost of finished goods and work-in-progress should include: raw materials, labour and attributable overhead costs. Other production costs not attributable to the finished goods or work-in-progress should be expended in the period incurred.

10. The historical cost of work-in-progress should be determined by aggregating the actual cost of direct material, direct labour and attributable overhead based on normal production capacity. Abnormal costs due to inefficiency, spoilage or wastage should not be included in the value of stock.

11. Where the intrinsic value of a product appreciated by virtue of storage over time, e.g. timber, wines and spirits such storage costs should be included as part of the product cost and reflected in the value of stock.

12. The valuation of arable stock should be based on cost where adequate record-keeping and appropriate cost accounting system exist; otherwise, valuation should be based on net realizable value.

13. Reasonable provision for deterioration or normal spoilage should be made for perishable farm products.

14. Arable Stocks have three distinct operational stages: Tillage in-ground (growing crops) and harvested crops. Where practicable, costs should be accumulated separately for each stage.

15. The cost of plantation crops on hand at the end of the year should be determined by one method specified in paragraphs 33 and 35 above.

16. One or more of the following methods should be used where appropriate in valuing livestock:

a) Cost Method

b) Net Realisable Value

c) Appraisal Value

Whatever method that is adopted should be applied consistently

DISCLOSURE

1. Where differing method of valuation have been adopted for different types of stocks, the amount included in the Financial Statements and the methods used in respect of each type should be stated.

2. Enterprises should classify, in a manner appropriate to their business, items of stocks so as to indicate the amounts held in each category. For example, raw materials, work-in-progress, finished goods, spare parts and stocks.

3. Any change in the basis of valuation from that used in the previous period. Should be disclosed in accordance with IAS 1.

PART 5

NOTES ON LEGAL REQUIREMENTS

1. The requirements of its Standard are complementary to any disclosure requirements of the Companies Act 1968 and relevant regulations.

PART 6

COMPLIANCE WITH INTERNATIONAL ACCOUNTING STANDARD No. 2

1. The requirements of this Standard are substantially in line with the requirements of International Accounting Standard No. 2 – Valuation and Presentation of Inventories in the Context of the Historical Cost System.

EFFECTIVE DATE

1. This Standard becomes operative for Financial Statements covering periods beginning or after January, 1987.

IAS 4 STOCKS

This is similar to IAS 2 and SSAP 9.

Cost: Cost includes expenditure in bringing the product or service to its present location and condition and conversion costs.

Historical cost comprises the cost of purchase and the other incidental costs incurred in order to bring the items of stocks to their present condition and location.

Net Realizable Value:

Situations where net realizable value will be less than Cost are:

1. Where there is an increase in costs or a fall in selling price

2. Physical deterioration of stocks

3. Obsolescence of products

4. Selling products at a loss

5. Errors in production or purchasing

ARABLE CROPS

Under this, substantial costs, including First-time land clearing and stumping, are capitalised.

Valuation Stage

1. Tillage's-like accumulated costs for labor and usage machinery

2. In group crops-tillage, labor, seedling and disease control

3. Valuation of harvest crops = input cost.

PLANTATION PRODUCTS

The major problem with the determination of the value of a plantation product is that a plantation does not usually start to produce until after a long gestation period. So these costs are considered: Land preparation, planting, pruning and development costs. All these costs are accumulated to maturity and they are amortised over the estimated productive life of the plantation.

LIVESTOCK

Two major problems are associated with the valuation of livestock, these are:

1. Determining the actual number and their existence especially animals that graze and

2. Identifying the various stages of their development

The three approaches to the valuation of livestock are:

1. Cost Approach: The value is based on the actual cost incurred on each category of livestock.

2. Net Realizable Value: the value is based on the expected returns allowing for the costs of fattening, preparation for sale and selling

3. Appraisal Value: the value is determined by a professional valuer considering the current market value, the mortality factor and the relative marketability of the breed or class of stock.

VALUATION METHODS ALLOWED BY IAS 4

1. First In First Out (FIFO)

2. Average Cost

3. Specified Identification

4. Standard Cost

5. The Adjusted Selling Price Method

The standard does not support these bases:

1. Latest Purchase Price

2. Last In, First Out (LIFO)

3. Base Stock

Illustration 1

State and explain these concepts in valuation of stock

1. Cost method
2. Net Realizable Value
3. Market Value

Solution 1

Cost is expenditure incurred in bringing the product or service to its present location and condition.

Net Realizable Value is estimated selling price (net of trade discount) less all further costs to completion and less all costs to be incurred in marketing, distributing and selling but without deduction for administration.

Market value – the prevailing selling price in the open

market.Stocks are valued at the lower of cost or net realizable

value.

Illustration 2

Ewekoro Limited processes and sell a single product, purchase of raw materials during the year were made at a regular rate of 1000 tons at the beginning of each week. The price was $100 per ton 1st January, 2016, and $150 per ton with effect from 1st July, 2016. It remained constant from then until the end of the year, 31st December, 2016. In addition to this price, a custom duty and Port charges of $10 a ton was paid through the year. Transport from the docks to the factory cost $20 per ton.

Variable costs of processing were $25 per ton. There was capacity to process 1,500 tons per week and the fixed production cost for all levels of activity up to this capacity level were $30,000 per week. One ton of raw material is processed into one ton of finished product and sold, at a delivered price of $240 per ton, by sales force whose cost was fixed at $3,000 per week. Average delivery costs to customers were $7.50 per ton.

At the beginning of the year, there were no stocks, stock at the close of year were: raw materials 5,000 tons, finished products 2,000 ton. It is expected that the current costs and prices of 31 December, 2016 will continue during 2017.

You are to:

1. Calculate the value of stock at 31 December, 2016, on a basis acceptable under IAS 2 and IAS 4.
2. Draft an accounting policy statement on stock for the company for insertion in its annual accounts.
3. Calculate the value of raw materials stock on a LIFO basis

4. Comment upon the relative merits of FIFO, any other based recognized under IAS 2 and IAS 4 for valuing stock and LIFO (ICAN November, 2017).

Solution 2

EWEKORO LIMITED

VALUATION OF STOCK AT 31 DECEMBER,2016

Raw Materials	
Raw materials cost – (5000 tons x $150	750,000
Customs Duty and Port Charges (5,000 x $20)	50,000
Transportation (5,000 tons x $20)	100,000
Value of Raw Material Stock	900,000
Finished Products	
Raw Material Cost (2,000 tons x $150)	300,000
Customs Duty and Port charges (2,000 tons x $25)	20,000
Transportation (2,000 tons x $20)	40,000
Variable COST OF PROCESSING (2,000 tons x $25)	50,000
Fixed Overhead (2,000 tons x $20)	40,000
Value of finished Products	450,000

Workings

Fixed overhead per unit = $30,000 + 1,500 tons = $20.00

Accounting policy on stock and work-in-progress: Stocks are stated at lower cost on a First In, First Out basis and net realizable value. Cost of materials comprises supplier's invoice, freight and other charges incurred to bring the materials to their location and condition. Finished goods include direct materials and labour costs together with appropriate overheads based on normal activity levels.

Valuation of Raw Materials Stock, using LIFO basis

Purchase cost (500 tons $100.00)	500,000
Customs Duty and Port charges (5,000 x $10)	50,000
Transportation (5,000 tons x $20)	100,000
Relative merits of Stocks Valuation basis	650,000

1. FIFO

   a) It is an actual cost system

   b) It is acceptable to the Inland Revenue

   c) Its prices approach current market value

   d) It is administratively clumsy

   e) Comparison between jobs is difficult

2. Weighted Average Cost

a) It is acceptable to Inland Revenue

b) It is less complicated.

c) It makes job's comparison possible

d) No unrealistic stock profit occurs

3. LIFO

a) It is an actual Cost System

b) Production cost based fairly closely on current prices

c) Stock valued at the oldest prices

d) It is administratively clumsy on job comparison

4. Standard Cost

a) It gives rise to profit and losses

b) It is simple to apply

c) Practically difficult in carrying at a reasonable and acceptable standard price

d) Facilitates cost comparison.

CHAPTER SIX
ON CONSTRUCTION CONTRACTS IAS 11

PART 1

INTRODUCTION

1. The main issues involved in accounting for Construction Contracts are the timing, measurement and recognition of revenue and the net assets created during the construction.

2. Costs a Construction Contract may start to accumulate even before the contract is won. It is, therefore, necessary to determine the accounting treatment that should be accorded to such costs as soon as there is convincing evidence that the contract will be won.

3. The treatment of these costs may significantly affect the reported result of an accounting period and on the assets and liabilities of the reporting enterprise. Unless a correct treatment of such cost is adopted, it may lead to a wrong appraisal of the profitability of the Construction Contract.

4. The period for the execution of a Construction Contract depends on the nature, type and size of the contract. Some contracts run for only a short period of time, so it may be more prudent to recognize the profit on such a contract only upon completion. Some other contracts, however, may extend over two or more accounting periods of the enterprise, in which case, a meaningful basis has to be adopted for the determination of the proportion of profit that has been earned at each accounting date, the value that needs to be reported in the financial statement as work-in-progress in the books of the contractor. Most of the provisions of this Statement apply to the Contractor.

5. This statement does not cover:

a) Contracts that deal with research into the development of new products;

b) Service contracts that fall under job under-costing;

c) Property development projects including those often referred to in this country as contractor financed projects; and

d) The Employer can easily determine the treatment of construction contracts in the books of the Employers (Contractee) because of the value of any Construction Contract through the analysis of cash outlays and the liabilities accrued on the contract.

PART 2

DEFINITIONS

1. The following items are used in this Statement with meaningful specified:

2. Construction Contract refers to the execution of building and civil engineering projects, mechanical and electrical engineering installations and other fabrications normally evidenced by an agreement between two or more parties.

3. Short-term Construction Contract refers to a contract which is expected to be completed within twelve months.

4. Long-term Construction Contract refers to a contract which is expected to take more than twelve months to complete.

5. Revenue Realizable means that the portion of the work responsible for generating the revenue has been performed and therefore the revenue relating thereto has been earned.

6. Revenue Realizable means accounting for revenue in the financial statements when it has been earned.

7. Percentage-of-Completion Method of revenue recognition This is a method under which revenue is apportioned to each accounting period on the basis of the proportion of the contract executed during the period to the total value of the contract.

8. Completed-contract Method of Revenue Recognition Under this method, revenue is only recognized when the contract is completed.

9. Deferred costs relate to aspects of a contract that are not immediately certifiable contractor to enable construction work to start.

10. Under-billing arise where the rates used for progress billing for payments are lower than those used for revenue recognition.

11. Over-billing arise where the rates used for progress billing for payment are higher than those used for revenue recognition.

12. Contract Certification. This is a process by which the project Architect/Engineer issues a certificate to prove the value of work done on a construction contract at a particular date.

PART 3

EXPLANATORY NOTES

1. The main accounting problems associated with construction contracts are the timing, measurement and recognition of revenue and assets created during construction. The value assigned to work-in-progress has an effect on the Profit and Loss Account and the value reported as a current asset on the Balance Sheet. It also ensures that proper matching of costs with revenue.

2. In practice, two methods are generally used for accounting for construction contracts, namely:

a) The Completed Contract Method

b) The Percentage-of-Completion Method

Both methods used, depending on the circumstances of each contract.

THE COMPLETED-CONTRACT METHOD

1. Under the completed-contract method, revenue is recognized when the contract is completed. Costs incurred on the contract and billing are accumulated until the contract is completed. No interim charges and credits are made to profit and loss account.

2. Sometimes, there are costs to be incurred at the end of the contract that may not be material to warrant the contract being uncompleted. Such costs are provided for and the Contract is treated as completed. In the construction industry, this is referred to as the practical completion stage.

3. Usually, the completed-contract method for long-term contracts is used in enterprises in a situation where there are no dependable estimates or where there are inherent uncertainties that make forecasts unrealizable. Under the point at which the contract is identified to be completed, revenue is recognized.

4. The completed-contract method appeals to many enterprises because the income reported in the accounts is the final result of the contract rather than an estimate of the result to date. The revenue at this point is terminal.

5. The major drawback of the completed-contract method when applied to long term-contract is that periodic revenue is subject to distortion. Revenue prior to completion is not reflected in the accounts of the reporting enterprise even if operations on the contract are uniform over the contraction period.

6. Under the completed-contract method, although profit is not recognized prior to the completion of the contract, foreseeable losses on the contract are often charged in the accounts in the period they are identified.

THE PERCENTAGE-OF-COMPLETED METHOD

1. Under the percentage-of-completion method, costs that are incurred on contracts are accumulated on an asset account. The proportion of revenue in relation to the work done, may be ascertained by one of the following two methods:

a) The percentage of estimated total revenue that the incurred cost to date bears to the estimated total costs.

b) The percentage of total contract value that the engineering and architectural work done to date bears to the Engineering and Architectural estimate of the whole contract.

2. Where the percentage-of-completion method is used, it is used to establish that the revenue is not overstated by computing the estimated total cost of completion and comparing it with the total estimated revenue.

3. The percentage of completion method is used when:

a) There is a contract in which the following terms are included:

(i)   The goods or services to be provided and received

(ii) The frequency of inspection of work-in-progress and the certification procedures for billing purposes;

(iii) The manner of billing for work done and the terms of payment.

b) The contractor has an adequate estimating process and the ability to estimate reliably both the cost of completion and the percentage of contract executed.

c) The contract has a cost accounting system that adequately accumulates and allocates costs to final works consistent with his estimating process.

4. The percentage-of-completion method is considered to give a measure of activities performed in each accounting period and the resultant revenue thus, revenue is adequately matched with cost in the accounting period.

GENERAL

1. There are several types of contracts. This includes:

a) Fixed Sum (lump sum) contract – The contractor undertakes or agree to execute specific projects or works in consideration for a fixed sum. It excludes variation, escalation, etc.

b) Cost-plus a Fixed rate contract – Allows for reimbursement of agreed costs incurred plus a fixed fee or a percentage uplift on the agreed costs incurred.

c) Re-measure-contract – Allows final contract price to be determined by the measurement of final quantities.

d) Variation-Price Contract – contains one or more clauses regarding;

(i) Price variation that allows adjustments to base price;

(ii) Work variation for additional work order from an employer;

(iii) Prolongation that takes care of additional work order costs resulting from delays not caused by the contractor.

2. In general, costs of contracts begin to accrue with pre-contract cost which are expenses in the period incurred or deferred and charged to the contract where there is reasonable assurance that the contract will be won.

3. Some enterprises defer general and administrative expenses related to the contract but cannot be immediately allocated to it until it is completed. This is to avoid being overburdened in periods in which revenue is not recognized. Other enterprises expenses them in the year incurred as long as the operations of the year can absorb them.

4. When a contract is in a very advanced stage of completion, and the estimated cost to completion is small in relation to the work already done, the contract is often regarded as completed and provision is made for the cost to completion.

CHAPTER SEVEN
STATEMENT OF ACCOUNTING STANDARD
IAS 6

ON EXTRA-ORDINARY ITEMS AND PRIOR YEAR ADJUSTMENTS

PART 1

INTRODUCTION

1. Two opposing views that have considerable support for the determination of operating income in the year are the Current Operating Performance Concept and the All-inclusive Concept. Recently, there has been considerable diversity of views as to what constitutes extraordinary and unusual items, prior year adjustments and how they should be treated in accounts.

2. The primary objectives of this Statement are:

a) To examine the issues involved in the determination of operating income in any given accounting period and;

b) To prescribe the accounting treatment of extraordinary and unusual items and prior year adjustments and their appropriate disclosure in financial statements.

PART 2

DEFINITIONS

1. The following terms are used in this Statement with the meanings specified: -

a) Exceptional items are those that, though normal to an enterprise's activity are abnormal due to their infrequency of occurrence and size e.g. abnormally high bad debts.

b) Extraordinary items are those that occur outside the ordinary activities of an enterprise and are not expected to re occur frequently

c) Prior year adjustments are items of revenue and expenses that were recorded this year but would have been recorded in a prior year or years if all of the facts had been known at that time. These do not include adjustments for differences between actual and accounting estimates.

d) Ordinary activities of an enterprise are normal product lines or day-to-day activities of an enterprise.

PART 3

EXPLANATORY NOTES

1. Two problems are associated with extraordinary items: their precise identification and treatment in financial statements.

2. For proper classification of an enterprise's extraordinary revenue, expense, or cost items, proper analysis of the ordinary activities of an enterprise is usually undertaken. Material items that are infrequent and fall outside the normal activities of the enterprise are classified as extraordinary.

3. What items are regarded as extraordinary will depend on industry norm. for example, a company in the oil industry will treat an income or loss resulting from the sale of its buildings as an extraordinary item. On the other hand, a property holding company may treat equally material gain or loss on the sale of a building as an exceptional item.

4. The treatment of an item as extraordinary in the Profit and Loss Account depends on the reporting concept adopted by the reporting entity. A reporting entity may either choose the Current-Operating-Performance-Concept or the All-Inclusive Concept.

CURRENT-OPERATING-PERFORMANCE CONCEPT

1. Under the current operating performance concept, the profit and loss account segregates the result of activities into two parts, i.e., those that are from ordinary activities of an enterprise and those that are not.

2. Revenue and expenses from ordinary activities of an enterprise are matched thereby providing the current operating performance of the enterprise.

3. Similarly, non-operating items which include revenue and expenses not associated with the ordinary activities of an enterprise are matched and reported separately.

4. Exceptional items are sometime reported separately in the Profit and Loss Account to highlight their effects on the results of operations during the period.

5. Exceptional items are taken to reserved or retained earnings so as not to distort the result of operations during the period.

6. One of the major advantages of this method of presentation of result of operations is that it makes it easy to evaluate the performance of management in terms of the main line of activities and other sideline activities. Because information is presented in such a way that attention can easily be drawn to certain sections that may have special significance to users, some financial analysts favor this format.

7. Under the current operating format, the Profit and Loss Account is complicated Besides, it is better for internal management reporting and control purposes than for external reporting.

8. This concept is rarely used for external reporting especially in its strict sense. A modified version is often presented.

ALL-INCLUSIVE CONCEPT

1. Several variations of all-inclusive concept are in use, depending on the amount of detail an enterprise wishes to provide. Some enterprises present a non-segregated profit and loss account showing the total revenues and expenses. This is a single-step format and widely used these days by large enterprises.

2. The single-step format sacrifices detailed information for simplicity and this makes it easy for readers to follow.

3. On the other hand, some enterprises present segregated profit and loss accounts that clearly show total revenues (including a section for other income), expenses, extraordinary items (net of applicable taxes), and a section for Retained Profits/Reserves. The Statement of Retained Profits/Reserves excludes extraordinary items but includes prior year adjustments.

4. The all-inclusive concepts seem to be favored by the majority of users because the net profit or loss for the year represents all the regular and extraordinary earnings or losses for the year irrespective of the source. Where there is consistency in presentation of financial information, trends in earnings can be easily established and overall performance of the enterprise can be judged.

EXTRAORDINARY ITEMS

1. Extraordinary items are revenue and expense items of an enterprise that are distinguished because they are both unusual in nature and infrequent in occurrence. An item that is identified as extraordinary is usually abnormal and unrelated to the ordinary activities of the enterprise.

2. For proper distinction to be made, due consideration is usually given to the lines of business which the enterprise is engaged, the environment in which the enterprise operates, the industry norm, and the government regulations affecting the industry.

3. The past occurrence or event in an enterprise usually provides sufficient evidence for the classification of an item as either extraordinary or ordinary.

4. Certain gains or losses are reported as extraordinary items because they are unusual in nature, occur infrequently and are unrelated to the ordinary activities of an enterprise. Examples of such items include: -

    a) Profit or loss arising from trade investment

    b) Profit or loss arising on the sale of a segment, line of business or subsidiary,

    c) Profit or loss arising on the expropriation of an assets or nationalization of assets of an enterprise;

    d) Redundancy costs relating to discontinued products or business line. Costs relating to the closure of branches are not normally regarded as extraordinary items.

5. Extraordinary items are usually reported net of their associated taxes. The taxes of these items are rarely reported as part of the tax charge for the year.

PRIOR YEAR ADJUSTMENTS

1. Prior year adjustments occur as a result of either the correction of fundamental errors that were previously made in the accounts or of the wrong application accounting principles or a change in an accounting policy.

2. Usually, when errors are detected before accounts are finalized or published, such errors are corrected. In some cases, errors may escape detection in one period or to be discovered in another. The correction of such errors may require adjustment of past, present and future account balances.

3. Adjustments of accounting estimates are usually not classified as prior year adjustments and therefore are part of income or loss in the current and subsequent years. Examples of this category of adjustments are: changes in the estimate of useful lies of fixed assets, or net realizable value of stock believed to be obsolescence. Any change in an accounting estimate is not usually treated as an extraordinary item although it could be treated as an exceptional item.

4. Changes in accounting estimates occur frequently in practice because, on the financial statements may be finalized, important events or conditions may be dispute or uncertain. Where the outcome of such events or conditions and fairly predictable, provision is usually made for such events or conditions.

5. When an accounting principle that is different from the one previously used is adopted, a change in accounting principle occurs. For example, a change from reducing-balance-method of deprecation to a straight-line method is a change in accounting principle.

6. When an accounting principle is generally treated by including the portion that relates to the year in the profit and loss account of the current year, the cumulative balance is taken to Retained Earnings/Reserves.

7. Misapplication of accounting principle may occur due to the careless mistake of an employee. For example, where a fixed asset is mistakenly treated as an expense for the period, a misapplication of accounting principles has occurred. Such an error is fundamental and therefore, affects the balances of accounts in the past and current year.

8. A fundamental error is usually corrected by making appropriate adjustments to the opening retained profits figure and other affected account balances.

9. Prior Year Adjustments are usually reported net of associated taxes.

RETAINED PROFITS/RESERVES

1. Retained profits usually form a detachable part of the Profit and Loss Account Depending on the concept being used, extraordinary items are either reported as a part of the profit and loss account (all-inclusive concept) or reported in the Retained Profits Account (the Current-Operating-Concept). The practice of reporting extraordinary items in the Retained Profits Account is unusual.

2. No matter the concept used, prior year adjustments are reported in the Retained Profit Account.

FINANCIAL STATEMENT PRESENTATION

1. Exceptional and Extra ordinary items are usually shown on the face of the profit and Loss Account; the former forms part of normal activities and the latter is shown after: "Profit Tax and Before Extraordinary Items".

PART 4
THE ACCOUNTING STANDARD

EXTRA ORDINARY ITEMS AND PRIOR YEAR ADJUSTMENTS

The accounting Standard comprises paragraphs 37 – 49 of this statement. The standard should be read in the context of all other parts of this statement and of the preface to the Statement of Accounting Standards published by the NASB.

1. A reporting entity should adopt the All-inclusive-concept of reporting

2. A multiple step format that is appropriate for an enterprise or industry should be used and should normally include:

   a) Profit after Tax and before extraordinary items.

   b) Extraordinary items

   c) Profit after extraordinary items

3. Retained profit/reserves should form part of the profit and loss account and should be clearly identified. All prior year adjustments should be reported in the retained profits/reserves account net of associated taxes.

4. Items should be treated and reported as extraordinary only if they are unusual in nature. Infrequent in occurrence and unrelated to the ordinary activities of the reporting enterprise.

5. Extraordinary items should be reported separately in the appropriate section of the profit and loss account, net of their associated taxes. Such taxes, where material should be disclosed in the Notes to the Accounts.

6. Exceptional items should be separately reported as a part of the results of ordinary activities.

7. Errors that result from the use of incorrect accounting estimates including those of estimated tax should be treated in the current year, as part of the result of ordinary activities.

8. A change in accounting principle should be reported by including in the profit and loss account of the current year, only the portion that relates to the year, and the cumulative amount resulting from a change to the new accounting principles should be taken to Retained Earnings.

9. Errors in misapplication of accounting principle, when discovered should be corrected by adjusting the appropriate accounts including Retained Profits/Reserves.

10. Prior year adjustments should be reported in the net of associated taxes.

DISCLOSURE IN FINANCIAL STATEMENTS

1. Extraordinary items, net of associated taxes, should be disclosed in the appropriate section of the Profit and Loss Account.

2. Prior year adjustments, net of the associated taxes, should be disclosed in the Retained Profits/Reserves section of the Profit and Loss Account.

3. Exceptional Items, gross of any associated taxes, should be disclosed in the Profit and Loss Account.

PART 5

NOTES ON LEGAL REQUIREMENTS

1. The requirements of this Standard are complementary to any disclosure requirement of the company Act 1968 and related regulations.

PART 6

COMPLIANCE WITH INTERNATIONAL ACCOUNTING STANDARD No. 8

1. The requirements of this Standard accord substantially with the requirements of the International Accounting Standard No. 8 – Unusual and Prior Period Items and Changes in Accounting Policies.

EFFECTIVE DATE

1. The Standard becomes operative for financial statements covering period beginning on or after 1st January, 1988.

Part 5

This standard meets the International Accounting Standard No. 8 requirements and is effective from 1st January, 1988.

ON FOREIGN CURRENCY

CHAPTER EIGHT
CONVERSIONS AND TRANSLATIONS
IAS 21

PART 1

INTRODUCTION

Organizations or individuals in Nigeria often engage in business dealings, governments, enterprises of individuals in other countries. These dealings may involve the payment, receipt or transfer of foreign currency or the creation of foreign currency assets and liabilities.

1. In each transaction with a foreign party, the invoice price is usually quoted in terms of a foreign currency which is not necessarily the domestic currency of that party. For the transaction to be reflected in the Nigeria Enterprise accounts, the amount must be converted into Naira.

2. Transactions between parties in different countries generally require one party to purchase some foreign currency in order to settle its obligations. Between the date of the initial transaction and the final settlement, there may be fluctuations in the exchange rate, which may result in a gain or loss.

A Nigerian company maintaining a branch office in a foreign country or holding an equity interest in a foreign company must translate the accounting expressed in foreign currency into Naira before the financial statements be consolidated or combined.

1. The primary objectives of this statement are to provide uniform account treatment for:

a) Foreign exchange transactions and,

The translation by a Nigerian enterprise of the financial statements of its foreign branches, subsidiaries, associates or joint ventures based in a country.

PART 2

DEFINITIONS

1. The following terms are used in this statement with the meanings specified:

a) Foreign Currency is any other than the domestic currency, the Naira.

b) Conversion is the process of expressing a foreign currency amount in Naira at an appropriate rate of exchange. (see appendix).

c) Translation is the restating of accounting balances of foreign operations at their equivalents in Naira.

d) Exchange Rate is the rate at which a country's currency is exchanged for another country's currency. Some exchange rates that are used in practice are presented below:

(i) Official Exchange Rate is that established by the appropriate governmental agency for eligible transactions. A country may have several official rates, each designated for use for a particular economic activity and which also reflects governmental policies concerning desired economic goals. Before the introduction of the Foreign Exchange Markets in September, 1986. The Central Bank of Nigeria provided the only official exchange rate in Nigeria.

(ii) Spot Rate is the exchange rate prevailing on a particular day. This is usually the rate used to settle accounts at the end of the day for immediate delivery of currency. In Nigeria, each Authorized Dealer has Spot Rate determined either from bidding on Foreign Exchange Market or from negotiated rates on funds from other sources.

(iii) Closing Rate of Exchange is the exchange rate ruling at the balance sheet date

(iv) Forward Rate is the rate quoted or agreed upon now for future delivery of currency between the parties involved.

e) Reporting Currency is the currency in which financial transactions are recorded and financial statements are presented. For Nigeria enterprises, the reporting currency is the Naira.

f) Foreign Operations refer to the business activities based in a country other than Nigeria, of a branch, subsidiary, associates or joint venture of a Nigerian enterprise. These may or may not form an integral part of the activities of the parent body in Nigeria. Foreign Operations form an integral part of Nigerian Enterprises. It has no separate cash flows.

g) A foreign Entity is said to exist where the activities of a branch, a subsidiary and associated company or a joint venture do not form an integral part of activities of the related enterprise in Nigeria.

h) Monetary items are monies held and items to be received or paid in money other assets and liabilities are Non-Monetary Items.

i) Foreign Currency Loan is an obligation repayable in foreign currency.

j) An authorized dealer in foreign currency is either a banker or a non-bank corporate organization appointed by the Federal Minister of Finance.

PART 3
EXPLANATORY NOTES

GENERAL

1. Some Nigerian enterprises have business dealings with their counterparts in other parts of the world. Such dealings may involve the importation or exportation of goods and services and the borrowing or lending money.

2. These business dealings give rise to the receipt. Payment or transfer of foreign currency between the parties. The foreign currency that is remitted to meet these financial obligations may be that of a country other than those of the parties concerned. Conversion to a third currency may thus be necessary.

When an enterprise in Nigeria exports goods or renders services to a foreign company, the bill forwarded to the foreign company may be made out in Nigeria (Naira)or foreign currency such as the Pound Sterling or the United States Dollar.

If the bill is in Naira, and the foreign company pays the bills in Naira transaction is treated like any other normal domestic transaction.

Where the foreign company is billed in a foreign currency, the payment received may be lodged into a foreign currency domiciliary account or sold to an authorized dealer. In both cases, the payment is converted at the exchange rate ruling at the date of receipt.

If the exchange rate in effect at the date of the receipt of payment is the same as it was at the date of sale, no exchange gain or loss has occurred; if however the rates at these dates are not the same, an exchange gain or loss occurred and it is recognized.

Suppose a Nigerian enterprise imports goods or receives services from a foreign company, and the bill is made in Naira. In that case, the transaction is treated as though it was a domestic transaction.

CONVERSION

Transactions in foreign currencies are normally converted at the rates ruling on the transaction dates.

Exchange gains or losses may arise on conversion and they usually require recognition in the Profit and Loss Account.

Usually, gains or losses on transactions arise because of the movement in foreign exchange rate between the date of initial transaction and the date of settlement. Such gains or losses on conversion are taken to the Profit and Loss Account as part of the operation of the period.

At the Balance Sheet date, balances in foreign currencies including domiciliary accounts are converted into Naira using closing rates. However, that rate is used when a balance is settled at a contracted rate. All differences arising on conversion are usually taken to the Profit and Loss Account, except differences on long-term foreign currency monetary items, which may be deferred and taken to the Profit and Loss Account on a systematic basis over the remaining lives of the monetary items concerned. However, losses on such items are not usually deferred if it is reasonable to expect that exchange loses will reoccur on the same items in future.

TRANSLATION OF THE ACCOUNTS OF FOREIGN OPERATIONS

1. Several methods of translating foreign currency account balance representing assets, liabilities, revenues and expenses of foreign operations, are in use:

i. **Closing Rate Method:** All assets and liabilities are translated at the rate ruling at the Balance Sheet date. This method is sometimes also referred to as the Current Rate Method.

ii. **Temporal Method:** Under this method, current assets and liabilities are translated at the rate ruling on the balance sheet date, and non-current assets and liabilities are translated at the applicable historical rates on the dates they were acquired or incurred. This method is sometimes referred to as the Current-Non-Current Method.

iii. **Monetary, Non-Monetary Method:** Under this method, monetary assets and liabilities are translated at the rates ruling at the balance sheet date and non-monetary assets and liabilities at the historical rates ruling at the dates they were acquired or incurred. Assets and liabilities are regarded and classified as non-monetary.

2. Foreign operations may be conducted through a branch, a subsidiary, an associate or a joint venture. Depending on the relationship, foreign operations may or may not form an integral part of the activities of the related enterprise resident in Nigeria.

3. Usually, before the accounts of a foreign branch, a subsidiary, an associate or a joint venture of a Nigerian enterprise are translated to combine or consolidate the financial statements, the relationship between them are carefully analyzed. The nature of the relationships between each of the foreign entities will determine whether the temporal method or the closing Rate Method of translation is to be used.

4. Suppose the accounts of any foreign branch, subsidiary associate, or venture are not in conformity with the Statements of Accounting Standard. In that case, such accounts are adjusted to conform with the Nigerian Standards before combining or consolidating them with the accounts of the Nigerian parent enterprise.

5. Currently, most enterprises in Nigeria tend to carry out their foreign-based business activities through branches. However, because of exchange control restrictions, such branches usually maintain separate cash flows. The actual movement of funds between the branches and their Head Offices in Nigeria tend to be infrequent and mainly in an outward direction. In such circumstances, it is usual to translate the accounts of such foreign operations using the closing rate method.

6. In those special cases where foreign operations are carried on as an integral part of the activities of the parent enterprise in Nigeria with no separate cash flow being maintained by the foreign operations, the

accounts of such foreign operations are sometimes translated using either the Closing Rate Method or the Temporal Method.

7. In some enterprises, revenue and expense accounts for their foreign operations are translated at year end, under the Closing Rate Method, using the simple average of opening and the closing rates. If the activities of the foreign operations are seasonal, a weighted average exchange rate is sometimes used.

8. Some enterprises using the closing rate method translate both fixed assets and their associated depreciation charges into Naira at the rate ruling on the balance sheet date. Sometimes, a weighted average exchange rate is used for additions or retirements, or the average exchange rate is used for additions or retirements of fixed assets at different times.

9. A few enterprises use the Monetary, non-monetary Method. A clear distinction is usually made between monetary assets and liabilities. Monetary items are translated at the rates ruling on the balance sheet date. On the other hand, non-monetary assets and liabilities are translated at the historical rates ruling at the date they were acquired or incurred.

10. Accruals and prepayments resulting from services rendered or received are usually translated to the reporting currency at the Closing Rate. Any exchange differences between the rate ruling on the translation date and settlement date are usually taken to the Profit and Loss Account.

11. Exchange gains or losses may arise on translation and usually require recognition in the Profit and Loss Account, Revenue Reserve Account or Capital Reserve Account. However, exchange gains or losses resulting from translating the accounts of foreign entities that do not form an integral part of the activities of the Nigerian parent enterprise are sometimes taken to Revenue or Capital Reserve.

12. Suppose a foreign branch, a subsidiary, or an associated company operates as an integral part of the operations of its Nigerian enterprise. In that case, the financial statements of such a branch, a subsidiary, or an associated company are translated using another temporal method.

13. Exchange gains or losses on such transactions are taken to the Profit and Loss Account as a part of the results of the operations of the period.

DEVALUATION

1. Where there is a devaluation of foreign currency as a result of acute depreciation or outright devaluation by the relevant government, this fact is usually recognized in the accounts as an exceptional event.

2. Where there is no means of hedging against exchange losses as a result of severe depreciation or formal devaluation and where liabilities resulting from recent acquisition of assets invoiced in foreign currency are affected, the exchange differences may be included as part of the cost of the asset provided that the adjustment carrying amount does not exceed the lower of replacement cost the amount recoverable from the use of sale of the asset.

RESTRICTIONS OF FOREIGN EXCHANGE REMITTANCE

1. Where there are restrictions on the remittance of the profits of a foreign operation the related Nigerian enterprise may not treat such profits as part of its earnings until received and if the operations form an integral part of the operations, the related Nigerian enterprise, combination or consideration become inappropriate in the circumstance.

2. Sometimes, a long-term receivable or payable is settled by a series of installment spread out over a period of years, and the portion of the long-term receivable or payable relating to each installment is considered to have a separate life accordingly, any exchange gain or loss is calculated only for each portion of the long-term receivable or payable and amortised over its particular remaining life.

3. The life of a long-term monetary asset or liability may be changed by renegotiation of its terms or by refinancing. If the negotiated refinanced loan is in the same currency as that of the original loan, any unamortised balance or unrealised exchange gains or losses at the date of renegotiation or refinanced may be amortised over the lesser of:

a) The remaining life of the original assets or liability; and

b) The life of the renegotiated or refinanced asset or liability. Any gains or losses arising from changes in exchange rates occurring subsequent to the date of renegotiation or refinancing relating to the negotiated refinanced loan are often amortised over its remaining life.

DISCLOSURE PATTERNS

1. At present, the information disclosed by enterprises in Nigeria is not uniform for instance, some enterprises do not disclose:

a) Their accounting policies with respect to foreign exchange conversion and transactions.

b) The effects on the accounts of significant movements in exchange between the year end and the time the accounts are finalized.

c) The net total gains or losses in the Profit and Loss Account arising from changes in exchange rates.

PART 4
ACCOUNTING STANDARD

FOREIGN EXCHANGE CONVERSIONS AND TRANSLATIONS

The Accounting Standard comprises paragraphs 37-47 of this Statement. The Standard should be read in the context of all other parts of this Statement and of the Preface to Statements of Accounting Standards published by the NASB.

1. A reporting enterprise should state its accounting policy with respect to foreign Exchange Conversions and Translations. Such an accounting policy should form an integral part of financial statements as prescribed by IAS 1.

2. Since the Naira is the reporting currency and unit of measuring transactions in foreign currencies should be converted into Naira at the rates of exchange ruling at the dates of such transactions. Differences arising at the dates of settlements should be taken to the Profit and Loss Account.

3. At the Balance Sheet date, balances of foreign currencies should be converted into Naira using the closing rate. However, when a balance is settled at a contracted rate, that rate should be used. All differences on long term foreign currency monetary items which should either be written off or deferred and taken to the Profit and Loss Account on a systematic basis over the remaining lives of the monetary items concerned. However, loses on such items should not be deferred if it is reasonable to expect that exchange losses will recur on the items in future.

TRANSLATION OF FINANCIAL STATEMENTS OF FOREIGN OPERATIONS

Financial Statements of a foreign entity should be modified, where necessary to meet the accounting Standards set in Nigeria before consolidation or combination with the accounts of the related Nigerian enterprise.

The financial statements of a foreign entity should be incorporated in the accounts of the related Nigerian enterprise using the Closing Rate method as follows:

1. Assets and Liabilities, both monetary and non0monetary should be translated in the closing rate;

2. The exchange differences resulting from translating the opening net investment in the foreign entity at an exchange rate different from that at which it was previously reported should be taken to a Capital Reserve Account;

3. Income Statement items should be translated either at the closing rate or at the exchange rates at the date of the transactions. Differences arising from translating income statement items at exchange rates other than the closing rate whilst translating balance sheet items at the closing rate should be taken to Income or Revenue Reserves;

4. Any exchange differences arising from other changes to shareholder interest account in the foreign entity should be recognized in the appropriate shareholder interest account such as Share Capital Reserve or Revenue Reserve.

5. In those special cases, where a foreign operation is carried on as an integral part of the activities of the parent enterprise in Nigeria with no separate cash flow being maintained by the foreign operations, the assets, liabilities and capital accounts of such a foreign operation should be translated using either the Temporal Method or the Closing Rate Method Revenue and expense accounts should be translated using the average exchange rate, under Temporal Method or the Closing Rate Method.

6. A parent enterprise should not treat the profit of its foreign operations, the remittance of which is restricted, as part of its earnings until received.

7. When there is no means of hedging against foreign exchange losses as a result of severe depreciation or formal devaluation and where liabilities resulting from recent acquisition of assets invoiced in foreign currency are affected, the exchange difference may be included as a part of the cost of the asset provided that the adjusted carrying the amount does not exceed the lower of replacement cost or the amount recoverable from the use of sale of the asset.

8. Sometimes, a long-term receivable or payable is settled by a series of installments spread over a period of years. The portion of the long-term receivable or payable relating to each installment should be considered to have a separate life. Accordingly, any exchange gain or loss should be calculated for each portion of the long-term receivable or payable and amortised over its particular life.

9. The life of a long-term monetary assets or liability may be changed by renegotiation of its terms or by refinancing. If the negotiated or refinanced loan is in the same currency as that of the original loan, any unamortised balance of unrealised exchange gains or losses at the date of renegotiation or refinancing should be amortised over the lesser of:

a) The remaining life of the original assets or liability; and

b) The life of the renegotiated or refinanced asset or liability. Any gains or losses arising from changes in exchange rates occurring subsequent to the dates of renegotiation or refinancing, relating to the negotiated or refinanced loan should be amortised over its remaining life.

DISCLOSURE

In addition to the disclosure required by IAS 1, Disclosure of Accounting Policies, and IAS 2, Information to be Disclosed in Financial Statements, the following Disclosures should be made in appropriate sections financial statements of a Nigerian enterprise:

1. The accounting policy with respect to treatment of foreign exchange conversions translation;

2. The treatment given to foreign exchange gains/losses;

3. The net total gains or losses arising from changes in foreign exchange rates taken to the Profit and Loss Account;

4. Restriction, if any, on repatriation of investments or returns thereon to Nigeria.

5. Post balance sheet rate movement on transactions that have significant impact on the Profit and Loss Account and Balance Sheet items should be Notes to the Accounts.

6. The number of gains or losses deferred.

APPENDIX

DIFFICULTIES IN ESTABLISHING A SINGLE FOREIGN RATE

At present, fortnightly, bidding for foreign exchange is held in the official Foreign Exchange Market (FEM) and each successful bank at the bidding is compelled to self-foreign currency won at a fixed small percentage over the particular price it bid for the foreign currency. As a result, at any point in time, the selling rates for foreign currency under FEM vary from bank to bank.

Apart from the foreign currency purchased by banks under FEM and which they can sell only for stipulated transactions, the bank are allowed to purchase foreign currency ("Autonomous Fund") at any rate they wish to subject the restriction that they cannot resell it at more than a fixed percentage over the price at which they purchased the particular fund concerned. Since no averaging of purchased price is permitted, a bank has to match every specific purchase of foreign currency with specific sales of the funds concerned. As a result, apart from the fact that at any point in time, each bank may be applying more than one rate for transactions in autonomous funds on a particular day.

This at present, each bank has its own FEM rate determined at fortnightly bidding. Similarly, each bank has its own rate derived from autonomous funds. In the circumstance, it becomes rather difficult for enterprises to have and the NASB to select and recommend a single rate ruling on a particular date.

IAS 6 EXTRA-IORDINARY ITEMS AND PRIOR YEAR ADJUSTMENT

This is similar to IAS 8 and SSAP 6

This IAS is very important hence the following shows questions set in the past. As they are similar questions, they are given similar solutions.

IAS 6 are in: (i)   Question 2(c) ICAN PE 1 May, 2021

1. ICAN November, 2018 Question 2

2. ICAN May, 2023, Question 4

Illustration 1

Distinguish between:

1. Exceptional Items

2. Extra-Ordinary Items

3. Prior Year Items

4. Prior Year Adjustment

Illustration 2

Babyface Limited has a turnover of $12 million and pre-profit of $2 million before taking account of the following items:

1. Cost of $1.5 million incurred in terminating production at one of the company's factories.

2. Provision for an abnormally large debt of $1million arising in a trading contract.

3. Profits of $300,000 on sales of Plant & machinery written off in a previous year when production of the particular product ceased.

4. An extra $200,000 contribution by the Company to the employee's pension fund.

You are required to:

a) Indicate whether items (i) to (v) above should be treated as exceptional, extra ordinary or normal trading transactions with reference to IAS 6 (ICAN November, 2018. Question 2).

IAS 6 Question 3

The following are some happenings in some companies. State the type of items with reference to IAS 6.

1. The company will provide an extra $110,000 towards the end of service benefit scheme introduced early in the year. This sum represents 12% of the payroll of the company's employees who are members of the Scheme, which must be set aside for that purpose as from that year.

2. Provision for bad debt of $150,000 arising on the death of one of the major local distributors of the company's production.

3. On 2nd February, 19 x 3 a loss of $175,000 was made on disposal of all insurance claims on a Machinery which was involved in a fire accident in November, 19 x 2. The last financial year was 19 x 2 December, 31.

4. Costs of $250,000 incurred in demolition and terminating production at one of the branches.

5. Additional Depreciation of $420,000 relating to previous year as a result of the mis-posting of the cost of an item of Machinery into stock account.

6. Taxation under-provision in respect of previous year's profit arising from the change in the company's income tax rate was $27,000.

7. The discovery of fraud in Stocks of $220,000 for items that were supposedly supplied to the company and included in the year-end valuation of one of the branches, but were in fact never supplied although all documentations showed evidence of full delivery.

Solution1

1. Exceptional items are those that though normal to activity of an enterprise are abnormal e.g. Abnormal high bad debts.

2. Extra-ordinary items – are those that occur outside the ordinary activities of an enterprise and are not expected to recur frequently e.g., the discontinuance of a significant part of the business, the sale of an investment not acquired with the intension of resale, writing off because of unusual events or developments during the period and the expropriation of assets.

3. Prior Year Items: These are items of revenue and expenses that were recorded this year but would have been recorded in a previous year.

Prior year items are two types: Adjustable and non-adjustable items.

Prior year adjustable items are expenses that were recorded this year but would have been recorded in a prior year if all of the facts had been known. They do not include adjustments for differences between actual and accounting estimates.

Infact, they are material adjustments applicable to prior items year arising from changes in accounting policies and from the correction of fundamental errors.

Solution 2

Babyface Limited

1. Cost of $1.5 million incurred in terminating production Extra ordinary items.

2. Provision for an abnormally large-debt of $1 million-This normal trading event which material hence called Exceptional item.

3. Profit of $300,000 on sale of Plant and Machinery written off in a previous year – Extra-ordinary item.

4. An extra $200,000 contribution by the company – Exceptional item

Solution 3

1. Provision for an extra $110,000 = Exceptional item

2. Bad debts provision of $150,000 = Abnormal hence exceptional

3. Loss of $175,000 on insurance claims = both prior year adjustment item and exceptional item

4. Cost of terminating production in a branch =   Extra-ordinary item

5. Additional depreciation of $120,000 for previous year = Prior year adjustment item

6. Taxation under provision - normal adjustment item.

7. Fraud in stocks – $220,000 = If current year, exceptional item – but if previous year, prior year adjustment.

CHAPTER NINE
STATEMENT OF ACCOUNTING STANDARD
IAS 8

ON ACCOUNTING FOR EMPLOYEES' RETIREMENT BENEFITS

PART I

INTRODUCTION

1. Many charitable organizations, government and business establishments provide retirement benefits for their employees. Retirement benefits can consist of monthly payments to former employees or a lump sum upon attainment of a specific retirement age and may include additional payments in case of death or disability. Depending on the terms of retirement benefits plan, some employers bear the entire cost of a retirement plan whilst other employers contribute a proportion of the cost of plan with the employee bearing the remaining fraction.

2. Some retirement plans evidenced by a well-articulated document forming a part of the total employment contract of the employees. Some plans are not so clear and can only be inferred from the employers' policies practices. In some countries, laws prescribe the minimum benefits payable to a qualified employee to protect the employee.

3. The main issue involved in accounting for retirement benefits are the determination of the:

a) Amount due to employees before or after the plan implementation date.

b) Amount of funding required in order to meet employees' entitlements upon retirement and

c) Amount of information to be disclosed in financial statements.

4. The primary objectives of this statement are to narrow the differences in the methods or manner used in:

a) Measuring the amount of retirement obligations under retirement benefits plans

b) Allocating the cost of the plan and recognizing resulting gains or losses to the accounting periods, and

c) Disclosing the plan and the effects of the plan implementation on the reporting enterprise as accurately as possible.

5. This statement will not cover:

a) Benefits resulting from termination indemnities:

b) Long-term leave benefits;

c) Redundancy plans or strictly gratuitous schemes, health and welfare or bonus plans; and

d) National insurance benefit schemes, government pension schemes and social arrangements such as National Provident Fund.

PART II

DEFINITIONS

1. In this statement, the following terms are used as described below:

2. Provident, pension, retirement benefit scheme, are contracts, formal or informal between employers and employees specifying what benefits accrue to employee upon the attainment of a specified age or length of service and other obligations and responsibilities of the two parties.

3. A funded retirement scheme is one in which the employer agrees to make periodic payments to an agency usually an insurance company, bank or a trustee that manages the plan.

4. Funding is the process of making irrevocable periodic payments towards a plan to meet future obligations for the payment of retirement benefits.

5. Unfunded schemes is one in which there is no specific periodic payment towards a plan.

6. A qualifying scheme meets all the requirements of the joint Tax Board as to the employers' and employees' contribution and investment of trust funds with respect to status.

7. Contributory schemes are those that require employers and employees to contribute to the scheme.

8. Non-contributory schemes are those that require no contributions from the employees.

9. Vested benefits refer to the portion of retirement benefits that have accrued to the employee whether or not he remains employed by the enterprise.

10. Self-administered scheme is one in which the investment and management of the scheme are undertaken in-house.

11. Beneficiaries are those employees covered by a scheme or persons nominated by them as recipients of the benefits.

12. Net asset available for benefits refer to the excess of assets over liabilities.

13. Actuarial assumptions refer to the set of assumptions as to rates of mortality of employees, interest, inflation, etc., used by the actuary in arriving at any actual calculations or valuations.

14. Actuarial value of assets is the value determined by the actuary based on estimated futures income, proceed of sales or redemption of assets.

15. Actuarial value of liabilities is the estimated value of expenditures of the fund.

16. Actuarial deficiency is the excess of actuarial value of assets over the actuarial value of liabilities.

17. Actuarial surplus is the excess of assets' actuarial value over liabilities' actuarial value.

18. Provident fund is a scheme in which the employee receives a lump-sum upon cessation of membership in the scheme.

19. Pensionable service may include years of service before, during and after introduction of scheme.

20. A normal retirement age is the earliest age a fund beneficiary is entitled to receive benefit under the scheme without regard to disability or ill-health provision that may allow for early retirement.

21. Transfer payment is payment made to another scheme when a beneficiary of the former scheme changes employment.

22. Top hat scheme is a scheme planned for top executives or directors of an organization to augment the benefits received from the general scheme.

PART III

EXPLANATORY NOTES

1. In the recent past, employee retirement costs of pension plan costs have become an important portion of the operating costs of many business enterprises. Consequently, the manner in which such costs are calculated and accounted for may have a significant effect on the reported profits of business enterprises and may result in lack of comparability between the results of such enterprises from one period to the other.

2. Employee retirement schemes or pension plans are usually designed with the aim of providing enough funds for current or former employees. Such entitlements may include widow's or orphan's and disability benefits.

3. A pension plan or retirement scheme means a formal or informal contract between employer and employees specifying what benefits accrue to employees upon the attainment of a specified retirement age. Other obligations and responsibilities of the parties under the contract are usually specified. Under this kind of arrangement, there may also be conditions for membership qualification. A formula for calculating the amount receivable by an employee or his beneficiaries and a commencement date for an employee to qualify for benefit may also be given.

4. Gratuitous payment or arbitrary amounts decided only on or after an employee's retirement do not constitute a pension plan or retirement scheme for this statement. However, any scheme that systematically provides retirement benefits to employees after leaving employment will be considered a pension scheme.

5. Sometimes, company practices may provide conclusive evidence that a plan in effect although such a plan may not be in writing. The provisions f this statement cover such a situation and refer to unfunded plans, insured plans, trust fund plans, defined-contribution plans and defined-benefit plans.

6. Different obligations are assumed by different employers For example, some employers may take direct responsibility for meeting the benefits specified in retirement plans. In such a situation, any

deficiency in funding of the plan is made up by the company. (This is also known as define-benefits plan).

7. Retirement benefits can be determined in either of two ways, namely;

a) As a function of years of service and earnings

b) As a function of accumulated contribution

8. In this first case, a retirement benefit plan can be either a defined contribution plan, the employer and often the employees make contributions to a fund or plan at intervals and in specified amounts. The fund or plan generated earnings that enhance its value.

9. When needed, actuarial advice may be obtained if the fund is to provide a future benefit based on present contributions and projected investments earnings. Usually, contributions that incorporate actuarial factors do not discharge employers from their obligations under the scheme.

10. When a pension scheme is introduced or an improvement is made on an old scheme, pension entitlements are often granted to employees who have been working before the new scheme or the improvement as though the new scheme or the improvement had been applicable from the commencement of their service or some other agreed period. Past service liability is therefore recognized and the funding thereof usually can be spread over a number of years.

11. Under a benefit-based scheme, any subsequent increase in the pay of employees will include a proportionate increase in past service liability to reflect the under-funding. Thus, any current pay increase creates two liability components i.e. past service liability and current pension cost.

12. Disbursement of pension benefits may rest with:

a) An employer who administers his own scheme;

b) A life insurance company;

c) An agent or trustee;

d) An industry-wide pension fund; or

e) A combination of (a) to (d)

13. In order to qualify as a pension/provident fund scheme, certain condition stipulated by the Joint Tax Board must be met. Those schemes that qualify will gain tax advantages.

14. Retirement plans may provide for a measure or vesting, in which case, there is the passing over of rights to an employee either to pension benefits or to withdrawal privileges regarding the employer's contributions. The employee who remains with his employer until retirement is usually unaffected by vesting.

15. Benefits to beneficiaries of a plan may fall into two categories, those to which rights are vested and those that are yet to vest within the accounting period: At the end an accounting period; the liability of beneficiaries' benefits may include both. It is usually advisable to indicate which benefits are

vested and which are yet to be vested so that workers and readers of financial statements may assess the plan's ability to meet its obligations when workers withdraw from it or retire under the plan.

16. Under the advanced financing method, funds are provided on a regular basis during the active working life of employees. Payments into the funds are usually based on actuarial calculations and may be in the form of a lump sum or regular contributions. An advance funding may be fully under or over funded. Non-self-administered pension schemes are financed through the advance financing method, and therefore are funded.

17. Under pay-as-you-go system, the active working generation provides the funds for pensions of those who have retired.

18. In practice, a funded retirement benefit plan can be either a defined contribution plan or defined benefit plan each having its own characteristics. Under the defined contribution plan, the employees contribute to a fund or plan at intervals and in specified amounts. The fund or plan generates earnings that enhance its value. When needed actuarial advice may be obtained if the fund is to provide expected future benefits based on present contribution and projected investment earning. Usually, contributions that incorporate actuarial fact do not discharge the employer from their obligations under scheme.

19. For employers that wish to have a funded scheme, the services of an insurance company may be engaged. Insurance companies provide a wide variety contracts as far as contributory plans are concerned.

20. All parties to a retirement benefit plan are interested in its level of funding management. Beneficiaries are interested because they directly affect the level of funding whereas the employers are under moral and sometimes legal obligations to provide benefits to their retiring employees.

DETERMINATION OF RETIREMENT COST

1. Cost-based retirement scheme are relatively easy to compute since they; made up of past service and current costs arrived at on the basis of the form contained in the scheme. The two costs combined give the retirement exp-for the period.

2. In the case of benefit-based schemes, many factors are considered in actual computations when arriving at the estimated retirement costs for the period. Some factors that are considered include mortality rate, salaries, inflation, trend employment and the amounts of interest to be earned on the fund. Although the accountant may not be involved in actuarial computations, he is expected to be able to understand the actuarial assumptions made to assure himself they are realistic, consistent and defensible. The costs that are arrived at will reflect benefits that will accrue to employees.

3. Another aspect of benefit cost consideration is funding. While accounting retirement cost is concerned with the build-up of retirement benefits that are obligate during employees' working lives, funding deals with provision of cash and other considerations for discharging such obligations. A distinction beta accounting for and funding of retirement benefits is not always made in practice.

4. In order to properly match costs with re-venue generated, full retirement cost are accrued and charged to operations in the periods they- are general there are past service costs associated with employees, such costs are v& allocated on the basis of employees expected working lives.

5. Where a retirement benefit scheme is amended and there is a past service associated with the amendment, such cost is also usually allocated systematic and consistently to relevant accounting periods as in paragraph.

6. Often, introducing a new retirement scheme results in a lump sum benefits cost associated with past employee services. Some companies take the view that such past service costs, relate to past periods and, therefore reflect such costs as an adjustment to retained earnings. Other companies take the view that past service costs still relate to the current workforce. Years subsequent to the introduction of the scheme bear the past service costs.

7. If vested past service benefits are unaccounted for or only partially accounted for, such past service costs are often charged to operations, and a liability is recognized until funded. The liability is gradually liquidated with periodic funding in accordance with the provisions of the scheme.

ACTUARIAL COST METHODS

1. Many actuarial cost methods were developed for funding purposes, although some are also good for accounting purposes. The two broad categories of actuarial methods in use are Accrued Benefit Cost Method and Projected Benefit Cost Method.

a) Accrued benefit cost method - under this method, the amount assigned to the current year usually represents the present value of the increase in present employee's retirement benefits resulting from that years services. This method incorporates increases in the benefits of the individual employee as he approaches his retirement age. In most plans, the retirement benefits may be related to salary levels, which may increase from year to year. The aggregate retirement cost for the workforce increases with any increase in its average age.

b) Projected benefit cost method - under this method, the amount assigned to the current year usually represents the level of amount that will provide for the estimated projected retirement benefits over the service lives of either the individual employee or the employees group. Costs computed under this method tends to vary year by year depending on the actuarial assumptions made.

2. Some actuarial cost methods assign to subsequent years, the cost arising at the adoption or amendment of a plan. Other methods assign a portion of the cost to prior to the adoption or amendment of a plan and assign the remainder to subsequent years. At the adoption of a plan, the portion of cost assigned to subsequent years is known as normal cost. Past services are usually accrued for accounting purposes and a liability is established. Such a liability is through funding.

3. Often, a valuation is made at a later date after the adoption of a scheme in which additional costs may be assigned to the prior years. This cost is known prior service-cost which is accrued like past service cost as in paragraph 30.

4. Past service costs or prior service costs may be fully funded, partially funded or not at all funded, depending on the requirements of a scheme. It is usually more advantageous to fund past or prior service costs. Such costs are included in the accounts as part of current operating cost for accounting purposes.

5. Actuarial cost methods that are used arc those that measure retirement benefit employees systematically from year to year. Therefore, methods that result in huge differences between actual employees' annual remuneration and actuarial calculation are avoided.

ACTUARIAL GAINS OR LOSSES

1. Actuarial gains or losses result from the divergence between actual remuneration of employees and that projected. Several factors can be responsible for tit divergence among which are assumptions about salary, turnover or employee's mortality rate, inflation and rate of return on investment earn-able by the fund. In order to recognize the differences between estimated future events, reviews are made periodically. These periodic reviews, usually between three and five years, help make actuarial assumptions more realistic.

2. The primary concern with respect 10 actuarial gains or losses is the time; recognize that in accounts. In practice, three methods are in use:

a) Immediate recognition in which gains are immediately taken as deductions from current or future retirement costs whilst losses treated as additions;

b) Spreading in which the net gains or losses are applied to currents, future costs either through the normal cost or through past service cost; and

c) Averaging in which case, an average is taken or net annual gain losses developed from past occurrences but projected on future events and applied to normal costs.

3. Unrealised appreciation and depreciation in the value of investments retirement benefit funds are often considered forms of actuarial losses. In practice, they are not consistently treated as deductions or as current or future retirement benefits expenses.

4. Some employee's retirement benefit plans make provision for employees to Ineligible immediately they are employed: some plans put restrictions on age or length of service before qualification, whilst the rest stats states condition conditions employees must meet before they qualify. Coverage may be detailed or broadly outlined. Depending on the provisions of the retirement benefit plans, actuarial calculation may exclude employees on the basis of age probability of retirement, disability or death.

5. If provisions are made for employees at the time of employment and actuarial assumptions turn to be unduly favorable, over-funding occurs in such a situation, the over-funding may reduce employees current retirement costs whilst any under-funded amount is added to the current retirement cost. It is safer to include all potential beneficiaries of a retirement benefit scheme and to make provision for turnover, mortality, inflation and other factors if funding fluctuations are minimized.

INSURED PLANS

1. Insurance companies always undertake insured plans. In such insured plans funding arrangements are often used for accounting purposes also Like the other methods already discussed, certain elements of pension cost account for the difference between the amount paid to an insurance company 'and the trial charged to the accounts during the period.

2. Defined benefit plans maintain a set of accounts ordinarily associated with business enterprises. Assets, liabilities and revenue accounts are often maintained and general-purpose financing statements are prepared and forwarded to employers and beneficiaries alike. For very large organizations operating trust and pension departments, a statement of source and application of funds may be included.

ASSETS

1. The assets of a defined benefit plan will include:

a) Contributions receivable (due from employers, employees).

b) Investments of the plan (these include equity or debt securities and real estate):

c) Cash and other monetary assets;

d) Other operating assets.

2. Defined benefit plan assets are usually measured at market value (not realizable value) or lower cost, unless there had been a subsequent revaluation. The lowest value is used because it provides beneficiaries and employers reliable information for evaluating the plan's ability to meet its obligations under the scheme.

3. Some plans invest in insurance policies in order to meet members' benefits. Such policies arc valued at their current net realizable values by actually determined assessment of the amount recoverable from the policies.

LIABILITIES

1. Liabilities of a defined plan will include:

a) Accounts payable or creditors

b) Borrowing;

c) Liabilities from members' vested benefits; and

d) Current pensioners' benefits.

2. Accounts payable and borrowing are easy to determine and do not create measurement problems. However, liability for members' benefits could create measurement problems.

3. In measuring liability for members' benefits, all benefits due to all beneficiaries of the plan resulting from their past and present services are expected to be considered. The liability so determined reflects

the fact that future sacrifice of economic benefits by reporting entity are expected to be made to meet the needs of the fund. The sacrifice is in the form of transfer of assets (cash and marketable securities) in order to fund the plan.

4. The liability of a defined benefit plan in respect of benefit payable is calculated on the basis of the present value of expected future payments which arise from membership of the plan or to the reporting date or balance sheet date. Actual assumptions are usually the basis for such calculations.

5. At the balance sheet date, liability for members benefit will include benefits which have been vested to members and those that nave not. Although vesting is a legal matter, for accounting purposes, future benefits are to be accrued. In order to have readers of financial statement to understand the financial position of a fund, it is advisable to disclose the vested and non-vested amounts separately

REVENUE

1. Revenues of the defined benefit plan

a) Investment revenue:

b) Contribution revenue,

c) Other items of revenue.

Investment revenue may include interest and dividends, property rentals and profit from sale of investments. Contributions from members, employers and others constitute the contributions revenue. Other revenue items will include insurance policy payments and short-term gains on investments or foreign currency conversions. All these items of revenue are reported in the Income and Expenditure Account of the Fund;

EXPENSES

1. Expense of defined plan will include:

a) General administration expenses;

b) Contribution paid or payable;

c) Investment related expenses

d) Benefit related expenses

All these expenses are usually incurred in maintaining the fund in transferring benefits to the beneficiaries. They encompass current expenses and those accrued for the purpose of showing benefits due to members in the future.

CHANGE IN ACCOUNTING METHOD

1. Where an enterprise changes from one acceptable method to the other, such a change is often disclosed in the Notes to the Accounts. If the change is from an old acceptable method to an unknown method, a

change in accounting policy may have occurred in which case IAS Disclosure of Accounting Policies will apply.

DISCLOSURE

1. Most enterprises in Nigeria do not disclose any information about the existence or non-existence of retirement or pension plans for their employees. The few that makes any disclosures do so in the Notes to the accounts. Users of financial statements would be better informed, if disclosures are made in the Notes to the Accounts of:

a) The existence of retirement or pension plans specifying the categories of employees that are covered by the plan or plans;

b) The company's accounting and funding policies;

c) Provision made for pension cost in the year;

d) The actuarial gains or losses in the year, if any, and how treated, and

e) Whether separate accounts are prepared for the scheme.

PART IV
ACCOUNTING STANDARD

EMPLOYEE RETIREMENT BENEFITS

The accounting Standard comprises paragraph 56-76 of this statement. Standard should be read in the context of all other parts of this statement and the preface to this statement of accounting standards published by the NASS.

1. This statement covers employee retirement schemes or provident pension plans in which there are formal or implied contracts between employers and employees specifying benefit or specific amounts due to employees upon die attainment of, a retirement age or due to disability, early leading or death. Furthermore, this statement's provisions cover unfunded plans, insured and uninsured plan trust fund plans, defined contribution plans and defined benefit plans.

2. A reporting enterprise should state its accounting policy with respect to funding of employee retirement benefits and this should be in. compliance with the provisions of IAS 1 - Disclosure of Accounts Policies.

3. In determining the costs of benefit-based plans or schemes:

a) Calculations should be made such that full retirement benefits are accrued to cover the active working lives of employees with reporting employer.

b) The basis for the calculations in (a) above should be constantly applied

c) The assumptions on which the calculations are based should be realistic and reviewed regularly.

1. When a pension or retirement scheme is introduced or and improvement is made on an old scheme, retirement entitlement due to the employees may be computed as though the new scheme or the improvement had been applicable from the commencement of their services. If there are past service costs associated with employees, such costs should be deferred and charged to current and future operations over a period not more than five years in a systematic and consistent manner.

2. Funds for retirement pension entitlements should be provided under the advance financing system. Pay-as-you-go system and unfunded scheme "are unacceptable because they fail to anticipate and provide in advance the entitlement of employees upon their retirement withdrawal or death.

3. A funded retirement benefits scheme or plan should be either a defined contribution plan or a defined benefit plan, with the characteristics of each properly documented and understood by the employees and employers. A funded retirement benefit scheme or plan may be self-administered or administered by a third party.

4. In order to match costs properly with revenues generated, full retirement benefit costs should be accrued and charged to operations in the period to which they relate.

5. Where vested past service benefits are unaccounted or only partially accounted for, such vested service costs should be. charged to current operations with a corresponding liability recognized. The liability should be reduced by related periodic funding payments until extinguished.

6. Since all actuarial cost methods cannot be used as a basis for accounting entries for retirement benefit costs, proper evaluation must be made of the method used by an enterprise Actuarial cost methods that should be used for the dual purposes should be those that measure retirement benefits of employees systematically from year to year.

7. Any adjustment in accrued benefit cost calculations brought about by actuarial revaluation should be included in the retirement benefit costs of the current period or spread over period not exceeding five years.

8. Where past service cost has been paid or reflected in the account in excess the amount charged to operations. The un-absorbed debit should be written out immediately to the income statement of the reporting entity. In the event of plan termination. Any unfulfilled obligation should be charged to income unless taken over by another plan.

TRUSTEES ACCOUNT

1. Under the defined benefit plan. Assets. Liability and revenue accounts should be maintained. General purpose financial statements should as income and expenditure account. Balance sheet and source and application of fund should be prepared and forwarded to the employers of their trustees, at least once in a year.

2. Assets of defined benefit plan should be measured at the market value cost. Whichever is lower. Unless current actuarial valuation is available.

3. Where a plan invests in insurance policies in order to meet members benefit such policies should be valued at their current net realizable value which is actuarial determined.

4. In the measurement of liability of member's benefit. All benefit due to beneficiaries either related to past or current services should be taken into consideration. Such liability created should be funded by the transfer of funds to the scheme within a period not exceeding five years.

5. The ability of a defined plan in respect of benefits, all benefits due to the beneficiaries either related to past or current services should be calculated on the basis of the present value of the expected future payments that arise from membership up to the reporting or balance sheet date. Relevant actual assumptions should be the basis for such calculations.

6. At the balance sheet date, liability for members benefits should include benefits which are vested for accounting purposes. All future benefits should be provided for and funded.

7. Revenues of a defined plan should include investment income proposed rentals profits from sale of investments, contributions from members, employers' insurance policy payments. Short-term gains on investment including foreign currency gains and losses and all other income. All the items should be reported in the revenue accounts of the fund.

8. Expenses of a defined benefit plan should include general administrative expenses, premiums paid or payable, investment-related expenses and other accruals with a view to reflecting due to members in the future. All these expenses should be shown in the appropriate sections of the fund's revenue accounts.

9. For a defined benefit plan, separate financial statements should be prepared in accordance with relevant statement of accounting standard and sent to the employers and employees or their trustees at least once a year.

DISCLOSURES

1. Every enterprise should disclose in the notes to the accounts the following information:

a) The existence of a retirement provident or pension plan and the categories of employees covered;

b) The accounting, actuarial and funding methods used and changes thereto, where a defined contribution or benefit plan exists; and

c) The provisions are made for retirement, provident, or pension costs for the year.

d) The standard meets the requirements of the International Accounting Standards Nos 19 and 36.

IAS 19
EMPLOYEES RETIREMENT BENEFITS

Illustration 1

Write short notes on:

a) Terminal funding

b) Past Service cost

Illustration 2

a) Distinguish between a "defined contribution" and a "defined benefit pension scheme", and

b) Explain the bases of accounting that should be applied in each case when determining the annual expenses of a company providing such scheme

Solution 1

a) Terminal Funding is a method of recognizing the projected cost of retirement benefits only at the time an employee retires.

b) Past service cost is the actuarial determined cost arising from the introduction of a retirement benefit plan or the making or improvement of such a plan.

Solution 2

a) There are two distinct types of pension schemes

In a defined contribution scheme, the employer will normally discharge his obligation by making agreed contributions to a pension scheme, and the benefits paid will depend upon the funds available from these contributions and investment earnings.

In a defined benefit scheme, the benefits to be paid will usually depend upon either the revalued carrier average or, more typically, the employee's final pay.

b) The accruals (matching) concept is used. In a defined contribution scheme, the employer's obligation at any point in time is restricted to the account of the contribution payable to date.

While in the defined benefit scheme, two basic approaches are used:

(i) The income approach aims to match the cost of pensions directly with the services received from the employee.

(ii) The balance sheet approach – Under this, the net actuarial pension liability or net asset at the beginning and end of the period is estimated strictly by reference to information relating to those points in time and the charge for the period from the change therein, adjusted for payments made during the period.

For more details read ICAN Newsletter titled the "Nigerian Accountant" Jan/March 20… IAS and IAS 19.

CHAPTER TEN
ACCOUNTING FOR DEPRECIATION
IAS 9

PART 1

INTRODUCTON

1. Property, plant and equipment, generally referred to as fixed assets are those tangible resources of an enterprise that are employed in its operations. Each item of fixed asset usually has a limited useful economic life during which it can be profitably used in the operation of the enterprise. Depreciation is the method of charging the cost of these fixed assets to operations. When the use of such fixed asset is no longer of economic benefit to the enterprise, the item is usually retired or disposed of.

2. This statement provides a guide for uniform and acceptable methods of determining and reporting depreciation on items of property, plant, and equipment, as well as whether such items are stated at their historical costs or revalued amounts.

3. The statements do not deal with depreciation on the following assets:

a) Regenerative natural resources such as forests, standing timber, cattle etc.

b) Non-regenerative resources include mineral deposits, oil and gas deposits, etc.

c) Real estate development property companies

d) Goodwill and other intangible assets such as trademarks, patents, etc.

PART 2

DEFINITIONS

1. The following terms are used in this statement with the meanings specified

a) Depreciation represents an estimate of the portion of the historical cost or revalued amount of a fixed asset chargeable to operations during an accounting period. In determining depreciation, cognizance is usually taken of the wear and tear on an asset resulting from use, affixion of time or obsolesce dictated by change in technology and market forces.

b) Depreciation Assets are items of property, plant and equipment with the following characteristics:

(i)   Have lives of over one year;

(ii) Are acquired primarily for use in producing of goods or services for an enterprise;

(iii) Have limited useful economic lives; and

(iv) Are not intended for sale in the ordinary course of business.

c) An Investment Property is an investment in Land or Building held primarily for generating income or capital appreciation and not occupied substantially for use in the operations of the enterprise.

d) Depreciate Value refers to that part of the net book value of a predicable asset that an enterprise can allocate to future operations through depreciation.

e) Estimated useful life of an Asset is the shorter of:

(i) The pre-determined physical life; and

(ii) The useful, economic life during which it could be profitably employed in the operations of the enterprise.

f) Residual Value of a Depreciable Asset is the estimated net amount recoverable from its disposal after its expected useful life.

g) Revaluation of Depreciable Asset is the process by which a new value is determined for a Depreciable asset having regard to its statement, the prevailing economic and market conditions at the time of the revaluation.

PART 3

EXPLANATORY NOTES

1. Depreciation is the systematic and period allocation of the historical cost or revalued amount less Estimated residual value of a loss value asset over its estimated useful life.

2. There are some common misconceptions about depreciation. It is sometimes wrongly believed that depreciation:

a) Is a valuation process attempting to determine the value or worth of a loss value asset;

b) May not be provided on an asset that is appreciating in value e.g. building; and

c) Is intended to provide enterprise with funds which to replace their assets.

3. Depreciation is not a valuation process because it is not the means by which a value or worth is assigned an asset. Also, depreciation does not necessarily provide an enterprise with funds to replace its depreciable assets. Because depreciation represents an estimate of that portion of the historical cost or revalued amount of a fixed asset chargeable to operations during an accounting period. It is the asset that may have occurred during the accounting period.

4. Some factors which are usually taken into consideration when estimating the useful economic life of a depreciable asset are:

a) Expected physical wear and tear due to usage;

b) Obsolescence due to change in technology, production requirements or consumer taste; and

c) Legal or other restrictions placed on the asset, for example, by a lessor or government.

5. Freehold land, having an indefinite life, is usually not depreciable

METHODS FOR CALCULATING DEPRECIATION

1. The method which is chosen for calculating depreciation on a depreciable asset may be based on the usage or contribution contemplated or on the passage of time. Usually, the nature of the asset determines the appropriate method to be used.

METHOD BASED ON PASSAGE OF TIME

1. Some depreciation methods based on the passage of time are:

a) Straight-line

b) Decreasing charge;

(i) Sum-of-the-year-digit;

(ii) Reducing balance

c) Annuity and sinking fund

2. Under the Straight-Line Method, the depreciable value of an asset is allocated equally to operations over the relevant years on the basis of the estimated useful economic life of the asset.

3. The Sum-of-Year-Digit and the Reducing Balancing Methods allocated the highest depreciation in the first years that an asset id in declining as the asset becomes older.

4. The Sum-of-Year-Digit Method provides for decreasing charges to operations through the application of fractions determined by adding the sum-of-years-digits of the asset's useful life in a reverse order.

5. The Reducing-Balance Method applies a constant depreciation rate to a declining net asset book value.

6. Annuity and sinking Fund Methods regard each item of property, plant and equipment as an investment expected to generate cash-in-flows and making a rate of return equal to or greater than the internal rate of return of the reporting enterprise. Under each method depreciation is equal to the excess of the cash-in-flow for the period over the return on the book value using the internal rate of return.

These two methods are really used in practice.

METHODS BASED ON LEVEL OF USAGE OR OUTPUT

1. Some depreciation methods based on the usage or output are:

   a) Service-hour; and

   b) Productive output

2. Under the service-hour method, the life span of the depreciable asset is determined by the total number of hours it can produce goods and services. The depreciable amount of the asset is divided by

the estimated total service hours to obtain an hourly depreciation rate which is then applied to the total hour of use during the period.

3. Under the productive output method, the life span of the depreciable asset is estimated in terms of the total number of units it can produce. The depreciable amount of the asset is divided by the estimated total number of units to obtain a unit depreciation rate which when applied to the total output for the period gives the depreciation expenses for the period.

GROUP OR COMPOSITE DEPRECIATION

1. In some cases, similar assets are collected and grouped as though they were a single asset, and a single rate is then determined using any of the above methods that are considered appropriate. This approach is adopted by organizations with small but highly valuable items such as tools and dice.

RETIREMENT OR DISPOSAL OF AN ITEM OF PROPERTY, PLANT AND EQUIPMENT

1. When an enterprise decides to retire or dispose of an item of property, plant and equipment, fractional depreciation calculated up to date of retirement or disposal is usually charged to the Profit and Loss Account. All the related accounting balances are eliminated from the Property, Plant and Equipment and Accumulated Depreciation Accounts.

DEPRECIATION ON REVALUED ITEMS OF PROPERTY, PLANT AND EQUIPMENT

1. When an item of Property, Plant and Equipment is revalued, the previously determined depreciation rate or an appropriately adjusted rate is usually applied to the new value in determining the current depreciation charge.

2. The depreciation charge based on the new value of an item of Property, Pant and Equipment is sometimes allocated between historical cost of the item and the surplus arising on the revaluation of the items and charged to income and the revaluation surplus accounts respectively. This practice, however, is generally considered unacceptable.

DEPRECIATION OF INVESTMENT PROPERTIES

1. Whilst An enterprise purchases property, Pant and Equipment for use in producing goods and services, investments in property are sometimes made for rental income and capital appreciation by non-property dealing enterprise.

2. Items of property pose some problems for non-property dealing enterprises. Some argue that properties should not be depreciated since they are held for income and capital appreciation, rather, they should be revalued yearly to reflect their current market values. The difference between the value at the beginning and the end may be treated as unrealised profit or loss and taken to Capital Reserve or the Profit and Loss Account, respectively.

3. Some enterprises take initial revaluation surplus on an item to a special Revaluation Account. Any subsequent gains or loss are taken directly to Owner's Equity except losses whose effects more than wipe out the previous gains. Such losses are taken to the Profit and Loss Account.

4. Other enterprises take initial revaluation surplus on an item to a special Revaluation Account. Any subsequent gains are taken directly to the account whilst losses are taken to the Profit and Loss Account. An increase is only taken to the Profit and Loss Account if related to a previous decrease that has been put through the Profit and Loss Account.

5. There are those who argue that there should be no difference in the treatment of investment in properties and properties held for use in reproducing goods and services. They are of the view that all should be subject to depreciation since they are maintained in the books because of their income-generating potentials.

6. This Statement takes the view that the intention behind the holding of an item of property determines its classification and whether or not depreciation may be taken on it or not.

7. A property qualifies to be treated as an investment property if it is not occupying substantially for use in the operations of an enterprise. For the purpose of this statement, occupation of more than 15% of the property is regard as substantial investment properties may either be depreciated like other items of Property, Pant and Equipment or may be accounted for in the manner described in paragraph 26 and 29 set out above.

DEPRECIATION OF AN ITEM OF PROPERTY AS AN INVESTMENT PROPERTY

1. When a piece of property is reclassified as an investment property and it is decided to be accounted for as such, the property is usually removed from its group of depreciable assets. The related accumulated depreciation charged, to the extent that it is no longer required, is taken to the Profit and Loss Account. Any related revaluation surplus is usually transferred to capital reserve, not income or retained earnings.

CHANGE IN DEPRECIATION RATE

1. An enterprise may make a change in depreciation rate due to new information about the actual life of such an asset. Such a change is usually considered as a change in an accounting estimate. Accordingly, no restatement of the depreciation charged in the prior periods is required.

2. A change from one depreciation method to another may be necessitated by the desire to show better the true and fair view of the affair of an enterprise. Such a change is usually considered a change in an accounting policy.

DISCLOSURE

1. Enterprises in Nigeria generally disclose the following:

a) The accounting policies with respect to depreciation;

b) The aggregate amount charged by categories of depreciable assets;

c) The amount charged as depreciation in the period

d) Methods used in computing depreciation in the period

e) The aggregate accumulated depreciation is divided into major categories of depreciable assets.

PART 4

ACCOUNTING FOR DEPRECIATION

The accounting standard comprises paragraph 35-46 of this statement. The Standard should be read in the context of all other parts of this Statement and of the preface to the Statement of Accounting standard published by NASB.

1. The depreciable value of an item of property, plant and equipment should be either the historical cost or the revalued amount computed in accordance with IAS and this Standard.

2. The useful economic life over which the allocation of the depreciable value takes place should be determined after due consideration of:

a) Expected physical wear and tear due to usage;

b) Obsolescence due to changes in technology; production requirement or consumer taste and

c) Legal or other restrictions placed on the asset, for example, by a lessor or government.

3. Several methods for calculating depreciation are available. The methods that an enterprise selects should reflect the characteristics of the asset, its intended use, and its practice in the industry in which the enterprise operates. The only methods that currently meet these requirements are the Straight-Line and Reducing Balance.

4. Where a group of assets is depreciated as though it were a single asset, effort should be made to ensure that the applicable rate is representative, consistently applied and constantly reviewed to reflect internal changes in the group.

5. When an item of Property, Plant and Equipment is revalued, the previous determined depreciation rate or an appropriately adjusted rate should be applied to the new value to determine the current depreciation charge.

6. The depreciation charge so determined in paragraph 39 should be charged entirely to income and should not be charged partly to income and partly against revaluation surplus on the basis of a pro rata allocation between the historical cost of item and surplus which arose on its revaluation.

7. A piece of property qualifies to be treated as an investment property if it not occupies substantially for use in the operations of an enterprise. For the purpose of this statement, an occupation of more than 15% of the property should be considered substantial.

8. When there is an increase over original cost in the carrying amount of a depreciable asset or an investment property on a revaluation, an enterprise should take the increase to Capital Reserve as a revaluation surplus. Provided that the surplus had not been reversed or utilized earlier, any subsequent decrease in the revaluation of the same asset should be charged against the revaluation surplus. In case where the decrease is more than the previous increases, the difference should be charged to income. An increase on revaluation which is directly related to a previous decrease in carrying amount of the same asset that was charged to income, either through the charging of depreciation or arising from a revaluation should be credited to income to the extent that it offers the previously recorded decrease.

9. When a piece of property is classified as an investment property and it is decided to be accounted for as such, the property should be removed from its group of depreciable assets. The accumulated depreciation on it, to the extent that it is no longer required, should be taken to the Profit and Loss Account. Any related revaluation surplus should not be transferred to income or retained earnings but transferred to Capital reserve.

10. A change from one depreciation method to another should be considered a change in an accounting policy and should be treated in accordance with the provisions of IAS 1 – Disclosure of Accounting Policies, and IAS 6 – Extraordinary items and Prior Year Adjustments.

DISCLOSURE

1. A reporting enterprise should state its accounting policy with respect to depreciation.

2. In addition to the disclosure requirements of IAS 2-Information to be disclosed in Financial Statement and IAS 3-Accounting for Property, Plant and Equipment, the following disclosures are to be made in the Notes to the Accounts:

a) The amount charged as depreciation during the period

b) The effect of any change in depreciation rate on the period's operating results.

c) The book value and the amount that would otherwise have been charged by way of depreciation on any item of property, plant and equipment.

This statement meets the requirements of IAS Nos. 4 &25.

Illustration 2

Sekoni and Co. depreciate its plant and machinery on a straight-line basis for ten years irrespective of when such plant/machinery is bought or sold in the year.

2013	11,600
2014	6,200
2015	3,400
2016-2023	50,400
	71,600

As at 1st December, 2017 the written down values of the plant and machinery was $39,030. In 2014, plant and machinery bought was at a cost of $70. In addition, 2015 additional Plant amounting to $3,600 was bought and a machinery which cost $1,400 in 2022 was sold for $700.

The managing director agreed that a machine be purchased under hire purchase agreement in the same year. The machine had a cash purchase price of $5,820. The hire purchase agreement provided for its immediate payment of $1,500 on 1/11/25 and live half yearly installments of $1,000. The total payment due for the machine bought on hire is $6,500.

You are required to:

a) Calculate the depreciation for 2024 and 2025

b) Calculate the profit/loss on assets disposed off

c) Show the plant and machinery account for the year 2014 and 2015

d) Ascertain the hire purchases interest and apportion it over 2015, 2016 and 2017. (ICAN).

Solution to IAS 9

Solution 1

Depreciation means the permanent and continuing diminution in an asset's quality, quantity, or value from any cause whatsoever. It can also be defined as the allocation of the depreciable amount of an asset over its useful life. The methods of depreciation are: Straight line, reducing balance, sum of digits, annuity, investment revaluation, depletion unity and machine hour methods.

1. A provision is an amount set aside out of profits or other surpluses (or charged to Profit and Loss Account) to provide for depreciation, renewals or diminution in value of assets or to meet a liability.

2. Reserve is an amount set aside out of profit or other surpluses which is not designed to meet any liability, contingency, commitment or diminution in value of assets known to exist at the balance sheet date. Reserve are divided into Revenue and Capital Reserves.

Solution 2

SEKONI & COMPANY

a) Depreciation calculation for Plant and Machinery

Year purchased	At 1/1/24 $	Disposal $	At 321/12/24 $
2013	11,600	11,600	
2014	6,200	6,200	
2015	3,400	3,400	
2016-2023	50,400 (1,200)	49,200	
2024	5,900	5,900	
For 2017	**At/1/17**		**Depreciation**
2013	11,600	11,600	Fully depreciated
2014	6,200	6,200	Fully depreciated
2015	3,400	3,400	Fully depreciated
2016-2023	49,200 (1,400)	47,800	4,920
2024	5,900	5,900	590
2025	76,600	9,420	942
			6,452

PROFIT/LOSS ON ASSETS DESPOSED

	Cost $	Dep. $	NBV $	Sale $	P/L $
2014 Sales P & M	1,200	1,080(a)	120	70	(50)
2025 Sales P & M	1,400	560(4)	840	700	(140)
	2,600	1,640	960	770	(190)

Plant And Machinery					
1/1/24 Balance c/d	71,600	1986	Disposal		1,200
2024 Purchases	5,900	1986	Balance		76,300
	77,500				77,500
1/1/24 Balance c/d	76,300	1987	Disposals		1,400
2025 Purchases	3,600	1987	Balance c/d		84,320
2025 Hire Purchase	5,820				
	85,720				85,720
1/1/26 Balance	84,320				

Provision for Depreciation Plant & Machinery					
31/12/16	Disposal	1,080	1/1/86 b/d		32,570
31/12/16	Balance c/d	37,460	31/12/86		5,970
		38,540			38,540
31/12/17	Disposal	560	1/1/87 b/d		37,460
31/12/17	Balance c/d	43,352	31/12/87 P& L		6,450
		43,912			43,912
			1/1/88 Bal b/d		43,352

Hire Purchase Interest					
(i)	Deposit		1,500		
	Installments (1,000 x 5)		5,000		
			6,500		
	Less cash sale price		(5,820)		
			680		
(ii)	If apportion equally	2025	$226-66		
		2026	$226-67		
		2027	4226-66		
(iii)	If apportioned on basis of number of installment				
	Date install. No.		No. of Installment		
	1/1/87 5		$^{5}/_{15}$ x $^{680}/_{1}$ = 226.62		
	30/6/87 4		$^{4}/_{15}$ x $^{680}/_{1}$ = 181.33		
	31/12/87 3		$^{3}/_{15}$ x $^{680}/_{1}$ = 136.00		
	30/6/88 2		$^{2}/_{15}$ x $^{680}/_{1}$ = 90.67		
	31/12/88 1		$^{1}/_{15}$ x $^{680}/_{1}$ = 45.33		

CHAPTER ELEVEN
ACCOUNTING BY BANKS AND NON-BANK FINANCIAL INSTITUTIONS IAS 10

PART 1

INTRODUCTION

1. In recent times, national attention has focused on the banking industry and the accounting practices followed by banks due to the:

(a) Importance of the sector in the industrial and commercial development of the economy

(b) Inconsistence accounting policies and reporting practices which make comparison of performance difficult.

(c) Allegedly overstated profits reported by banks.

(d) Survival problems of troubled banks

(e) Probable 'share out' that may be ahead as a result of increased competition in the industry; and

(f) Resulting need to sustain public confidence in the banking sector.

2. This statement provides a guide for accounting policies and methods that banks should follow in preparing their financial statements. Improved accounting and reporting practices are important in ensuring reliable financial statements that are comparable across the industry.

3. This statement (part I) focuses on three main area s of concern relating to accounting practices followed by banks, namely:

(a) Income recognition

(b) Loss recognition; and

(c) Balance sheet classification

4. For the purpose of this statement, the term "bank" is used as defined by the Banking Act 1969, as amended, which applies to merchant and commercial banks.

5. This statement (part I) does not cover all aspects of banking activities nor the activities of financial institutions not covered by the Banking Act 1969, as amended. Part 2 will cover other aspects of banking activities and will be extended to cover noono0bank financial institutions.

PART 2

DEFINITIONS

The following terms are in this statement with the meanings specified below;

1. Credit risks include the loan contingencies attaching to all forms of credit which a bank may enter, e.g. Loans, Overdrafts, Leases, Guarantees, Acceptances and other similar items.

2. Risk Assets are funded credit risks.

3. Reported Credit represents the aggregate amount reported under loans, advances leases, and other risk assets.

4. Syndicated Loans are agreements between two or more lending institutions to provide a borrower with credit facility utilizing common loan documentation.

5. Loan Losses include bad debts written off provision made against losses arising on a bank's credit risks, losses on loans and advances considered doubtful of collection and all other loss contingencies attaching to a bank's credit risks. The provisions may be general or specific.

6. Loan Loss expenses is the amount charged to income in the current period in respect of loan losses.

7. Specific Loan Loss Provisions are the amount provided for specific loans and advances considered doubtful to recover.

8. General Loan Loss provisions are amounts provided against the as yet unidentified losses known to exist in any port-folio and relate to the balance of loan and advances that have not been subject to a specific loan loss provision.

9. Lease are a contractual agreement between an owner (the Lessor) and another party (the Lessee) that convey to the lessee the right to use the lessor's property for a period of time in return for a consideration usually periodic payment called rentals.

10. Operating Lessee are those in which the lessor, while giving the lessee use of the leased property retains practically at the risk, obligations and rewards of ownership (e.g. early obsolescence or appreciation).

11. Finance or capital Lessees are those in which ownership risks and rewards are substantially transferred to the lessee, who is obliged to pay such costs as insurance, maintenance and similar charges on the property. Usually the agreement is non-cancellable and the lessee has the option to buy the property for a nominal amount upon the expiration of the lease term.

12. Non-Performing Loans are those that are for a period of time not performing in accordance with the terms of the credit facility and are unable to meet principal and/or interest repayment obligations in full and this may be doubtful of collection.

13. Loan rescheduling includes restructuring, refinancing, or forming a new arrangement to pay interest and liquidate principal. With customers whose loan accounts had early been judged to be non

performing. Situations where additional credit facilities are granted to an existing non-performing loan and new payment terms are agreed upon also constitute loan rescheduling.

14. Credit-related Fee Incomes are fee incomes resulting from services that constitute an integral part of a credit facility. This includes all fees charged in connection with arranging a credit facility such as loan arrangement fees, legal costs, syndication fees and commitment fees, exclusive of interest charges. A credit related service should always be interpreted to constitute an integral part of a credit facility if a customer does not have a choice but to utilize for the service, the bank providing for the credit.

15. Non-Credit Related Fee Incomes include fees and commissions charged for banking services in which the bank retains no credit risk and includes commission on letters of credit and foreign exchange dealings, etc. Such fees can be contingent on the occurrence of a future events, e.g. underwriting commissions, or are earned in stages in accordance with a contract or on completion of a service.

16. Fixed Facilities are repayable per defined repayment terms and include term loans, installment credit and leases.

17. Revolving Facilities are facilities with no periodic or stage repayment terms but with specific upper limits, for example overdrafts and other revolving credits that are renewable periodically.

18. Off-Balance Sheet Engagements include letters of credit, bonds, guarantees indemnities, acceptances, trade related contingencies such as documentary credits etc.

PART 3

EXPLANATORY NOTES

1. Banks represents a significant and influential sector of the economy and play a major role in maintaining confidence in the monetary system. There is, therefore considerable and wide spread interest in their management and performance. The quality of their financial statements will help foster public confidence in the banks and evaluate their performance.

2. Following the recent deregulation of the banking industry in Nigeria, many new banks were licensed, and bank financial statements have attracted national attention because of the diversity in profitability, which is often attributed to differences in recognizing and recording financial transactions and their presentation in financial statements.

3. There is a need to ensure that banks financial statements are uniformly presented and that their contents are reliable, factual and comparable to assist the users in evaluating bank performance. Uniform presentation will also assist regulatory agencies to properly classify banks and to better regulate their operations.

ACCOUNTING POLICIES

1. Accounting policies provide well-articulated bases for the preparation of financial statements of which the type form an integral part.

2. Most banks, however, do not disclose all their accounting policies under captions and on separate pages, and they still present some individual items in the financial statements as part of the note.

3. The accounting policies most commonly disclose but only in general term include;

Determination of provision for loan losses;

a) Accrual of interest on non performing and doubtful loans

b) Translation and conversion of foreign currencies.

c) Valuation of investments

d) Deferred taxes; and

e) Depreciation of fixed assets and leased properties.

4. At present, most banks do not present accounting policies in specific term with respect to:

a) Off Balance Sheet engagements which give rise to contingencies commitments.

b) Specific and general loans provisions

c) Uncollectible debts; and

d) Income recognition, especially of interest on non-performing doubtful loans.

INCOME RECOGNITION

1. Banks generally derive revenues from interest income on loans and advanced commission on turnover, transfer fees, arrangement fees, syndication commitment fees, lease rental, income from commercial paper sale, exchange bankers' acceptances, and discount of bills. Banks also charge rendering other financial and trust services to their customers.

2. Banks generally recognize their revenue when they are earned or loose. However, many banks recognize credit-related fee income which is signed in relation to interest earned, when the credit facilities are granted, rate deferring such income recognition over the life of the related credit adjustment of the yield on credit. Some banks take account of the size credit related fee when negotiating the interest rate on the related facility as front ending income, which would otherwise be recognized over the tenor of the credit risk. This is not regarded as good practice.

3. In case of loans and advances, income is usually earned over the period of the outstanding credit at contracted yield, in proportion to the outstanding balances to the extent that collectability is not in doubt.

4. The timing of classification of loans and advances as non-performing, so as to put the related interest income in suspense, is a controversial issue. Will some banks take such interest income on non-performing loans into their interest suspense account others take it into interest income thereby overstating profit.

LOSS RECOGNITION

1. In the ordinary course of business, banks normally suffer some losses on loans, advances and other credits as a result of their becoming partly or wholly uncollectible. Such losses are usually recorded in the periods they are first recognized.

2. Banks usually make specific provisions for loans losses that have been identified as non-performing. In addition to specific provisions, some banks also make general provisions for loan losses.

3. It is the responsibility of bank management to assess its credit port-folio and make provisions for non-performing and doubtful credit risks. It I comparatively easy to identify fixed facilities which are non-performing but revolving facilities are more complex. Normally, the first indication that a revolving facility may be non-performing is where the account turnover is considerably less than anticipated or when interest is charged, which takes the balance above the credit limit.

4. The industry's standard of credit analysis and the detailed credit documentation available on customers' files vary widely. Further, loan losses are generally not assessed regularly and the criteria for the assessment are not usually clearly defined and consistently applied from period to period. This inadequacy of credit documentation, analysis and assessment of loan losses is not regarded as good practice.

BALANCE SHEET CLASSIFICATION

1. Banks follow several practices in classifying Balance Sheet items, resulting in favourable asst and liability presentation and sometimes border on "windows dressing". Usually, the objectives of such practices are to:

   a) Reduce reported credit

   b) Reduce reported deposit; and

   c) Enhance reported liquidity.

   These are not regarded as good practices.

2. There is diversity in the treatment of uncleared inter-branch and inter-bank items. Some banks treat them under other assets, liabilities of even cash, others treat them as cheque for collection.

TRANSFERS OF REPORTED CREDITS

1. Banks may borrow money, pledge their risk assets as collateral, and sell them with or without recourse.

2. In the case of sale of risk assets, the risks and rewards of title are passed on to the buyer. Where the sale is made without recourse, the principal is usually removed from reported credit, a profit or loss is recognized on disposal at the date the asset is sold and off-balance sheet contingency is recorded.

3. Practice varies where the sale is made with recourse to the seller, meaning that the reward of the risk asset is transferred to the buyer but the credit risk is retained. The selling bank may treat the transaction as secured borrowing recording the proceeds from the transfer as a liability. Alternatively, the transfer may be accounted for a sale, whereby the principal is removed from reported credit and usually included amongst off-balance sheet risk contingency. The profit on sale is usually amortised over the period of the related credit risk it proportion to the outstanding principal. Losses there are usually recognized as soon as they can be estimated. Determination of the appropriate accounting method would normally be influenced by the substance of the transfer and the extent to which the transferor retains or transfers the underlying credit risk.

4. The transfer of a risk asset sometimes attracts different accounting treatment in the financial statements of the parties involved. For example, a swap of placement of equal tenor and maturity may be presented by one bank as a secured borrowing whilst the other bank may treat the same item as a sale, thereby improving liquidity and reducing its reported credit.

5. Most banks in Nigeria account for all leases operating leases despite the fact that most of such leases are finance leases. Under this practice, the leased term using either the sum-of-digits or the straight-line method. This is not regarded as good practice.

6. Following the balance sheet treatment described in paragraph 28, the related lease rental income is recognized when due on a straight line basis over the lease term. This pattern of income recognition taking together with the depreciation method has the undesirable consequences of not recognizing lease finance income in a manner that provides a constant on the lessor's net investment.

7. Most banks follow the lease accounting method outlined in paragraphs 28 and 29 because of their concern that they may not be able to claim capital allowances on the leased assets if they are not showed as fixed assets on the balance sheet.

FINANCIAL STATEMENTS PRESENTATION

1. Banks normally prepare financial statements which provide information about their liquidity, solvency and risk that may attach to their assets, liabilities and off-balance sheet engagements.

2. Typical financial statements generally include:

a) Statements of Accounting Policies

b) Balance Sheet

c) Income Statements or Profit and Loss Account

d) Statement of Source and Application of Funds

e) Notes on the Accounts

f) Five Year Financial Summary

g) Statement of Value Added

3. Typically, each principal revenue source in the financial statement is stated separately to enable users assess the performance of that particular source of revenue. Similar each principal item of expenses is stated separately in the financial statements.

4. Assets and liabilities are generally grouped according to their nature and listed in order of their liquidity. Assets are usually listed as the most liquid in the form of cash and short-term funds to the most liquid in the form of fixed assets. Liabilities are similarly listed.

5. It is not desirable to offset an asset or liability by deduction of another assets or liability unless a legal right of set-off exists. Such offsetting reduced the usefulness of the balance sheet and is not regarded as good practice.

OFF BALANCE SHEET ENGAGEMENTS

1. Banks also center into transactions that are currently recognized as assets or liabilities in the balance sheet but which non-the-less give rise to credit risks, contingencies and commitments. Such transactions include letters of credit, bonds, guarantees, indemnities, acceptances, and trade-related contingencies such as documentary credits. These types of transactions are referred to as "off-Balance Sheet Engagements".

2. It is good practice for banks to disclose the nature and number of contingencies and commitments arising from different classes of off-balance sheet engagements.

PART 4

ACCOUNTING STANDARD

Statement of accounting standard 10 comprises paragraphs 38 to 72. The standard should be read in the context of paragraphs 1-37 of this statement and of the preface of the statements accounting standards, IAS and other relevant standards published by the Nigerian Accounting Standards Board.

ACCOUNTING POLICIES

1. A bank should articulate and disclose as an integral part of its financial statement all the significant accounting policies adopted in the preparation of its financial statements.

2. The accounting policies should be prominently disclosed under one caption rather than as notes to individual items in the financial statements.

INCOME RECOGNITION

1. On straight forward loans, overdraft and other risk assets, interest income should be recognized so to record a constant yield on the outstanding principal of the life of the credit at the interest rate applicable to the facility.

2. For discount products on which interest is often settled up-front in or arrears, the discount should be amortised over the product's life to give a constant yield on the outstanding principal.

3. Credit related fee income, where material and its collectability not in doubt should be deferred and amortised over the life of the related credit in proportion to the outstanding credit risk. Credit related fee income should be regarded as material in all situations where they constitute at least 10% of the projected average annual yield over life of the facility to which they relate. Related direct expenses should be deducted from the fees before deferral. Specific examples include:

a) Loan arrangement fees. Including legal fees and other up-front fees should be deferred and amortised over the life of the loan as an adjustment of yield. Where direct loan arrangement costs are significant, they should be deducted from the related fees before deferral.

b) In cases where a loan is syndicated, the bank should recognize loan syndication fees when the syndication is complete except to the extent that a proportion of the loan is retained. Where the yield on the portion of the loan retained by the syndicator is less than the average yield to the other syndication participants after considering any fees passed through by the syndicator, who should then defer the portion of the syndication fees to produce a yield on the portion of the loan retained that is not less than the average yield on the loans held by the other participants.

c) Commitment fees should be deferred and if the commitment is exercised, amortised over the life of the loan as an adjustment of yield or if the commitment on exercise, recognized in income upon expiration of the commitment. Exceptions would be:

(i) If the bank's experience with similar arrangement indicates that the likelihood that the commitment will be exercised is remote, the commitment fees should be recognized on a straight-line bases over the life of the facility or

(ii) If the commitment fees are determined retrospectively as a percentage of the unused facility in previous period, the fee should be recognized in income on the determination date.

4. In situations where credit related fee income is not material as defined in paragraph 42 above, the fees may be recognized at once provided all associated costs are expense in the same period.

5. Non-Credit Related Fee Income should be recognized as earned. Fees earned over a long period of time or in stages (and which are not contingent upon the occurrence of a future event) should be recognized when the related service is performed or upon the completion of contracted stages. Fees relating to a transaction in which some portions of related credit risk are retained, should be treated as in paragraph 42 above.

6. Lease Rental Income should be recognized systematically to record a constant yield on the lessor's net investments in the lease over its term. The yield should be adjusted in the appropriated period if the lease contains an interest rate variation clause.

7. Profits or losses arising on sale of loans or discount without recourse to the seller should be recognized by the seller when the transaction is completed.

8. Profits arising from sales on loans or discounts with recourse to the seller should be amortised by the seller over the remaining life. Losses should be recognized as soon as they can be reasonably estimated.

LOSS RECOGNITION

1. Banks should make provision for all losses as soon as they can be reasonably estimated. Losses can arise on any asset considered doubtful of being realised in full and can include loan loss provisions, provisions against diminution of the value of other assets and other loss contingencies.

LOAN LOSS

1. Banks should make provisions for loan loss after thoroughly reviewing all its credit risks, including loans and advances, lease and off-balance sheet engagements. The time at which a provision should be made against a credit risk is a matter of judgment, especially in the case of revolving facilities such as overdrafts. Each bank should develop a formal procedure in identifying non-performing facilities and evaluating loan losses and a systematic method of making provisions for loan losses. Each bank should consider other indications that a loss may arise on a credit risk, since for example, a loan may be doubtful or recovery even it is performing in accordance with its terms.

2. Paragraphs 51 to 55 set out rules which should be followed in determining provisions for loan and losses.

FIXED FACILITIES

1. Indications that a fixed facility is non-performing include a situation in which interest and/or principal repayments are in arrears of the facility terms.

In that case:

a) Interest overdue by more than 90 days (or a shorter period specified by regulatory authorities) should be suspended and recognized on a cash basis.

b) Principal repayments that are overdue by more than 120 days (or such shorter period as may be specified by regulatory authorities) should be fully provisioned and recoveries recognized on cash basis.

c) When individual principal repayments are subject to provision, banks should make provision against the outstanding principal repayments not yet due as follows

No. of days for which   Minimum percentage provision

Principal is overdue	required for principal not due
180 days	50%
360 days	100%

Where regulatory authorities stipulate shorter period or higher percentage than indicated above such shorter periods or higher percentages should be followed.

d) Where the facility is secured by a fixed legal charge over or by title to tangible property, the principal provisioning could cease the outstanding principal is less than a specified proportion of the estimated net realizable value of the security as follows:

(i) Where the principal repayment is overdue by more than one year, the outstanding unprovided principal should not exceed 50% of the estimated net realizable value of the security.

(ii) Where the principal repayment is overdue by more than two years, there should be no outstanding unprovided portion of the credit facility irrespective of the estimated net realizable value of security held.

(iii) In both (i) and (ii) above, where regulatory authorities stipulated shorter periods of lower percentages, such shorter periods or lower percentages should be followed.

e) Where a facility is secured by a floating charge or by an un-perfected or equitable charge over tangible property, it should be treated as an unsecured credit and no account taken of any security held in determining the provision for loans loss.

REVOLVING AND OVERDRAFT FACILITIES

1. Normally the first indication that a revolving or overdraft facility may be non-performing is when the turnover on the account is considerably lower than anticipated when the facility was arranged or when interest is charged which takes the facility above its credit limit.

In these circumstances:

a) A revolving facility should be classified as non-performing and unpaid interest suspended once 90 days (or such period as may be specified by regulatory authorities) elapses after exceeding the facility limit.

b) Where credit limits are not exceeded, each bank should have a systematic method for the identification of non-performing revolving credits. Once classified as non-performing, all unpaid interest in the facility should be suspended.

c) Once a facility is classified as non-performing, provision against principal and unpaid interest should be made in accordance with a systematic method to reduce the outstanding principal to the estimated net realizable value of any security held (following the criteria paragraphs 51 (d) and (e) above over a specified period.

2. In the case of revolving and overdraft facilities, where a loan rescheduling agreed with a customer, the rescheduling should be treated as a new facility. Provision should continue until it is clear that the

rescheduling is working. Interest previously suspended and, provisions against principal previously made should be recognized on cash basis.

Facilities Performing in Arrears

1. In many cases, short term cash flow difficulties result in a customer temporarily falling behind its facility terms. In these cases, provisions should be made in accordance with the principles set out in paragraphs 51 and 52 above. Once the facility begins to perform, interest previously suspended and provisions against principal previously made should be recognized on cash basis.

General Provisioning

1. Banks should make general loan loss provisions of at least 1% of risk assets not specified provided for, in addition to specific provisions to provide against the risk as yet unidentified losses which are known to exist in any portfolio using a systematic method which should be consistently followed from period to period.

Investment Securities

Long term investments in marketable securities should be stated at the lower cost and net realizable value. Market value should be disclosed.

Short term investments in marketable securities should be stated at the lower cost and net realizable value. The original cost should be disclosed.

Investments in securities for which there is no active market should be stated at lower cost and net realizable value.

BALANCE SHEET CLASSIFICATION

Lease

1. Banks should record the net investment in finance leases granted to customers as "advances under finance leases".

Incomplete Transactions

1. All transactions should be reported as having been completed unless the expense and delay associated with the analysis and proper classification of such items are out of proportion to the material of the record balance. The following items are often included in other assets and liabilities but were material and identifiable, should be treated asset out below:

a) Interest receivable from customers where not debited to customers should include in reported credit.

b) Interest received in advance, from customers where already debited to customer but not yet earned, should be deducted from reported credit.

c) Cheques in the course of collection which clear subsequently, should be shown as a component of the balance with the Central bank and also either in deposit liability or deducted from reported credit as appropriate.

d) Cheques in the course of collection which are subsequently dishonored should be reversed.

e) Cashier's cheques and other demand notes payable should be deducted cash with (CB), unless the demand note payable evidences a deposit, in which case it should be included in deposit liabilities.

f) Notes payable with fixed maturities should be included in deposit liability unless the maturity is over one year from the balance sheet date in which the repayment terms should be disclosed.

g) Cash collateral against advances should be separately disclosed.

h) Matured funds or deposits awaiting remittance should be reported as component of deposit liabilities.

i) Suspended interest should be deducted from outstanding credit as a component of the loan loss provision.

Disposals of Reported Credit

1. The seller should account for a transfer of reported credit without recourse to the seller as a disposal and risk asset excluded from the balance sheet.

2. A transfer of reported credit, with recourse to the seller, that purports that sales must satisfy the following conditions:

a) Control over the economic benefits of the asset must be passed to the buyer.

b) The seller can reasonably estimate its obligations under the recourse provision.

c) There must not be any repurchase obligations or options involved, except as stipulated by the recourse provisions.

Suppose the above conditions are satisfied and a transfer of reported credit with recourse to the seller is accounted for a sale. In that case, the contingency resulting from the recourse should be disclosed. If the above conditions are not met the transfer should be recorded as a borrowing.

DISCLOSURE

In addition to the disclosure requirements of IAS 2, Information to be disclosed in Financial Statements, banks should also disclose the following:

1. The statement of significant accounting policies should be included:

a) A brief description of the systematic method by which non-performing loans are identified, the method by which the provision for loan losses are provided for, and the bases upon which recoveries against provisions previously made and interest previously suspended are releases to income.

b) The nature of off-balance sheet engagements and the methods used to recognize income there on.

Income Statement

1. Each principal revenue item should be stated separately in a bank's financial statements to enable the user assess the contribution of that particular source of revenue.

2. The disclosure in the income statement and the notes to the financial statements should include but not limited to the following income and expense captions.

Income

1. Interest and discount income

2. Lease finance income

3. Fees for services rendered

4. Foreign exchange income

5. Commission income

6. Income from investments

Expenses

1. Interest expense

2. Loan loss expense, showing separately any release of provisions previously made

3. Commissions paid

4. Foreign exchange losses

5. General and administrative expenses

6. Diminution in asset values

A bank should disclose the following items in its financial statements:

1. Interest income split between bank and non-bank sources;

2. Interest expense split between bank and non-bank sources;

3. Credit-related fee income and expenses where such fees and expenses are treated as in paragraph 43.

4. A bank should not offset one revenue or expense by deducting another item of revenue or expense from it.

Balance Sheet

1. A bank should group its assets and liabilities in the balance sheet according to their nature and then list them in order of liquidity and maturity. The disclosures in the balance sheet and the notes to the financial statements should include but are not limited to the following assets and liabilities:

i.   Cash and short-term funds

ii.   Due from other banks

iii.   Bills discounted

iv.   Investments

v.   Advances under finance leases

vi.   Other assets

vii.   Fixed assets

Liabilities

i.   Deposits and current accounts

ii.   Due to other banks

iii.   Taxation payable

iv.   Dividend payable

v.   Other liabilities

vi.   Long-term loans

vii.   Shareholders' funds

1. Banks should provide in their financial statements a maturity profile of their risk assets and deposit liabilities into the following categories:

Under

1	-	1 month
3	-	3 months
6	-	6 months
Over	-	12 months

2. The above maturity profile should be based on the expected normal repayment periods of the assets and liabilities.

3. The amount of provision for loan losses, segregated between principal and interest, should be disclosed and deducted from the relevant asset category. Provision for losses of off-balance sheet engagements should be shown separately, and a component loss provision should be disclosed.

4. One item of asset or liability should not be offset by deducting another asset or liability unless a legal right of set-off exists.

Loans and Advances

1. A bank should disclose an analysis of loans and advances between performing and non-performing loans.

Off Balance Sheet Engagements and Contingencies

1. A bank should disclose the nature and amount of contingencies and commitments arising from the Off Balance Sheet engagements and analyse between the different contingencies. Off Balance Sheet engagements should not form part of Balance Sheet total and their disclosures in note form should distinguish between:

a) Direct credit substitutes, such as guarantees, acceptances and stand by letters of credit serving as guarantees;

b) Transaction related contingencies, such as bid bonds, performance guarantees and standby letters of credit related to particular transactions;

c) Short term self-liquidating trade-related contingencies resulting from the movement of goods and

d) Other contingencies.

Other Assets and Liabilities

1. In the Notes on the Accounts. A bank should disclose the major items that make up its "Other Assets" and "Other Liabilities"

Relation to Other Statement of Accounting Standard

1. This statement supplements the requirements set out in other statements of Accounting Standards. It has been framed on the basis that other statements of Accounting Standards apply to the financial statements of banks unless banks are specifically exempted from the scope of a Standard.

PART 5

Notes on legal Requirements

The requirements of this standards are complimentary to the requirements of the Banking Act of 1969, as amended. Companies and Allied Matters Decree of 1990, as amended and other relevant laws and regulations.

PART 6

Compliance with International Accounting Standard No. 30

The requirements of this Standard accord substantially with the requirements of International Accounting Standard No. 30 – Disclosures in the Financial Statements of Banks and Similar Financial Institutions.

Effective Date

1. This Standard becomes operative for financial statements covering period ending on or after 31 December, 1990.

Illustration 1

Define this terms:

1. Secret Reserve

2. Credit Risks

3. Income and Loss Recognition.

Solution 1

1. A Secret Reserve is a reserve which actually exists but is not disclosed in the Balance Sheet. It may take the form of a Hidden, Inner or Purely secret reserve.

Bankers create secret reserves by:

a) Inclusion of free reserves among current liabilities.

b) Crediting profits on realization of investments to a reserve and writing off losses.

Criticism of this Practice

1. Profits are actually higher than those disclosed

2. Hiding of severe decline in stability

3. Accounts not true and fair views.

a) Credit Risks

These include the loss contingencies attaching to all forms of credit which a bank may enter into e.g. overdrafts, leases, guarantees, acceptances and other similar items.

b) Income and Loss Recognition

Banks derive revenues from interest income loans and advances, commissions on turnover, transfer fees, foreign exchange etc. Banks recognize their revenues when they are earned realised.

Banks make specific provisions for loan losses that have been identified as non-performing. Banks make provision for all losses as soon as they can be reasonably estimated.

CHAPTER TWELVE
IAS 11/IFRS 20 ON LEASES

PART 1

INTRODUCTION

1. Leasing has in recent times in Nigeria become an attractive means of financing the acquisition and use of fixed assets such as land, buildings, place and equipment's. The attraction of leasing is heightened by the very high cost of fixed assets. The scarcity of foreign exchange to pay for imports and the relative ease of access to credit facilities for leasing.

2. At present financial statements published in Nigeria contain little or no information on lease transactions, some of which involve huge annual financial commitments. There is the need, therefore, to consider appropriate treatments and disclosure of lease transactions in the books of both the lessor and the leases.

This statement does not cover:

1. Lease agreements pertaining to exploration for or exploration of natural resources such as oil, gas, minerals and timbers;

2. Licensing agreements relating to intellectual properties such as motion, pictures, video recordings, manuscripts, patents and copyrights and

3. Leases are in favor of contract financing the development of landed property.

The primary objectives of this Statement are:

1. To ensure that published financial statements contain sufficient information about leases transactions to make it possible for users of such statements to determine the effects of leases commitments on the present and future operations of the reporting enterprises; and

2. To ensure uniform disclosure of terms and classes of leases in financial statements.

PART 2

DEFINITIONS

The following terms used in this statement with the meanings specified:

1. A lease is a contractual agreement between an owner (the lessor) and another party (the lessee) that conveys the right to use the leased asset for an agreed period in return for a consideration, usually periodic payments called rents.

2. In an Operating lease, the lessor, while giving the lessee the use of the leased property, retains practically all the risks, obligations and rewards of ownership (e.g., early obsolescence and appreciation).

3. Finance or Capital Lease is one in which ownership risks and rewards are transferred to the lessee, who is obliged to pay such costs as insurance, maintenance and similar charges on the property. Usually, the agreement is non-cancellable and the lessee has the option to buy the property for a nominal amount upon the expiration.

Other variants of Finance or Capital Leases are:

1. Leveraged Lease is a three-party lease involving a lender (often a financial institution) and the usual lessor and lessee. The lender supplies in most cases, the greater part of the purchase price of the leased asset.

2. Sales-Type Lease is one where the offeror or leader (the lessor) transfers substantially all the ownership risks and benefits of the property is greater or less than its carrying amount in the books of the lessor resulting in a profit or loss to the lessor who is often a manufacturer or dealer.

3. Direct Finance Lease is one which transfers substantially all the ownership risks and benefits of the property to the lessee and at the inception of the lease, the fair value of leased asset is the same as it carrying amount to the lessor (often not a manufacturer or dealer).

   a) Sale and leaseback are when the seller of the property leases it back from the buyer.

   b) Bargain Purchase Option is a provision in the lease agreement granting the lessee the option to purchase the leased property for a nominal sum considered lower than the likely prevailing fair value of the property at the time the option is exercisable. Given the attractiveness of the option, it is reasonably certain that the lease will exercise it.

   c) Fair Value is the amount that can be realised upon the sale of the property in a free market and in an arm's length transactions between knowledgeable parties.

   d) Inception of the Lease is the date both parties agree and make definite commitments to the principal lease agreement.

   e) Initial Direct Lease Costs are those incurred by the lessor directly attributable to a particular lease agreement. They include commissions, legal fees, documentation costs and stamp duty.

   f) Minimum Lease Payments are the payments over the lease term that the lessee is required to make or can make:

4. From the viewpoint of the lessee, minimum lease payments will normally include any full or partial guarantee by the lessee or his related party of a residual value of the leased asset at the expiry date. The amount of the guarantee is the minimum amount that could, in any event, become payable. Where the lessee has an option to acquire the equipment at the end of the lease the option payment, if the option is likely to be exercised, is part of the minimum lease payments.

5. From the viewpoint of the lessor, minimum lease payments will normally include any residual value guaranteed by the lessee or by a third party, unrelated to the lessor, who is financially capable of discharging the obligations under the guarantee.

6. Residual value of Lease is the estimated fair value of the leased asset at the end of the lease term.

7. The useful life of an asset is shorter than that of

   a) The predetermined physical life and

   b) The economic life during which it could be profitably employed in the operations of the enterprise

8. Unguaranteed Residual Value is the portion of the residual value of the leased asset that is not guaranteed by the lease or guaranteed only by a third party related to the lessor.

9. Credit Provider for Leased Asset is the third party in a leveraged lease who substantially finances the acquisition of the leased property.

10. Lessor's Investment in a Leveraged Lease is the Lessor's contribution to the acquisition cost of the leased asset plus initial direct cost less rental received.

11. Lease term is the duration of the lease which may vary from a few months to the entire expected economic life of the asset.

12. Non-cancellable Lease is one that the lease does not easily terminate except under one or more of the following conditions, where:

   a) There is an occurrence of some remote contingency

   b) The lessor agrees to cancel

   c) The lessee replaces the existing lease with another one with the same lessor

   d) The lessee pays a penalty which was meant to deter cancellation.

13. Contingent Rentals are increases or decreases in lease payments made by the lessee as a result of changes occurring after the inception of the lease.

14. Premium on Land and Building Transaction refers to the excess of the obligations of a lease over the combined fair value of both land and building in a lease transaction.

15. Gross Investment in the Lease is the aggregate of minimum lease payment under a finance lease from the point of view of the lessor and any un-gauranteed residual value accruing to the lessor.

16. Unearned Financed Income is the difference between the gross investment in the lease and the fair value of the leased assets at the inception of the lease.

17. Net Investment in the lease is the difference between the gross investment and the balance of the unearned finance income.

18. Rate of Interest Implicit the Lease is the discount rate that causes the present value at the beginning of the ease term of the minimum lease payments and any un-gauranteed residual value of the leased assert at the inception of the lease.

PART 3

EXPLANATORY NOTES

Provisions of a Lease Agreement

1. Lease agreements cover a variety of assets, both movable and immovable, as well as tangible and intangible. The provisions agreed by the lessor and the lessee are situation specific but most often include:

   Duration of lease tenor

   a) Rental payments which are periodic cash outlays. These may be made in fixed or variable amounts, increasing or decreasing as the case may be such payments may also be predetermined as a function of the usage of the assets. They are set at a level that enables the lessor to recover the initial investment plus a fair return on the investment over the asset's economic life.

   b) Restrictions may include prohibiting further acquisition of debt or using the asset for certain operations.

   c) Imposition of obligation for taxes insurance and maintenance. These obligations may be imposed on the lessor or lessee or shared.

   d) A Default clause always spells out what constitutes a default, the right of the lessor and the penalties impost under such a condition. For instance, the lessor may demand all past and future rent payments in case of a default, or he may have the right to sell and collect any shortfall between the sale price and the amount due.

   e) Termination provisions which often prohibit cancellations for effect it and the penalties for such action are included.

   f) Options which are available to the lessee where the lease runs its course. Examples are:

   (i) No option where the lessor takes back his asset with no lessee

   (ii) Bargain renewal option where the lessee has the choice to lease at lower than usual rental and

   (iii) Bargain purchase option where the lessee is given the choice to acquire the asset for a normal sum Hire purchase

2. Lenders are sometimes willing to lend to high-risk business or individuals only on the basis of long-term direct reduction loans. Direct reduction loans require the borrower to repay the principal and the interest uniform installments throughout the life of the loan. Thus, the principal borrowed is an example of a direct reduction loan, often associated with high risk.

3. Under the hire purchase plan, the economic ownership invested in the purchaser for the moment the agreement for hire purchase is entered into. The inclusion of the asset in the purchaser's books is thus appropriate. The obligations arising from the hire purchase agreement are recognized under facilities.

4. With hire purchase, the vendor retains the legal ownership of the asset sold until the entire cost of the asset is paid up. The asset, however, is no longer recorded as a part of the vendor's assets.

5. Assets usually traded under hire purchase are motor vehicle and home appliances. A wider range of assets is traded under other leasing types, such as commercial vehicles and computers. Generating sets, photocopies, printing machines, forklifts, earth-moving equipment and aircraft.

Classification of Leases

1. Leases are classified as either finance leases or operation leases as defined in paragraph 5 above.

2. Ownership property entails risks and benefits. Some of the risks include losses due to poor performance, obsolescence, idle capacity, losses in residual value and un-insured damage. Some of the benefits include the use of the asset as collateral, freedom to use the asset as one desires, and appreciation of value.

3. The main criterion for the classification of a lease as either a finance lease or an operating lease is whether the risks and benefits associated with a lease have been transferred substantially to the lessee or retained by the lessor.

4. A lease is said to qualify as a finance lease if the following conditions are met:

   a) The lease is non-cancellable, and

   b) Any of the following is applicable:

   (i) Lease term covers substantially (80%) more the useful life of the assets, or the net present value of the lease at its inception, using minimum lease payments and the implicit interest rate is equal to or greater than the fair value of the leased asset; or

   (ii) The lease has a purchase option which is likely to be exercised.

5. Any other lease that does qualify as a finance lease is usually treated as an operating lease.

Sub-Lease:

1. Sometimes a lease agreement permits the lessee to sub-lease to a third party who becomes a sub-lease. For the purpose of the new lease, the original lessee becomes the lessor. All or some of the obligations and the rights under the original lease are transferred to the new lessee.

2. The accounting treatment of a sub-lease is not different from that accorded a normal or original lease because there is a lessor and a lessee, respectively. The original lessee treats all the transactions pertaining to a sub-lease as lessor while the sub-lessees treat them as a lessee accordingly. The initial lessee continues to account for the original lease as a lessee.

3. Leases involving real estate require certain classification and accounting treatment by the lessees. The land, land, buildings, or equipment of a part of a lease agreement can be classified as either a finance lease or an operating lease. In Nigeria, the ownership of all land is vested in the State by virtue of a Land Use Act of 1978. Lease involving land in Nigeria are operating lease Capital Allowances on Qualifying Assets under Lease.

4. Only the lessor can claim capital allowances under lease in accordance with current tax legislation (CITA 1979 as amended) except in the case of the purchase transactions where the hire (the lessee) can claim capital allowance the exclusion of the lessor.

Accounting for Finance Lease By the Lessee

1. Under the finance lease, the lessee treats the lease transactions as if an was being purchased. That is like a financing transaction in which an asset is acquired and an obligation created.

2. The usual legal form of a lease agreement is such that the lessee does not acquire legal title to the leased asset. However, in the case of finance lease, the substance and finance reality are that the lessee acquires the economic benefits from the use of the leased asset for the major part of its useful life. Thus, the capitalization of finance lease at the accounts of the lessee is justified by consideration of substance over form.

3. Proponents of lease capitalization argue that by recognizing leases that are in essence purchase of assets as such, an enterprise's true economic resources and obligations are reflected in the accounts. Leaving them out usually results in understatement of assets employed and obligations incurred by an enterprise in generating revenues.

4. Proponents of capitalization argue that since the lessee does not legally own the assets, they should not be included among the lessee's assets. Besides proper disclosure of lease transactions in the notes to the accounts will provide the same information to users of financial statements.

5. The two alternative methods of accounting for finance leases by lessees are:

6. Record the leases as acquisition of assets and incurrence of liabilities or

7. Account for each lease payment as an expense of the period in which it is incurred.

8. In accounting for finance lease under the first method (24a), the lessee records an asset and a liability at an amount equal to the present value of the minimum lease payment during the term of the lease.

9. Where, however, the lessee is committed to guaranteeing all the residual value of the leased asset, the lessee records equal to the present value of the minimum lease payment during the term of the lease.

10. If the residual value is only partially guaranteed by the lessee or where no residual value is specified in the lease agreement, the lessee's interest in the leased asset id diminished by the amount of any un-guaranteed residual value expected to accrue to the lessor at the end of the lease term. Thus, the initial amount recorded by the lessee as at the beginning of the lease term, could be the fair value of

the asset at the inception of the lease minus the present value of the estimated unguaranteed residual value, if any, expected to accrue to the lessor at the end of the lease term.

11. In order to determine the discounted present value of leased assets and liabilities, two interest rates can be used:

   a)   Interest rate implicit in the lease, or

   b)   Lessee's incremental borrowing rate.

12. The interest rate implicit in the lease is the discount rate that causes the present value at the beginning of the lease term of the minimum lease payments and any unguaranteed residual value accruing to the lessor to be equal to the fair value of the leased asset at the inception of the lease. In practice, some form of approximation is sometimes used to simplify the calculations, e.g. sum of the years digit.

13. Lessee's incremental borrowing rate of interest is a substitute rate applicable to borrowed funds obtainable under similar security and for the same term by the lessee.

14. Each lease payment made by the lessee comprises two elements:

   a)   Interest expense, and

   b)   An amount that reduces the lease obligation.

   c)   The outstanding lease liability multiplied by the interest rate gives the interest expense.

15. Where the lease agreement contains a provision for the transfer of the assets, of the lessee, or contains a bargain purchase option, the leased asset is often amortised in a manner consistent with the lessee's normal depreciation policy.

16. If the lease does not provide for the transfer of ownership, the asset is amortised over the term of the lease or the useful life of the asset, whichever is shorter.

ACOUNTING FOR OPERATING LEASES BY THE LESSEES

1. With an operating lease, the lease assigns rent to the periods benefiting from the use of the asset and ignores, in the accounts, any commitments to make future payments. Appropriate accruals are usually made if the accounting period end between cash payment dates.

ACCOUNTING FOR FINANCE LEASES BY THE LESSOR

1. In recognition of the financing aspect of the investment in a financial lease a lessor usually records a lease payment receivable rather than a fixed asset is owned.

DIRECT FINANCE LEASES

1. In a direct finance lease, the lease contract usually establishes the lessor's right to receive a series of payments from the leases in return for providing the right to use the asset. At the beginning of the

lease term, the lessor recognizes the total minimum lease payments receivable plus any unguaranteed residual value expected to accrue to the lessor.

2. Unearned interest income in a finance lease is the difference between the lease rental receivable and the leased asset's fair value at the lease's inception. This amount is amortized systematically over the lease term.

3. The lessor's investment in the lease is represented by the lease rental receivable less the balance of unearned income and any provisions for items such as bad and doubtful debt.

4. The periodic minimum lease payment that is usually received is made up of no components:

   a) Interest income earned and

   b) An amount that reduces the lease rental receivable

The opening balance of lessor's investment multiplied by the interest rate gives the interest income earned for the period.

ACCOUNTING FOR OPERATING LEASES BY THE LESSOR

1. If the lessor classifies a lease as an operating lease, it means that he has retained the risks and benefits of ownership and, therefore, accounts for the leased property as a fixed asset.

2. The lease payments he receives periodically are accounted for as lease rental income.

3. Initial direct costs incurred with respect to operating leases are usually written off in periods incurred.

SALE LEASEBACK TRANSACTIONS

1. Under a sale and leaseback transaction, the owner of property (seller or lessee) sells the asset to another person and simultaneously leases it back from the new owner. The use of the asset is usually uninterrupted.

2. In a sale and leaseback transaction, the asset may be sold at a price equal to or greater than current market value. It is then leased back for a term approximating the useful life of the asset and for payments that are sufficient to cover the new owner's investment plus a reasonable return thereon.

3. A sale and leaseback lease can be classified as an operating or a finance lease depending on whether the lease met the criterion specified in paragraphs 14 and 15.

4. If the lease qualifies as a finance lease, the excess of sales proceeds over the carrying amount is usually deferred by the seller lessee and amortised over the term of the lease or the useful life of the asset, whichever is shorter.

5. Suppose the lease qualifies as an operating lease. In that case, there income generated by the seller lessee is usually deferred and amortised in proportion to the rental payment over the period of time the assert is expected to be used by the lessee.

6. Where the market value is less than the asset's net book value on a sale and leaseback date, the loss is usually recognized immediately.

SALES-TYPE LEASES

1. The primary difference between a direct finance lease and a sales type lease is the manufacturer's or dealer's profit (loss) resulting from the sale to the lessee. This is usually a means of promoting the sale of the manufacturer's product.

2. In order to account for sales-type lease, the following are needed;

   a) Gross investment in lease or lease payments receivable with residual value being zero

   b) Unearned interest income

   c) Sales price of the asset, and

   d) The cost of carrying value of the asset sold.

3. Each datum can be explained as follows:

   a) The lessor's gross investment in a lease is the undiscounted total return the lessor expects to receive from the asset.

   b) The unearned interest income is the difference between the investment in the lease and the present value of the minimum payment.

   c) The sales of the leased asset is the market value at the inception of the lease.

4. Sale type leases usually contain two profit elements:

5. The initial profit or loss on the transaction at the inception of the lease; and

6. The interest income to be earned over the lease term.

7. In view of the fact that this transaction is recognized by the lessor as sale, the cost or carrying amount of the asset is removed from the books. The profit or loss resulting from the finance lease set out in paragraph 36-37.

8. The treatment of lease payments receivable and unearned interest income follows the pattern for direct finance lease set out in paragraph 36-37.

OTHER RELATED ACCOUNTING MATTERS

INITIAL DIRECT COSTS

1. In an attempt to negotiate and execute a lease agreement, a lessor may incur initial direct costs. Where such costs are specifically identified with a lease, their treatment will be dictated by the type of lease.

2. The initial direct cost may be written-off immediately or allocated against the income over the lease term.

3. Under the sales type lease, the initial cost may be charged to cost of sales as a part of the sales promotion cost of the asset sold. There is usually no reason to amortise it over the life of the lease contract.

RE-APPRAISAL OF UNGUARANTEED RESIDUAL VALUE

1. Due to uncertainties associated with estimating residual values, it is usually advisable to have them reassessed periodically to confirm that they are reasonable and in live with the initial estimate. If a periodic reassessment reveals a value that is not in conformity with an initial estimate, a write-down or increase in the lessor's investment may be made.

CONTIGENT RENTALS

1. Contingent rentals are increases or decreases in the minimum rental payments due to changes in some factors occurring after the inception of the lease such as:

   a) Changes in hours of use of a leased asset

   b) Legislation

   c) Increase (decrease) in interest rate and

   d) Volume of sales

   Since these factors are not predictable or measurable at the inception of the lease, they do not usually form a part of the minimum lease payment. They account for the variations between the predetermined and the actual rental payment.

2. Due to the uncertainties associated with contingent rentals, they are usually written-off by the lessee in the period in which they are incurred and taken to income by the lessor when earned.

PART 4
ACCOUNTING STANDARD

ACCOUNTING FOR LEASES

The accounting standard comprises paragraphs 61-89 of this statement. The standard should be read in the context of paragraph 1-60 of this statement and of the preface to the statements of accounting standards published by the Nigerian Accounting Standard Board.

GENERAL

1. A reporting enterprise should state, in the appropriate section of its financial statement, its accounting policy with respect to leases.

2. A reporting enterprise should classify a lease as either a finance lease or an operating lease at the inception of a lease.

3. A lease qualifies as a finance lease if the following conditions are met:

   a) Lease is non-cancellable and

   b) Any of the following is applicable;

   (i) The lease term covers substantially (80% or more) the estimated useful life of the asset, or

   (ii) The net present value of the lease at its inception using the minimum lease payments and the implicit interest rate is equal to or greater than the fair value of the leased asset, or

   (iii) The lease has a purchase option which is likely to be exercised.

4. A lease that does not qualify as a finance lease as specified in paragraph 63 should be treated as an operating lease.

ACCOUNTING FOR LEASES IN THE FINANCIAL STATEMENTS OF LESSES

FINANCE LEASES

1. The reporting enterprise should account for a finance lease by recording the lease as an acquisition of an asset and the incurrence of a liability.

2. Where the lessee capitalizes lease right as above, the following should be determined:

   a) The initial value of the leased asset and the corresponding liability

   b) The amortization rate or amount; and

   c) The amount by which the lease liability is to be reduced.

3. At the beginning of the lease term, the lessee should record the initial asset and liability at amount equal to the fair value of the leased asset less the present value of an unguaranteed or partially guaranteed residual value, which would accrue to the lessor at the end of the term of the lease. The interest rate implicit in the lease is the discount factor to apply in calculating the present value of the unguaranteed residual value accruing to the lessor.

4. Where the lessee cannot determine the fair value of the leased asset at the inception of the lease or is unable to make a reasonable estimate of the residual value of the lease without which the interest rate implicit in the lease could not be computed, the initial asset and liability should be recorded at amount equal to the present value of the minimum lease payments using the lessee's incremental borrowing rate as the discounting factor.

5. The leased asset should be depreciated, or the rights under the leased asset should be amortised in a manner consistent with the depreciation of the lessee's own asset.

6. The minimum lease payment in respect of each accounting period should be allocated between finance charge and the reduction of the outstanding lease liability. The finance charge should be determined by applying the rate implicit in the lease to the outstanding liability at the beginning of the period. The "sum-of-years-digit" may be used as an approximation.

7. Contingent rentals should be written off during the period in which they are incurred.

OPERATING LEASES

1. The rental expense should be charged to the income account on a systematic basis in line with the time pattern of the user's benefit, not on the basis of the rental payments made by the user.

ACCOUNTING FOR LEASES IN THE FINANCIAL STATEMENTS OF THE LESSORS

FINANCE LEASES

1. An asset under a lease should be recorded in the financial statement of the lessor, not as property, plant and equipment, but as an investment in a lease.

2. At the inception of the lease, the lessor should recognize in the accounting simultaneously:

   a) Gross investment in the lease, and

   b) Unearned finance income from the lease.

3. The unearned finance income should be deferred and allocated to income of the lessor over the lease term based on a pattern reflecting a constant periodic range of return on the lessor's net investment outstanding.

4. Contingent rental should be recognized in the account of the period to which they relate.

5. Initial direct costs that are identifiable with direct financing leases should be taken to the income statement in the period in which the costs were incurred.

6. In sales-type leases, the manufacturer or dealer lessor takes the difference between the fair value of the asset at the inception of the lease and its carrying amount to the income statement.

7. Investment in leases should be reviewed periodically for recover-ability in same manner as other receivables, but having regard to the security, if any, by the lessor e.g. recourse to the leased asset.

8. Where a re-appraisal is made of the asset's residual value and this shows diminution, the resulting loss should be charged to the income statement. Gross investment in the lease should similarly be written down.

a) The amount and the major classes of assets being leased at the balance sheet date. Liabilities related to these leased assets should be separately disclosed from other liabilities while, differentiating between current and long-term portions of the liabilities.

b) Commitments for minimum lease payments with a term in excess of one year, in summary, stating the amount and the yearly future payments due.

c) Any significant financing restrictions, renewal or purchase options contingent rentals and other contingencies from leases.

DISCLOSURES IN FINANCIAL STATEMENT OF LESSORS:

The following disclosures should be made in financial statements of the lessor:

1. The gross investment in leases classified as finance leases, the related deferred income and the unguaranteed residual values of the leased assets should be disclosed at the balance sheet date.

2. The net investment in lease should be broken into current and non-current portions.

3. For assets under operating lease, the amount of assets under each category and the accumulated depreciation at the balance sheet date.

PART 5

NOTES ON LEGAL REQUIREMENTS

The requirements of this standard are complementary to any disclosure requirements of the companies and allied matter Decree 1990 and other relevant laws and regulations.

QUESTION ON IAS II

LEASES

1. Distinguish between the two types of leases.

2. Outline the recommended respective treatments in the book as of account of your company.

3. To set out the recommended respective disclosures in the published accounts of your company.

OPERATING LEASE:

1. Where the lessor classifies a lease agreement as an operating lease, it should be accounted for by the lessor as an item of property, plant and equipment. Accordingly, the periodic rentals that are receivable should be treated as income.

2. The depreciation of a leased asset by the lessor should be on the basis of lessor's normal depreciation policy for that class of assets leased out.

3. The initial direct costs associated with the operating lease should be incurred in the income statement.

ACCOUNTING FOR SALE AND LEASE-BACK TRANSACTIONS:

1. Where in a sale and lease-back transaction, an asset is sold at a price equivalent or greater than the current market value and it is leased back for approximating the useful life of the asset and for payments that sufficiently cover the new owner's investment plus a reasonable return thereon transaction should be classified as a finance lease by the seller lessee.

2. Suppose a sale and lease-back qualifies as an operating lease. In that case, that is when not meet the conditions of a finance lease profit generated by the seller should be deferred and amortised systematically over the life of the asset.

3. Where a sale and lease-back qualifies as an operating lease, that is when not meet the conditions of a finance lease profit generated by the seller should be deferred and amortised in proportion to the rental payment term of the lease.

4. Where the asset's market value is less than the carrying amount of the sale and leaseback transaction, the difference should be done immediately to the income statement of the seller lessee. Similarly associated with the transaction, e.g., professional free, should be done to the income statement.

DISCLOSURES IN FINANCIAL STATEMENTS OF LESSEES.

1. In addition to the disclosure requirement of SA 2 –INFORMATION DISCLOSED IN FINANCIAL STATEMENTS and IAS 3 ACCOUNTING PROPERTY, PLANT AND EQUIPMENT; the following disclosure made:

Solution to IAS II

IAS II is similar to IAS 17

Illustration/Solution

1. IAS 17 and IAS distinguishes between Finance Lease and Operating Lease.

2. Finance leases are those which transfer substantially all the risks and rewards of ownership of an asset to the lessee.

3. Typical characteristics of a financial lease are:

4. The rental repayable during the term of the lease will be sufficient to repay the lessor the cost of the equipment plus interest thereon.

5. The lessee will be responsible for the maintenance and insurance of the equipment through the lease.

6. The term of the lease is for the major part of the useful and economic life of the equipment.

Operating Leases are all leases other than finance lease.

The recommended treatments in Accounts:

7. A finance lease should be reflected in the Balance Sheet of a lease by recording an asset and a liability at amounts equal at the inception of the lease to the present value of the minimum lease payments or if lower at the fair value of the leased property. The minimum lease payments, the discount factor is the interest rate implicit in the lease.

8. Rentals should be apportioned between the finance charge and reduction of the outstanding liability.

9. The depreciation policy for leased assets should be consistent.

OUTSTANDING LEASES:

The charge to income under an operating lease should be the rental expenses, the accounting period, recognized on a systematic basis.

Recommended disclosure requirements.

FINANCE LEASE:

1. Disclosure should be made of the amounts of assets that are subject of finance leases and liabilities related to these lease assets should be shown separately.

2. Commitments for minimum lease payments under finance lease payments under finance leases and under non-cancellable operating leases:

3. Significant financing restrictions, renewal or purchase options.

CHAPTER THIRTEEN
AS 12
ACCOUNTING FOR DEFERRED TAXES

DEFINITIONS

The following terms are used in these statements with the meanings

1. Deferred Tax is the tax attributable to timing differences.

2. Timing Differences are differences between the taxable income and accounting income which arise because the periods in which some items of revenue and expenses are included in taxable income differ from the periods in which they are included in accounting income. Such differences originate in one period and reverse in one or more subsequent periods.

3. Permanent Differences are difference between taxable income and accounting income for a period that do not reverse in subsequent periods.

4. Tax Expense or Tax Savings is the amount of tax charged against or credited to the income of the period.

5. Accounting Income/Loss is the aggregate income or loss for the period as reported in the income statement, including unusual and extraordinary items but before deducting related income tax expense or adding related income tax saving.

6. Taxable Income (Tax Loss) is the amount of income or loss for a period, determined according to the rules prescribed by the relevant tax authority.

BASES OF PROVIDING FOR DEFERRED TAXES

The objectives of providing the deferred taxes is to ensure that the tax expense reported in an income statement of a particular period reflects the tax effects of revenue and expenses included in the pre-tax accounting income of the period. Permanent differences are not taking into consideration as they do not affect other periods.

In providing for deferred taxes, three major bases are commonly in use. These are the nil provision basis, the full provision basis and the partial provision.

Under the nil provision basis, tax effect of timing differences are ignored completely. Only the tax payable in respect to the accounting period is changed to income in that period, and no provision is made for deferred taxes. Proponents of this treatment hold the view that since tax liability arises only on taxable income and not on accounting, there is no need to provide for deferred taxes.

The full provision basis takes into account all the timing differences. Support for this view is based on the principle that financial statement of a particular period are expected to recognize the tax effects of all the transactions occurring in that period.

Under the partial provision basis, the tax effects of some timing differences are excluded from the computation of deferred taxes when there is reasonable evidence that those timing differences will not reverse for some considerable number of years. Supporters of the view argue that deferred tax has to be provided only where it is probable that tax will become payable as a result of the reversal of timing differences.

The partial provision has one major advantage over the other two bases discussed above. Under this method, the deferred tax provisions are based on assessing the ultimate tax liability.

METHOD OF COMPUTATION

The tax effect of timing differences (deferred tax) is usually computed as the difference between the tax computed after taking into account the transaction given rise to the timing difference and the tax computed without including such transaction.

As tax rates change over time, giving rise to the question of what rate to use in computing deferred taxes, the choice either the deferral or the liability method becomes fundamental to the method to computation of deferred taxes.

DEFERRED METHOD

Under the deferred method, deferred taxes are determined on the basis of the tax rate in effect when the timing differenced originate. No adjustments are made later to account for subsequent tax rate changes. Reversals of the tax effects of timing differences are accounted for using the tax rate current at the time the timing differences arose. For practical purposes, the rate used may be either average rate to date, or a rate determined through first-in-first out (FIFO) approach.

A basic argument against the deferral method is that under this method, the balance of deferred taxes may not represent the actual amount of additional taxes payable or receivable in the periods that timing differences reverse.

LIABILITY METHOD

Under the liability method, the deferred tax amount is computed using the tax rate expected to be in force during the period in which the timing differences reverse. Usually, the current tax is used as the best estimate of the future tax rate unless changes in tax rates are known in advance.

Under this method, the deferred tax provision represents the best estimate of the amount that would be payable or recoverable if the relevant timing differences reverse.

Thus, the difference between income tax expense and income tax payable for the period is directly adjusted on the deferred tax balance.

When accounting for timing differences results in a debt balance, prudence require that such debt be carried forward in the balance sheet only if there is a reasonable expectation of realization; this, if sufficient future taxable income will be generated in the period in which the timing differences will reverse.

POSITION OF THE STANDARD

Deferred tax should be computed using the liability method.

The tax effects of timing differences should be shown separately from the items or transactions to which they relate.

Provision for deferred taxes should be made except where there is a reasonable evidence that the timing differences will not reverse for some considerable period (at least three years) ahead. There should also be no indication that these timing differences will likely reverse after this period.

Deferred taxes relating to ordinary activities should be shown separately as part of the tax on extra-ordinary items.

The potential tax saving from tax loss available for carry-forward to future periods should not be included in the net income unless there is reasonable certainty that there will be future taxable income against which the loss will be relieved within the limited period allowed by the tax laws.

PART 1

INTRODUCTION

1. Profits and other gains of business organizations are sometimes recognized in one accounting period but brought into taxation in another period. In this situation there is need to consider deferred taxes and how to account for them properly in the financial statements of the related periods.

2. This statement deals with accounting for deferred taxes on income recognition and assessment. It related primarily to the deferred tax aspects of companies income tax, capital gains tax and petroleum profits tax in Nigeria.

3. Primary objective of the statement is to provide a guide for unity and acceptable methods and bases used in:

   a) Providing for deferred taxes;

   b) Computation of deferred taxes; and

   c) Presentation in the Financial Statements

4. Statement does not cover royalties; excise duties and sales taxes are indirect taxes charged and payable on production or sales such are usually not subject to timing differences with respect accounting and tax treatments except to the extent that a portion that is produced remains unsold at the end of the accounting of such differences are easily accounted for through appropriate components.

PART 2

DEFINITIONS

1.   The following terms are used in this statement with the meaning specified:

a) Deferred tax is the tax attributed to timing differences.

b) Timing Differences are differences between the taxable income and accounting income which some items of revenue and expenses are included in taxable income differ from the periods in which they are included in accounting income. Such differences originate in one period and reverse in one or more subsequent periods.

c) Permanent Differences are difference between taxable income and accounting income for a period that do not reverse in subsequent periods.

d) Tax Expenses or Tax Savings is the amount of tax charged against or credited to the income of the period.

e) Accounting Income/Loss is the aggregate income or loss for the period reported in the income statement, including unusual and extra-ordinary items but deducting related income tax expense or adding related income tax saving.

f) Taxable Income (Tax Loss) is the amount of income or loss for period determined according to the rules prescribed by the relevant tax authority.

PART 3

EXPLANATORY NOTES

1. Generally, the amount of tax payable in any particular period does not directly relate to the amount of income or loss shown on the income statement. This is so because the tax authorities compute the taxable income for a period based on a set of rules different from the generally accepted accounting principles followed while preparing the income statement.

2. Both the degrees of recognition and disclosure of deferred taxes in financial statements vary widely in Nigeria. Some subsidiaries of oversea companies (FIFO) approach

3. Operating in Nigeria tend to make provision for deferred taxes in compliance with the requirements of the parent's home country. Other international and major Nigerian companies tend to

acknowledge deferred tax but generally made no provision for it. These companies usually mention the liability for deferred taxes by way of footnotes.

PERMANENT DIFFERENCES

1. One reason for permanent differences is that certain items are considered to be properly included in the calculation but must be excluded from the other. For example, donations other than those specified in sections 20 and 21 of Companies Income Tax Act, 1979 are not allowable deductions in determining taxable income. Similarly, certain items of income that are properly included in the income statement are not subject to tax, such as interest arising on certain government securities. Differences such as these are described as permanent differences.

TIMING DIFFERENCES

1. A good example of timing differences is where the depreciation rate used to determine accounting income. Also, exercising intangible development cost by taking hundred percent deduction in the year the expenditure is incurred instead of the normal depreciation spread for accounting purposes is another example.

2. The incorporation in the balance sheet of the revaluation of an asset including an investment ion an associated or subsidiary company, could create a timing difference because the profit or loss that would result if the asset is realised and its revalued carrying amount, would be taxable, unless the disposal of the revalued asset and of any subsequent replacement asset would not result in a tax liability after taking account of any expected roll-over relief.

BASES OF PROVISING FOR DEFERRED TAXES

1. The objectives of providing for deferred taxes is to ensure that the tax expenses reported in an income statement of a particular period reflects the tax effect of revenue and expenses included in the pre-tax accounting income of the period permanent differences are not taking into consideration as they do after other periods.

2. Three major bases are commonly used to provide for deferred taxes. They are the nil provision basis, the full provision basis and the partial provision basis.

3. Under the nil provision basis, the tax effect of timing differences are ignored completely. Only the tax payable in respect to the accounting period is charged to income in that period, and no provision is made for deferred taxes. Proponents of this treatment hold the view that since tax liability arises only on taxable income and not on accounting income, there is no need to provide for deferred taxes.

4. The full provision basis takes into account all the timing differences. Support for this view is based on the principle that financial statement of a particular period are expected to recognize the tax effects of all the transactions occurring in that period.

5. Under a partial provision basis, the tax effects of some timing differences arc excluded from the computation of Deferred taxes when there is reasonable evident that those timing differences will not reverse for some considerable number of years. Supporters of the view argue that deferred tax has to be provided only where it is probable that tax will become payable as a result of the reversal of timing differences.

6. The partial provision basis has one major advantage over the other two bases discussed above. Under this method, the deferred tax provisions are based on assessing the ultimate tax liability.

METHOD OF COMPUTATION

1. The tax effect or timing differences (deferred tax) is usually computed as the difference between the tax computed after taking into account the transaction given rise to the timing difference and the tax computed without including such transaction.

2. As tax rates change over time, giving rise to the question of what rate to use in computing deferred taxes, the choice either the deferral or the liability method becomes fundamental to the method of computation of deferred faxes.

DEFERRAL METHOD

1. Under the deferral method, deferred taxes are determined on the basis of the tax rates in effect when the timing differences originate. No adjustments are made later to account for subsequent tax rate changes. Reversals of the tax effects of timing differences are accounted for using the tax rate current at the time the timing differences arose. For practical purposes, the rate used may be either an average rate to date, or a rate determined through first-in-first out (FIFO) approach.

2. A basic argument against the deferral method is that under this method, the 'balance of deferred taxes may not represent the actual amount of additional taxes payable or receivable in the periods that timing differences reverse.

LIABILITY METHOD

1. Under the liability method, the amount of deferred Sax is computed by using the tax rate expected to be in force during the period in which the timing differences reverse. Usually, the current tax rate is used as the best estimate of the future tax rate unless changes in tax rates are known in advance.

2. Under this method, the deferred lax provision represents the best estimate of the amount which would be payable or recoverable if the relevant timing differences reverse.

3. Thus, the difference between income tax expense and income tax payable for the period is directly adjusted on the deferred tax balances.

4. When accounting for timing differences results in a debt balance, prudence require that such debt be carried forward in the balance sheet only if there is reasonable expectation of realization; that is,

if sufficient future taxable income , ill be generated in the period in which the timing differences will revere.

TAX LOSSES

1. The Nigerian Tax Laws provide that tax losses of current period may be as if to reduced or eliminate tax to be paid in future periods. However, in the case of cessation of business, such losses may be used to reduce or eliminate payable in the current period. The Companies Income Tax Act, 1979 maximum carry forward period of four years. The use of a current to reduce or eliminate tax payable or paid is not allowed except in the year of cessation of business.

2. Tax losses result in tax savings provided there is taxable income against where the losses could be relieved. Consequently, such potential tax savings related to a tax loss carry-forward may be included in the income statement.

3. Since the tax laws limit the period over which a tax loss may be carried for offset against future taxable income, only the related timing differs that will reverse during the limited period are considered computing deferred taxes and treated either as a debit balance or as a debit to the deferred account.

4. The tax savings result from offsetting, and a tax loss is included in the net income.

FINANCIAL STATEMENT PRESENTATION

1. There are two methods of presenting the tax effect of timing differences in the financial statements:

a) Net-of-tax method; and

b) Separate line-item method.

NET-OF-TAX METHOD

1. Under this method, the tax effects of timing differences (determined by either the deferral or liability method) are not reported separately. Instead, they are reported as adjustments to the carrying amounts of specific assets or liabilities and the related revenues or expenses.

2. Whilst the net-of-tax method equally recognizes that the value of assets and liabilities is affected by tax consideration, it fails to distinguish between a transaction and its tax effects. The method is generally discouraged.

SEPARATE LINE-ITEM METHOD

1. Under this method, the tax effects in die financial statements are shown separately from item or transactions which they relate. The main advantage of this method is that it distinguishes between an item and its tax consequences.

PART IV

ACCOUNTING STANDARD ON ACCOUNTING FOR DEFERRED TAXES

Statement of Accounting Standard 12 comprises paragraphs 32 to 41. The standard should be read in the context of paragraphs 1 to 31 of this statement and the preface to the Statements of Accounting Standards and other relevant standards published by the Nigerian Accounting Standards Board.

1. Deferred tax should be computed using the liability method.

2. The tax effects of timing differences should be shown separately from the items or transaction to which they relate.

3. Provision for deferred taxes should be made except where there is reasonable evidence that the timing differences will not reverse for some considerable period (at least 3 years) ahead. There should also be no indication that these timing differences will likely reverse after this period.

4. The provision for deferred tax liabilities should be reduced by any deferred tax debit balances rising from separate categories of timing differences. A debit balance in deferred tax account should not be carried forward as an asset unless there is a reasonable expectation of realization.

5. The provision for deferred tax liabilities should be reduced by any deferred tax debit balances arising from separate categories of timing differences. A debit balance in deferred tax account should not be carried forward as an asset unless there is a reasonable expectation of realization.

6. Deferred taxes relating to ordinary activities should be shown separately as part of tax on profit or loss resulting from ordinary activities.

7. Deferred tax relating to extra ordinary items should be shown as part of the tar on extra ordinary items. The potential tax saving from tax loss that is available for carry forward to future periods should be included in the net income unless there is reasonable certainty that there will be future taxable income against which the loss will be relieved within the limited period allowed by the tax laws.

DISCLOSURE.

1. Deferred tax balance should be presented in the balance sheet separately from the share holders' interest. In case of a debit balance, it should be shown as an asset.

2. The disclosure required in paragraph 36 and 37 above may be shown either the face of the income statement or as notes.

3. The total amounts of any deferred taxes, both current and cumulative, is provided for should be disclosed by way of a note and analyzed into their many components.

PART 5

NOTE ON LEGAL REQUIREMENTS

1. The requirements of this standard are complementary to any disclosure requirements of the Companies and Allied Matters Decree (No. 1) or any other relevant laws and regulations.

PART 6

COMPLIANCE WITH INTERNATIONAL ACCOUNTING STANDARD No. 12

1. The requirement of this Standard is substantially in line with the requirements of the International Accounting Standard No. 10-ACCOUNTING FOR TAXES ON INCOME as they relate to deferred taxes.

2. EFFECTIVE DATE

3. The Standard becomes operative for financial statements covering periods beginning on or after 1st January, 1993.

IAS 12, EXPOSURE DRAFT 12 AND SSAP 24 & SSAP 15:

DEFERRED TAXATIONS

Illustration 1

1. Discuss the justification for providing for deferred taxation

2. Explain the meaning of the term timing differences and permanent differences.

3. Summit International Breweries Account as at 31st October, 20 showed these:

   a) Capital Allowance exceed book depreciation by $504,000

   b) An expenses of $80,000 incurred in perfecting a debenture trust deed was disallowed.

   c) Interest on loan to finance building under construction $450,000 was capitalized for accounting purposes but claimed as an expense in the tax return.

Determine whether they are permanent or timing differences. (ICAN May, 20...).

Solution 1

1. Deferred taxation is an accounting convention which is introduced in order to apply the accruals concept to income reporting where timing differences occur.

2. Permanent differences arise because certain types of income may be tax free (e.g. Franked investment income) and certain expenditure, although quite properly charged against accounting profits, is not allowed as a deduction from taxation profits e.g. donation.

3. Timing differences arise because certain items are included in the accounts of a period different from that in which they are dealt with for taxation purposes. They originate in one period and may reverse in later periods.

4. Originating timing differences occur when the profits assessable to tax are less than the profits reported in the accounts in any given year.

5. Reversing timing differences occur in subsequent years when the profits assessable to tax are greater than the reported for the year in the accounts. Originating timing differences can be divided into short-term and long-term timing differences.

6. Short-term reverses in the next accounting period while long-term reverses over a period exceeding one year.

   a) Excess of capital allowance over depreciation by $504,000. This timing difference will affect deferred taxation.

   b) An expense of $80,000 incurred in perfecting a debenture trust was disallowed. This is a permanent differences and it will enter deferred taxation.

   c) Interest on loan to finance building. This is originating time difference and it will enter deferred taxation.

Illustration 2

ABC Limited prepares its accounts annually to March 31. For the year ended March 31, 20XX, the following taxation details appeared in its accounts:

1. Income tax at 40% based on the year's profits: $450,000

2. Deferred taxation account balance in the previous year: $650,000 (previous year: $450,000)

Required:

1. Explain the following terms:
   a) Timing differences
   b) Permanent differences

2. Present the notes to the published profit and loss account with respect to taxation for the year that ended March 31, 20XX.

3. Draft an appropriate note for inclusion in the accounts regarding deferred taxation. (ICAN PE II, May 20, Q6)

Solution 2

Explanation of Terms

and (ii) See Solution to Illustration 1 .

Taxation Note

Taxation:

1. Based on profit for the year at 40% = $450,000

2. Add: Deferred tax provision = $200,000

3. Total as per profit and loss account = $650,000

Taxation is calculated on the adjusted profit for the year in accordance with standard tax laws.

Deferred Taxation

The company does not make provisions for deferred taxation, as it is expected that the timing differences relating to excess capital allowances and depreciation charges will not reverse in the foreseeable future. Deferred taxation can be accounted for using the Deferral Method or the Liability Method.

Illustration 3

The timing differences for a company over three consecutive years were as follows:

Year	Timing Difference (Originating)	Timing Difference (Reversing)	Net Timing Difference	Corporation Tax Rate (%)
1	$20,000	-	$20,000	50%
2	$35,000	($5,000)	$30,000	40%
3	$5,000	($15,000)	($10,000)	35%

Required:

Show, with workings, the debits or credits in the Deferred Tax Account for each of the three years using:

1. Deferral Method

2. Liability Method

Solution 3

1. Deferral Method

Year	Net Timing Difference ($)	Tax Rate (%)	Deferred Taxation (DFR) ($)
1	$20,000	50%	$10,000
2	$30,000	40%	
Balance	$50,000	44% (Average)	
3	($10,000)	50% (FIFO)	$5,000
		44% (Average)	$4,400
Balance	($10,000)		$5,000
(FIFO)	($40,000)	50%	$12,000
(Average)	($40,000)	44%	$17,600

2. Liability Method

Year	Net Timing Difference ($)	Tax Rate (%)	Deferred Taxation ($)
1	$20,000	50%	$10,000
2	$30,000	40%	$12,000
Rate Adjustment	($20,000)	(50% - 40%)	$2,000
Balance	$50,000	40%	$22,000
Rate Adjustment	($50,000)	(40% - 35%)	$2,500
3	($10,000)	35%	$2,500
Balance	$40,000	35%	$14,000

FORMAT OF ACCOUNTING ENTRIES ON TAXATION

Profit on ordinary activities before tax

Less

Taxation on profit on ordinary activities

Profit on ordinary activities after tax

Extra ordinary items (less tax)

Profit for the financial year

Less

Appropriations

Retained Profit for the year

The breakdown of the heading taxation

Taxation

Corporation tax on profit in the year at X%

Over/under provision in previous year

Tax credits on dividends received

Irrevocable Corporation

Overseas Taxation relief

Overseas taxation

Transfers to/from deferred taxation

IAS 9 Research and Development Activities

This is similar to SSAP 12

Illustration 1

1. How does a standard define:

a) Pure Research

b) Applied Research

c) Development

Solution 1

Research is original and planned investigation undertaken with the hope of gaining new scientific technical knowledge and understanding.

1. Pure Research – work directed primarily towards the advancement of knowledge.

2. Applied Research – work, other than development cost, directed primarily at exciting pure research.

3. Development is the translation of research findings or other knowledge in a planned design for the production or substantially improved.

Development cost can be deferred if:

1. The product or process clearly defined and the cost attributable thereto can be separately identified.

2. Technical feasibility of the products to process has been demonstrated.

3. Management has induced its intention to produce and market or use the product or process.

4. A clear indication of a pure market.

5. Adequate resources exist to complete the project.

Illustration 2

1. Set out the circumstances under which development costs can be deferred and amortised. (ICAN May 20…, Q30).

2. State how research and development cost are treated in accounts

3. State the disclosure requirement of IAS.

Solution 2

For conditions disclosure see solution to the above question 1.

Where development expenditure is deferred, its amortization should begin with commencement of commercial production and then be written off over the period in which the product is expected to be sold or used.

Disclosure requirements

1. Disclose total research and development cost.

2. The movement in and the balance of unamortised deferred development cost should be disclosed.

IAS 10 – CONTINGENT LIABILITY AND POST BALANCE SHEET

Define:

1. Contingency

2. Post Balance Sheet event

Solution

1. Contingency is a condition or situation the ultimate outcome of which gain or loss will be confirmed only on the occurrence or non-occurrence of one or more uncertain future events e.g. legal cost of future and guarantors' liability.

2. Post Balance Sheet event- these are those events both favorable and unfavorable that occur between the Balance Sheet and the date on which the financial statement are authorized for issue.

IAS 20 = Government Grant

Illustration 1

State the two approaches in accounting for government grant.

Solution

These are:

1. Capital approach

2. Income approach

Under capital approach, a grant is credited directly to shareholders interest. The reasons for those are that government grants are finance device and since they are not earned. Under income approach, a grant is taken to income over one or more periods. The reasons are that government grants are receipts. Secondly, they are gratuities through compliance and thirdly, they are extension of fiscal policies.

These grants are presented using two methods:

1. Grant as a deferred income, recognized in the income statement on a systematic and rational basis.

2. Deducts the arriving at the carrying amount of an asset.

Government grants are repaid if certain conditions are not fulfilled. For this, the grant can be charged in the current income or deducted in arriving at the carrying amount of an asset.

Disclosure of government grant

1. The Accounting policies

2. The nature and extent of the grant

3. The effect of the receipt or repayment

4. Contingencies like unfulfilled conditions

IAS 22 – Business Combination

Illustration 1

What is business combination? State the methods of accounting for it.

Solution

A business combination is the result of the acquiring of control of one or more enterprises for another enterprise or the uniting of interest of two or more enterprise. This may limit to minority and goodwill acquisition.

The two methods are:

1. The purchase method

2. The pooling of interest method

Water purchase method, the buyer accounts for the cost of an acquisition by restating identifiable assets and liabilities acquired at fair value at the date of acquisition. This may result to goodwill.

Under pooling of interest method, the object is to account for the pooled enterprises as though the separate businesses were continue as before, though now jointly owned. There is no goodwill.

IAS 23 – Capitalization of borrowing cost

Illustartion 1

What is borrowing cost? Justify the capitalization of the cost.

Solution 1

Borrowing costs are interest costs incurred by an enterprise in connection with the borrowing of funds. This includes amortization of discount, premium on issue of debt foreign currency differences and auxiliary costs.

The argument for:

1. Borrowing cost are similar to other costs

2. failure to capitalize initial costs of acquisition reduces current earnings.

3. It results in a greater degree of comparability.

Argument against:

1. Borrowing costs are incurred to support the whole of the enterprise's activities.

2. Capitalization makes the same asset have different carrying amounts

3. Interest costs fluctuate.

Capitalization occurs when such costs are significant to the enterprise and there is expenditure on assets. Borrowing costs are capitalised by applying a capitalization rate to this expenditure.

IAS 24 – Related Party

Illustration

What is a related party?

Solution

Related Party

Parties are considered to be related if one party has the ability to control the other party or exercises significant influence over the other party in making financial and operating decisions.

Related Party Transaction: A transfer of resources or obligations between related parties, regardless of whether a price is charged.

Miscellaneous Accounts

1. Distinguish Between the Following Terms:

    a) Accounting and Bookkeeping

    b) Real and Nominal Accounts

    c) Capital Income and Revenue Income

    d) Accruals and Prepayments

    e) Provisions and Reserves

2. You are required to prepare a Two-Column Cash Book, Ledger Posting, and Trial Balance

Transactions:

May 1 – Started business with capital in cash $100

May 2 – Paid rent by cash $10

May 3 – F. Lean lent us $500, paying by cheque

May 4 – We paid B. Menta by cheque $65

May 5 – Cash sales $98

May 7 – N. Mercy paid us by cheque $62

May 9 – We paid B. Burton in cash $22

May 11 – Cash sales paid direct into the bank $53

May 15 – G. Morton paid us in cash $65

May 16 – We took $50 out of the cash till and paid it into the bank account

May 19 – We repaid F. Lean $100 by cheque

May 22 – Cash sales paid direct into the bank $66

May 26 – Paid motor expenses by cheque $12

May 30 – Withdrew $100 cash from the bank for business use

May 31 – Paid wages in cash $97

3. Three-Column Cash Book and Bank Reconciliation Statement

May 1 – Opening Balances:

a) Cash in hand $211

b) Cash in bank $3,984

May 2 – We paid cash of the following by cheque after deducting a 5% discount each:

a) T. Adams $80

b) C. Bibby $260

c) D. Clarke $440

May 4 – C. Potts pays us a cheque for $98

May 6 – Cash sales paid direct into the bank $49

May 7 – Paid insurance by cash $5

May 9 – The following persons paid us their accounts by cheque after deducting a 2.5% discount each:

a) R. Smiley $160

b) J. Turner $640

c) R. Pimlott $520

May 12 – Paid motor expenses by cash $100

May 18 – Cash Sales $98

May 21 – Paid salaries by cheque $120

May 23 – Paid rent by cash $60

May 28 – Received a cheque for $500 as a loan from R. Godfrey

May 31 – Paid for stationery by cheque $27

Solution

To create a Two-Column Cash Book, Ledger postings, and a Trial Balance based on the provided transactions, we'll start with the Two-Column Cash Book, followed by the Ledger postings, and finally the Trial Balance.

Two-Column Cash Book

Cash Book (May)

Date	Details	Cash (Dr)	Cash (Cr)	Bank (Dr)	Bank (Cr)
May 1	Capital	100			
May 2	Rent		10		
May 3	Loan from F. Lean			500	
May 4	Payment to B. Menta		65		
May 5	Cash Sales	98			
May 7	Payment from N. Mercy			62	
May 9	Payment to B. Burton		22		
May 11	Cash Sales			53	
May 15	Payment from G. Morton				65
May 16	Cash to Bank				50
May 19	Repayment to F. Lean			100	
May 22	Cash Sales			66	
May 26	Motor Expenses		12		
May 30	Cash from Bank	100			

Date	Details	Cash (Dr)	Cash (Cr)	Bank (Dr)	Bank (Cr)
May 31	Wages		97		
Total		298	296	781	50

Ledger Posting

Cash Account

Date	Details	Debit ($)	Credit ($)	Balance
May 1	Capital	100		100
May 5	Cash Sales	98		198
May 15	G. Morton	65		263
May 30	Cash from Bank	100		363
May 2	Rent		10	353
May 9	B. Burton		22	331
May 31	Wages		97	234
Total		298	129	234

Bank Account

Date	Details	Debit ($)	Credit ($)	Balance
May 3	F. Lean	500		500
May 7	N. Mercy	62		562
May 11	Cash Sales	53		615
May 16	Transfer from Cash	50		665
May 19	Repayment to F. Lean		100	565
May 22	Cash Sales	66		631
Total		731	100	631

Trial Balance (As of May 31)

Account	Debit ($)	Credit ($)
Cash	234	
Bank	631	
F. Lean (Loan)		500
B. Menta		65
B. Burton		22
G. Morton		65
N. Mercy		62
Wages	97	
Rent	10	
Motor Expenses	12	
Total	1,067	1,067

Three-Column Cash Book and Bank Reconciliation Statement

Three-Column Cash Book (May)

Date	Details	Cash (Dr)	Cash (Cr)	Bank (Dr)	Bank (Cr)
May 1	Opening Balance	211		3,984	
May 2	T. Adams (after 5% discount)		76		
May 2	C. Bibby (after 5% discount)		247		
May 2	D. Clarke (after 5% discount)		418		
May 4	C. Potts			98	
May 6	Cash Sales			49	
May 7	Insurance		5		
May 9	R. Smiley (after 2.5% discount)			156	
May 9	J. Turner (after 2.5% discount)			640	
May 9	R. Pimlott (after 2.5% discount)			508	
May 12	Motor Expenses		100		
May 18	Cash Sales	98			
May 21	Salaries				120
May 23	Rent		60		
May 28	Loan from R. Godfrey			500	
May 31	Stationery				27
Total		309	1,021	6,045	247

Bank Reconciliation Statement

Bank Reconciliation Statement (as of May 31)

Particulars	Amount ($)
Balance as per Cash Book	6,045
Add: Cheques issued but not presented	(sum of outstanding cheques)
Less: Deposits not credited	(sum of uncredited deposits)
Adjusted Balance	(reconcile)

Notes

Adjust the figures in the Bank Reconciliation Statement based on actual outstanding cheques and uncredited deposits.

B. The figures for discounts and payments need to be calculated according to the given percentages for items in the Three-Column Cash Book.

1. Concept vs. Convention in Accounting

2. Difference Between Concept and Convention in Accounting:

   a) Concepts are fundamental principles, such as the accrual concept, going concern, and matching principle.

   b) Conventions are accepted accounting practices, such as consistency and materiality.

   c) IAS I Accounting Policies: Consistency, Prudence, Accrual, and Substance Over Form.

3. A Trial Balance Will Always Balance – Discuss.

   a) A trial balance ensures that total debits equal total credits, but errors like omissions or compensating errors can still occur.

5. **Prepare Trial Balance, Trading, Profit & Loss Account, and Balance Sheet (June 30, 2020)**

Account	Debit ($)	Credit ($)
Sales		50,000
Rent	560	
Insurance	290	
Purchases	35,600	
Salaries and Wages	3,400	
Packing and Postage	560	
Rates	210	
Sundry Expenses	390	
Carriage Inwards	110	
Carriage Outwards	205	
Stock (June 30, 2019)	7,800	
Debtors	8,400	
Creditors		3,900
Cash at Bank	890	
Cash in Hand	80	
Buildings	20,000	
Machinery	6,000	
Motor Vehicles	3,980	
Drawings	4,500	
Capital		39,081

Adjustments at June 30, 2020:

1. Closing Stock $9,663

2. Expenses Owing: Carriage Inwards $33

3. Prepaid Expenses: Insurance $14, Rent $40, Packing and Postage $28

Solution:

Trial Balance for Fidelis (December 31, 2018)

Account	Debit ($)	Credit ($)
Capital Account		20,500
Purchases	46,500	
Sales		60,900
Repairs to Buildings	848	
Motor Car	1,050	
Car Expenses	318	
Freehold Land & Buildings	10,000	
Balance at Bank	540	
Furniture & Fittings	1,580	
Wages & Salaries	8,606	
Provision for Depreciation (Motor Car)		150
Provision for Depreciation (Furniture & Fittings)		120
Discount Allowed	1,061	
Discount Received		810
Drawings	2,400	
Rate & Insurance	218	
Bad Debts	353	
Provision for Bad Debts (Jan. 1, 2018)		
Trade Debtors	5,213	
Trade Creditors		4,033
General Expenses	1,586	
Stock in Trade (Jan. 1, 2018)	6,300	
Total	**86,659**	**86,659**

The following matters are to be taken into account:

1. Stock in trade 31 December, 2018, $8,800

2. Wages and salaries outstanding at 31 December 2018, $318

3. Rates and Insurances paid in advance at 31 December 2018, $45

4. The provision for bad debts is to be reduced to $100

5. During 1992, Fidelis withdrew goods, valued at $200 for his own use. No entry has been made in the books for the withdrawal of these goods.

6. The item "repairs to buildings" $848 includes $650 respect of alterations and improvements to the building.

7. One-third of the car expenses represents the cost of Fidelis' motoring for private as distinct from business purposes.

8. Depreciation of 10% on freehold land and building, 5% each on motor car, furniture, and fittings.

Required:

Prepare a **Trading Profit and Loss Account** for the year and a **Balance Sheet** as on 31st December, 2018. To prepare the Trading Profit and Loss Account and the Balance Sheet for both scenarios, we will follow standard accounting practices. Let's break it down step by step for each case.

5. Trading, Profit & Loss Account, and Balance Sheet (June 30, 2020)

SOLUTION

Trading Profit and Loss Account for the Year Ended June 30, 2020

Trading Account

Particulars	Amount ($)
Sales	50,000
Less: Cost of Goods Sold	
Opening Stock	7,800
Add: Purchases	35,600
Less: Closing Stock	(9,663)
Cost of Goods Sold	(33,737)
Gross Profit	16,263

Profit and Loss Account

Particulars	Amount ($)
Gross Profit	16,263
Less: Expenses	
Rent	560
Insurance (adjusted)	290 - 14
Salaries and Wages	3,400
Packing and Postage (adjusted)	560 - 28
Rates	210
Sundry Expenses	390
Carriage Outwards	205

Particulars	Amount ($)
Carriage Inwards (adjusted)	110 + 33
Total Expenses	5,500
Net Profit	10,763

Balance Sheet as at June 30, 2020

Assets	Amount ($)	Liabilities and Equity	Amount ($)
Non-Current Assets		Equity	
Buildings	20,000	Capital	39,081
Machinery	6,000	Drawings	4,500
Motor Vehicles	3,980		
Current Assets		Current Liabilities	
Closing Stock	9,663	Creditors	3,900
Debtors	8,400	Expenses Owing	33
Cash at Bank	890		
Cash in Hand	80		
Total Assets	49,706	Total Liabilities & Equity	49,706

6. Trading Profit and Loss Account and Balance Sheet for Fidelis (December 31, 2018)

Trading Profit and Loss Account for the Year Ended December 31, 2018

Trading Account

Particulars	Amount ($)
Sales	60,900
Less: Cost of Goods Sold	
Opening Stock	6,300
Add: Purchases	46,500
Less: Closing Stock	(8,800)
Cost of Goods Sold	(44,000)
Gross Profit	16,900

Profit and Loss Account

Particulars	Amount ($)
Gross Profit	16,900
Less: Expenses	
Repairs to Buildings (adjusted)	848 - 650
Wages & Salaries (adjusted)	8,606 + 318
Car Expenses (adjusted)	318 / 3
Rates & Insurance (adjusted)	218 - 45
General Expenses	1,586

Particulars	Amount ($)
Bad Debts (adjusted)	353
Discount Allowed	1,061
Total Expenses	12,161
Net Profit	4,739

Balance Sheet as at December 31, 2018

Assets	Amount ($)	Liabilities and Equity	Amount ($)
Non-Current Assets		Equity	
Freehold Land & Buildings	10,000	Capital Account	20,500
Furniture & Fittings	1,580	Drawings	2,400
Motor Car	1,050	Provision for Bad Debts	100
Current Assets		Current Liabilities	
Trade Debtors	5,213	Trade Creditors	4,033
Balance at Bank	540		
Cash in Hand	-		
Closing Stock	8,800		
Total Assets	28,183	Total Liabilities & Equity	28,183

Notes:

Adjustments and calculations for expenses were made based on the additional information provided.

Ii. Ensure that all figures are checked for accuracy and that any unmentioned items are accounted for as per standard accounting principles.

Iii. The net profits calculated in both cases reflect the earnings after all expenses have been accounted for.

ILLUSTRATION 7

The bank column in the cash book of G. Golden for the month of December 2016 appears as follows:

Cash Book

2016	Debit ($)	Credit ($)
Dec. 27	Balance b/d	200
Dec. 27	Balance b/d	1,600
Dec. 29	J. Peel	60
Dec. 28	J. Jacobs	105
Dec. 31	M. Johnson	220
Dec. 30	M. Coutts	15
	Balance c/d	560
	Total	2,280

Bank Statement

Date	DR ($)	CR ($)	Balance ($)
Dec. 27	Balance b/f		400 CR
Dec. 29	Cheque		60
Dec. 30	J. Jacobs	105	
Dec. 30	Credit Transfer		70
Dec. 31	Bank Commission	20	

Required:

1. Write up the new Cash Book

2. Prepare a **Bank Reconciliation Statement** as on 31 December, 2016.

SOLUTION

To create the new Cash Book and prepare the Bank Reconciliation Statement for G. Golden as of December 31, 2016, we will first write the Cash Book with the correct entries based on the information provided. Then, we will reconcile the differences between the Cash Book and the Bank Statement.

1. New Cash Book for December 2016

Cash Book

Date	Details	Debit ($)	Credit ($)
Dec. 27	Balance b/d	200	
Dec. 27	Balance b/d	1,600	
Dec. 28	J. Jacobs	105	
Dec. 29	J. Peel	60	
Dec. 30	M. Coutts	15	
Dec. 31	M. Johnson	220	
	Total	2,300	
	Balance c/d		560
	Total		560

2. Bank Reconciliation Statement as of December 31, 2016

Bank Reconciliation Statement

Particulars	Amount ($)
Balance as per Bank Statement	400 CR
Add: Cheques deposited but not yet credited	105
Add: Credit Transfer	70
Less: Outstanding Cheques	60
Less: Bank Commission	20

Particulars	Amount ($)
Adjusted Balance	525

Explanation of Entries

1. Cash Book: The totals for the Debit column (Cash Inflows) is calculated at $2,300. The credit column (Cash Outflows) shows a balance carried down of $560.

2. Bank Reconciliation Statement:

   a) The balance as per the Bank Statement is $400 CR.

   b) Add amounts for cheques that have been deposited but not yet appeared in the bank statement (e.g., J. Jacobs and the Credit Transfer).

   c) Subtract amounts for outstanding cheques and bank commissions.

Conclusion

After preparing the new Cash Book and the Bank Reconciliation Statement, it is clear how the Cash Book and the Bank Statement relate to one another. The adjusted balance reflects the true amount available in the bank after accounting for outstanding items.

Illustration 8

The Bank columns in the cash book of Ojah for the month of December, 2014 are as follows:

Cash Book

2014	Debit ($)	Credit ($)
Dec. 5	I. Hunt	308
Dec. 24	L. Mason	120
Dec. 29	K. Kilner	124
Dec. 31	G. Corrie	106
Dec. 31	Balance C/d	380
	Total	1,038

Bank Statement

Date	DR ($)	CR ($)	Balance ($)
Dec. 1	Balance b/f		709 O/D
Dec. 5	Cheque		308
Dec. 14	P. Dennis	140	
Dec. 24	Cheque		120
Dec. 29	K. Kilner: Trade is Credit	124	
Dec. 29	United Trust: Standing Order	77	
Dec. 31	Bank Charges	49	

Required:

1. An Adjusted Cash Book

2. The Reconciliation Statement at the end of the year.

Solution

Prepare the Adjusted Cash Book and the Bank Reconciliation Statement for Ojah for the month of December 2014, The Cash Book is modify based on the information provided and then reconcile the discrepancies with the Bank Statement.

1. Adjusted Cash Book for December 2014

Adjusted Cash Book

Date	Details	Debit ($)	Credit ($)
Dec. 5	I. Hunt	308	
Dec. 14	P. Dennis		140
Dec. 24	L. Mason	120	
Dec. 29	K. Kilner	124	
Dec. 29	United Trust		77
Dec. 31	G. Corrie	106	

Date	Details	Debit ($)	Credit ($)
Dec. 31	Bank Charges		49
	Total	658	266
	Balance C/d		380
	Total		380

2. Bank Reconciliation Statement as of December 31, 2014

Bank Reconciliation Statement

Particulars	Amount ($)
Balance as per Bank Statement	709 O/D
Add: Cheques deposited but not yet credited	0
Less: Outstanding Cheques	0
Less: Bank Charges	49
Adjusted Balance	758 O/D

Explanation of Entries

1. Adjusted Cash Book: The total for the Debit column (Cash Inflows) is $658, and the total for the Credit column (Cash Outflows) is $266. The balance carried down is $380.

2. Bank Reconciliation Statement:

a) The balance as per the Bank Statement is 709 O/D (overdrawn).

b) There are no cheques deposited that have not been credited yet, nor any outstanding cheques.

c) The Bank Charges of $49 are deducted from the balance.

Conclusion

After preparing the Adjusted Cash Book and the Bank Reconciliation Statement, we see how the Cash Book balances relate to the Bank Statement. The adjusted balance reflects the true position of the bank account after accounting for bank charges and ensuring all transactions are included.

Illustration 9

The following is a summary of a cash book as prepared for the month of December, 2017:

Cash Book Summary

Receipts ($)	Payments ($)
1,469	Balance b/f 761
Balance carried forward 554	Payments 1,262
Total	**2,023**

All receipts are banked, and payments are made by cheque. Upon investigation, the following discrepancies were found:

1. Bank Charges of $136 and payments entered in the Bank Statement had not been entered in the cash book.

2. Cheques drawn amounting to $267 had not been presented to the Bank for payment.

3. Cheques received totaling $762 had been entered in the Cash Book and paid into the Bank but had not been credited by the Bank until January 1988.

4. A cheque for $22 had been entered as a receipt in the cash book instead of as a payment.

5. A cheque for $25 had been debited by the Bank in error.

6. A cheque received for $80 had been returned by the Bank and marked 'No funds available.' No adjustment had been made in the cash book.

7. All dividends receivable are credited to the bank account. During December, amounts totaling $62 were credited by the Bank but had no entries in the Cash Book.

8. A cheque drawn for $6 had been incorrectly entered in the Cash Book as $66.

9. The balance brought forward should have been $771.

10. The bank Statement as of 31 December, 2017, showed an overdraft of $1,162.

Required:

1. Show the adjustments required in the Cash Book

2. Prepare a Bank Reconciliation Statement as on 31 December, 2017.

SOLUTION:

To address the discrepancies identified in the cash book summary for December 2017, we will first make the necessary adjustments to the Cash Book. Then, we will prepare the Bank Reconciliation Statement as of December 31, 2017.

1. Adjustments Required in the Cash Book

Original Cash Book Summary

1. Receipts: $1,469

2. Payments: $1,262

3. Balance b/f: $761

4. Balance c/f: $554

Discrepancies to Adjust:

1. Bank Charges of $136: This needs to be added to payments.

2. Cheques drawn amounting to $267: This will be ignored in the Cash Book as it does not need adjustment.

3. Cheques received totaling $762: These should be noted as deposits not yet credited, but won't be adjusted in the Cash Book until credited by the bank.

4. Cheque for $22 entered as a receipt: This needs to be adjusted as a payment.

5. Cheque for $25 debited by the Bank in error: This will be added as a receipt in the Cash Book.

6. Cheque for $80 returned by the Bank: This needs to be deducted from receipts.

7. Dividends receivable of $62 credited by the Bank: This will be added as a receipt in the Cash Book.

8. Cheque drawn for $6 entered as $66: This will reduce the payments by $60.

9. Balance brought forward should have been $771: This should be corrected.

10. Bank overdraft of $1,162: This indicates the actual bank position but does not require an adjustment to the Cash Book.

Adjusted Cash Book Summary

Description	Amount ($)
Original Receipts	1,469
Add: Dividends Receivable	62
Add: Error in Bank Debit	25
Less: Returned Cheque	(80)
Less: Cheque Marked as Receipt	(22)
Total Receipts	1,454
Original Payments	1,262
Add: Bank Charges	136
Less: Error in Cheque Entry	(60)
Total Payments	1,338
New Balance b/f	771
Balance c/f	554

2. Bank Reconciliation Statement as of December 31, 2017

Bank Reconciliation Statement

Particulars	Amount ($)
Balance as per Bank Statement	(1,162) O/D
Add: Cheques received not credited	762
Less: Outstanding Cheques	(267)
Add: Error in Bank Debit	25
Adjusted Balance	(642) O/D

Explanations:

1. The Adjusted Cash Book reflects the necessary changes to receipts and payments based on the discrepancies identified.

2. The Bank Reconciliation Statement reconciles the overdraft shown in the bank statement with the adjustments made.

Conclusion:

This reconciliation highlights the differences between the cash book and the bank statement, ensuring that all transactions are accurately reflected

CHAPTER FOURTEEN
RS 9, 28 / IAS 4 INVESTMENTS

PART 1

INTRODUCTION

1. Organizations, in the course of their business operations, apply all or some of their resources in acquiring assets to be held for capital appreciation, income generation, or other purposes such as securing trading advantages.

2. Many financial statements published in Nigeria do not disclose adequate information about the investments field by the reporting enterprises, this statement therefore seeks lo provide a guide for the accounting treatment of investment transactions and their disclosure in the financial statements.

3. This statement deals primarily with situations where the size of the investments does not enable the investor to exercise significant influence or control over the financial and operating decisions of the Investee companies.

4. This statement does not cover:

a) Stocks/Inventory covered in IAS No.3

b) Property, Plant and Equipment covered in IAS No.3,

c) Accounting for Lease IAS No. 11,

d) Investment in pension benefit plans and Life Insurance; Enterprises

e) Investment in subsidiaries and associates,

f) Investment in Joint Ventures,

g) Goodwill, Patents, Trademarks and similar Assets.

5. The statement focuses on three main forms of investments, namely;

a) Short-term investment (current investments)

b) Long-term investments, and

c) Investment properties.

DEFINITIONS

1. The following terms are used in this statement with the meanings specified below;

a) Investments are assets acquired by an enterprise for purpose of capital appreciation or income generation without any activities in the form of production, trade, or provision of services.

b) Short-term investments are readily realizable investments intended to be held for not more than one year.

c) Long-term investments are investments other than short-term investments.

d) An investment Property is an investment in land or building held primarily for generating income or capital appreciation and not occupied substantially for use or in the operations of the investing enterprise or another enterprise in the same group as the investing j enterprise. A property is deemed to be substantially occupied if the owner or another enterprise in the same- group occupies more than 15% of the lettable space.

e) Carrying Amount means the amount at which the asset is recorded in the books of account on a particular date in relation to an asset.

f) Market Value is the amount obtainable from the sale of an investing in an active market such as the Stock Exchange.

g) Fair Value is the amount for which an asset could be exchanged a knowledgeable willing buyer arid a knowledgeable willing seller is an arm's length transaction.

h) Marketable means that there is an active market value or an indicator of such value could be obtained.

EXPLANATORY NOTES

NATURE OF INVESTMENTS

Business organizations often employ funds not immediately needed in the conduct of regular operations advantageously without any activities being involved in the form of trade, production or the provision of services. Such investments could be in the form of equity securities, debt securities or investment in tangible assets such as land and building. However, some organizations have as their primary business the making of such investments.

CLASSIFICATION OF INVESTMENTS

For Balance Sheet purposes, investments are usually classified as short-term investments (current investments) or long-term investments.

SHORT-TERM INVESTMENTS

Short-term investments are investments held temporarily in place of cash and which can be converted into cash when current financing needs make such conversion desirable. In order to be classified as short-term, an investment must be readily realizable. In addition, it must be the intension of management to hold such an investment for not more than one-year Short-term investments may be in ordinary' shares, preference shares, bonds, treasury bills, commercial 1 papers, bankers' acceptances etc.

VALUATION OF SHORT-TERM INVESTMENTS

There is a wide difference in practice as lo the carrying of short-term investment. Some organizations carry such investments at:

a) Cost

b) Market value, or

c) Lower of Cost and Market Value (LCM).

COST

Valuation of short-term investments at cost requires that such investments be recorded at the date of acquisition and carried at cost unless their market value becomes less than cost by a substantial amount and the decline in market value is due to a permanent condition. Subsequent to such decline, recoveries in market value are not recognized in the accounts because the reduced carrying value is viewed as cost for future accounting purposes. Cost frill include such charges as .brokerages, fees, duties, etc. relating directly to the acquisition.

MARKET VALUE

1. Under the market value method of valuation, the investment portfolio is revalued at the end of each accounting period at market value poses two problems:

a) Determination of the market value of the securities at the end of each accounting period, and

b) The method of recognizing the holding gain or loss that may result.

Supporters of the market value method argue that since they are easily realizable stores of wealth or cash substitutes, the organization is not concerned with the cost of such items but the cash it could realize from their disposal. It is further argued that reporting investments at cost will enable management to recognize income at its discretion by selling selected investments, repurchasing them immediately, and reporting the resulting profit in the income statement. This will increase the reported income even though its transactions have not changed the organization's economic position.

LOWER OF COST AND MARKET VALUE (LCM)

Another method of valuing marketable securities is the Lower of Cost and Marks Value (LCM). Under the LCM method, short-term investments are carried as portfolio. Portfolios of short-term investments are carried at their aggregate acquisition cost unless their aggregate market value is lower, in which case t& portfolio is carried at the market value and the unrealised loss is recognized.

The amount by which aggregate cost exceeds aggregate market value (the unrealised loss) of the short-term equity investment portfolio is accounted as unrealised loss and charged to income for the period.

Proponents of the Lower of Cost and Market Value (LCM) method argue that it makes for a prudent balance sheet amount. If also prevents situations v temporary swings in stock market prices, which may reverse, are brought into the accounts merely as a result of the choice of a particular balance sheet data.

Critics of this method argue that the use of portfolio basis results in unrealised losses being offset against unrealised gains.

LOWER OF COST AND MARKET VALUE (MODIFIED)

Under this method, short-term investments are valued at lower cost and market value, on an item-by item basis. This approach avoids setting off unrealised losses against unrealised gains as is the case under the portfolio basis.

LONG-TERM INVESTMENTS

Long-term investments exist where management decides to employ funds over a long period of time to earn income. Classification of an investment as long-term must be justified no only by management intention but also by the circumstances of the individual case. Long-term investments may include debt and equity securities.

CARRYING AMOUNT OF LONG-TERM INVESTMENTS

1. The current market value of long-term investments is less immediate relevance as the management of an enterprise does not intend, or is unable to secure that value by their disposal. As such, long-term investments are carried at historical cost, less provision for impairments in their value. Alternatively; they may be carried at current market value. Where a long-term investment is carried at current market value, it is not appropriate to account for any increase in the current value a realised profit for the period. Instead, the amount of any increase is accounted for as a surplus on revaluation reserve.

2. Where management decides to earn1 long-term investments at market value such value is expected to be kept up to date. In order words, enterprises are expected to carry long-term investments at either current value or historical cost.

3. When a permanent decline in value of an investment occurs, the earning amount is usually reduced to recognize the loss. Such a reduction is charged to the income statement for the period. However, to the extent that decrease in carrying amount offsets a previous increase for the same investment, which has been credited to revaluation surplus and not subsequently reversed or utilized, it is charged against revaluation surplus.

4. When an investment has been written down as in paragraph 22 above, the new-earning amount is deemed to be the new basis for subsequent accounting purposes. Reductions in carrying amount

may be reversed when there is an increase, other than temporary; in the value of the investment, or if the reasons for the reduction no longer exist.

5. In the case of investments in debt securities, it would be appropriate to amortised any discount or premium arising on acquisition over the period to maturity so that earnings from the investment would reflect a constant yield based on acquisition cost which may be higher or lower than the coupon rates. The amortised discount or premium are credited or charged to income as though it were interest and added to or subtracted from the carrying amount of the security. The resulting carrying amounts are then regarded as cost.

6. Where dividends received represent a distribution of earnings retained i the business prior to the acquisition of the stock by the investor, the amount received relating to he pre-acquisition period is usually deducted from the cost of the investment. This distinguished from post-acquisition dividends which are credited to the income, statement.

7. Where interest received on dated stocks includes interest accrued before the dale of purchase, the relevant amount is usually credited to acquisition cost and the portion of interest relating to post-acquisition period of interest relating to post-acquisition period is credited to income statement.

8. An increase in the carrying amount of a long-term investment arising from revaluation is usually credited directly to owners' equity as a revaluation surplus However, an increase on revaluation, which is directly related to a previous decrease in earning amount for the same investment as that charged to income as in paragraph 22 above, is credited to income but only to the extent that offsets the decrease previously charged to income

INVESTMENT PROPERTIES

1. Investment properties represent an enterprise's interest in land and building held primarily for their investment potentials and not occupied substantially the enterprise itself or a member of its group of companies. A property deemed to qualify as an investment property if not more than 15% of the lettable space is occupied by the owner or another enterprise in the group.

2. Since investment properties, by definition, are not employed in the business operational purposes and their disposal would not normally affect manufacturing or trading operations of the enterprise, the current value of such investment and changes in the market value are more important than the calculation of depreciation.

3. Investment properties are usually carried in the balance sheet at their market values and revalued periodically on a systematic basis. At present, most enterprises account for their investment properties in accordance with IAS Accounting for Depreciation. However, some carry their investment properties in the balance sheet at market value revalued periodically and systematically.

GAINS AND LOSSES ON SALE OF INVESTMENTS

1. When an investment is sold, the gain or loss on the sale is usually taken to the income statement of the period of sale. Such gain or loss is computed as the difference between the proceeds of sale net of expenses and its carrying amount.

2. If the investment sold had previously been revalued and the increase in the carrying amount has been credited to and still remains in a revaluation surplus account within the owners' equity, the amount of the increase is transferred to income.

3. When only part of an enterprise's holding of a particular investment is disposed off, the carrying amount of the part sold will be calculated on the basis of the average carrying amount of the total holdings,

TRANSFER OF INVESTMENTS

1. Where long-term investments are re-classified as short-term investments transfers are made at lower of cost and market value. If the investment was previously revalued, any remaining revaluation surplus is reversed on the transfer.

2. Investments re-classified from short-term to long-term are each transferred at historical cost less provision for impairment in their values or at market value if they were previously stated at that value.

PART IV
ACCOUNTING STANDARD

ACCOUNTING FOR INVESTMENTS

The accounting Standard comprises paragraphs 36-59 of this statement. The standard should be read in the context of paragraph 1-35 of this statement and of the preface to the statements of Accounting Standards published by the Nigerian Accounting Standard Board.

CLASSIFICATION OF INVESTMENTS

1. A reporting enterprise should classify its investments into short-term, long-term, and investment properties.

SHORT-TERM INVESTMENTS

1. Short-term investments should be valued at the lower of cost and market the earning amount should be determined on an item-by-item basis.

2. The amount by which cost exceeds market value (unrealised loss) should be charged to the income statement for the period.

3. Realised gains and losses on disposal of short-term investments should be included in the income statement for the period of disposal.

LONG-TERM INVESTMENTS

1. Long-term investments should be carried at cost or at a revalued amount.

2. When there has been a permanent decline in value of an investment, the carrying amount of the investment should be written down to recognize the loss such reduction should be charged to the income statement. Reductions in carrying amount may be reversed when there is an increase, other than temporary, in the value of the investment, or if the reasons for the reduction no longer exist

3. An increase in earning amount arising from the on of long-term invests should be credited to owners' equity as revaluation surplus. To the exist a decrease in earning amount offsets a previous increase, for the same inv that has been credited to revaluation surplus and not subsequent re-utilized, it should be charged against that revaluation surplus rather than income.

4. An increase on revaluation which is directly related to previous carrying amount for the same investment that was charged to income, such should be credited to the extent that it offset the previously recorded decrease.

5. When a reporting enterprise receives dividends representing distributive earnings retained hi the business prior to acquiring stocks in an investment company, such dividends should be treated as deductions from the cost of investment.

6. When a reporting enterprise receives interest on dated stocks which include interest accrued before the date of purchase, the relevant amount should be credited to acquisition cost and the portion of interest relating to the post-acquisition period should be credited to income statement

7. When an investment has been written down as in paragraph 40 - 44 above, the new carrying is deemed to be the new basis for subsequent accounting purposes.

8. Any discounts or premiums arising on acquisition of debt securities should be amortised over the period to maturity so that earnings from the investment will reflect a constant yield based on acquisition cost. The amortised discount.

LONG-TERM INVESTMENT

1. Long-term Investment should be carried at cost or at a revalued amount

2. When there has been a permanent decline m value of an investment, the carrying amount of the investment should be written down to recognize the loss. Such a reduction should be charged to the income statement. Reductions in earning amount may be reversed when there is an increase, other than temporary, in the value of the investment, or if the reasons for the reduction no longer exist.

3. An increase in carrying amount arising from the revaluation of long-term investments should be credited to owners' equity as revaluation surplus. To the extent that a decrease in carrying amount

offsets a previous increase, the same investment that has been credited to revaluation surplus and not subsequently reversed or utilized should be charged against that revaluation surplus rather than income.

4. An increase in revaluation, which is directly related to a previous decrease in the carrying amount for the same investment that was charged to income, should be credited to the extent that it offsets the previously recorded decrease.

5. When a reporting enterprise receives dividends that represent a distribution of earnings retained in the business prior to acquisition of stock in an investee company, such dividends should be treated as deductions from the cost of the investment.

6. When a reporting enterprise receives interest on dated stock which includes interest accrued before the date of purchase, the relevant amount should be credited to acquisition cost and the portion of interest relating to post-acquisition period should be credited to income statement.

7. When an investment has been written down as in paragraphs 40-44 above, the new carrying amount is deemed to be the new basis for subsequent accounting purposes.

8. Any discounts or premiums arising on acquisition of debt securities should amortised over the period to maturity so that earnings from the investment would reflect a constant yield based on acquisition cost. The amortised discount or premium should be credited or charged to income as though it were interest and added to or subtracted from the earning amount of the security. The resulting carrying amount should then be regarded as cost.

INVESTMENT PROPERTIES

1. Every enterprise should have a policy on accounting for investment proportion either in accordance with IAS 3 and IAS 9, or in accordance with this standard as stated below.

2. Investment properties should be carried in the balance sheet at the market values and revalued periodically systematically at least once every three years.

3. Investment properties should not be subject to periodic charges for depreciation.

4. A decrease in carrying amount of an investment property should be treated in the manner specified in paragraphs 41 and 46. An increase in carrying amount should be treated in accordance with paragraphs 42 and 43.

TRANSFER OF INVESTMENTS

1. Where long-term investments are re-classified as short-term investment transfers should be made at the lower cost and market value. If the investment was previously revalued, any remaining revaluation surplus should be removed on the transfer.

2. Investments re-classified from short-term to long-term should be transferred at historical cost less provision for impairment in their value or at market value if they were previously stated at that value.

DISCLOSURES

1. A reporting enterprise should state, in the appropriate section of its financial statements, its accounting policies with respect to investments.

2. When investments include securities of quoted companies, the aggregate market value of securities as well as their corresponding carrying amounts should be disclosed.

3. A reporting enterprise should disclose in its financial statements significant amounts included in income in respect of:

   a) Interest, dividends and rentals on short-term investments, long-term investments and investment properties.

   b) Profits and losses on disposal of short-term investments.

   c) Profits and losses on disposal of long-term investments, and

   d) The amount by which aggregate cost exceeds market value (the net unrealised loss).

4. An enterprise should disclose any significant restrictions on the realizability of investments or the remittance of investment income and proceeds of disposal.

5. An enterprise whose main business is the holding of investments should show an analysis of the portfolio of investments.

6. A reporting enterprise should disclose the names of the persons making the valuation of its investment properties or other long-term investments for which relative market does not exist, their professional qualification, the dates and source of valuation. Where the person making the valuation are employees or officers of the company or group which owns the properties, this fact should be disclosed.

GENERAL REQUIREMENTS

1. The requirements of this standard are complementary to any disclosure requirements of the Companies and Allied Matters Decree of 1990 and other laws and regulations.

PART VI
COMPLIANCE WITH INTERNATIONAL ACCOUNTING STANDARD NO. 25

1. The requirements of this Standard substantially align with the requirements of International Accounting Standard No. 25, Accounting for Investments.

EFFECTIVE DATE

1. This standard becomes operative for Financial Statements covering periods beginning on or after January 1, 1994.

IAS 25-Investments

Question

What is investment?

Solution

An investment is an asset held by an enterprise for the accreditation of wealth through distribution such as interest, loyalties, dividends and rentals. fair capital acquisition trading relationships.

A current investment is an investment that is by its nature readily realizable and intended to be held for not more than one year.

For accounting treatment, see questions and Solutions on IAS 3, IAS 9 and IAS 4

CHAPTER FIFTEEN
VALUE ADDED TAX DECREE 1994
ARRANGEMENT OF SECTIONS

PART ONE

IMPOSITION, ETC, OF VALUE ADDED TAX

PART TWO

ADMINISTRATION

PART THREE

RETURNS, REMITTANCES, RECOVERY AND REFUND OF TAX

DECREE No. 102 (IST DECEMBER 1993) COMMENCEMENT

THE FEDERAL MILITARY GOVERNMENT hereby decrees as follows:

(Note that each country differs,The above is from Nigerian tax system)

PART ONE

IMPOSITION, ETC, OF VALUE ADDED TAX

1. There is hereby imposed and charged a tax to be known as Value Added Tax (in this Decree referred to as 'the tax') which shall be administered in accordance with the provisions of this Decree.

2. The tax shall be charged and payable on the goods and services (in this Decree referred to as 'taxable goods and services') listed in column A of Schedule 1 and 2 to this Decree at the rate specified in column B of the said schedule.

3. The goods and services listed in schedule 3 to this Decree.

4. The tax shall be computed at the rate specified in column B of the Schedule 1 and 2 to this Decree, of the value of all taxable goods and services as determined under section 5 and 6 of this Decree.

5. For the purpose of this Decree, the value of taxable goods and services shall be determined as follows, that is:-

    a) If the supply is for a money consideration, its value shall be deemed an amount which with the addition of the tax chargeable is equal to the consideration:

    b) If the supply is for a consideration not consisting of money, the value of supply shall be seemed to be its market value

    c) Where the supply of taxable goods or services is not the only means of which a consideration is money relates the supply shall be deemed such part of consideration as is properly attributed to it.

    d) For the purpose of this Decree, the open market value of supply of taxable goods or services shall be taken to the amount that would fall to be taken as its value under subsection (1) (b) of this section if the supply where by such consideration in money as could be payable by a person in transaction at arm's length.

6. The value of imported taxable goods for this Decree shall be the amount that is equal to the price of the goods so imported and shall includes:-

    a) All taxes, duties and other charges levied either outside or by reason of importation into Countries other than the tax imposed by this Decree;

    b) All costs by way of commission, parking, transport and insurance up to the port or place of importation.

PART TWO

ADMINISTRATION

1. The tax shall be administered and managed by the Federal Board of Inland Revenue (in this decree referred to as 'the Board')

2. The Board may do such things as it may deem necessary and expedient for the assessment and collection of the tax and shall account for all amounts so collected in accordance with the provisions of this Decree.

3. A manufacturer, wholesaler, importer and supplier of taxable goods or services (in this Decree referred to as 'taxable person') shall, within six months of the commencement of the Decree or six months of the commencement of business, whichever is earlier, register with the Board for the tax.

4. A person who is registered under section 8 of this Decree (in the Decree referred to as 'a registered person') shall keep such records and book for all transaction, operations imports and other activities relating to taxable goods and services as are sufficient to determine the correct amount of tax under this Decree.

PART THREE

RETURNS, REMITTANCES, RECOVERY, AND REFUND OF TAX

1. A taxable person shall pay to the supplier the tax on the goods and services purchased by or supplied to him.

a) The tax paid by a taxable person under subsection (1) of this shall be known as input tax.

2. A taxable person shall on supplying taxable goods or to his accredited distributor, agent, client or consumer, as the case may be, collect the tax on those goods or services at the rate specified in the section of this Decree.

a) The tax collected by a taxable person under subsection of this section shall be known as output tax.

3. A taxable person shall render to the Board, on or before the 14th day of the month following that in which the purchase or supply was made a return of all taxable goods and services purchased or supplied by him during the preceding month in such manner as the Board may from time to time determine.

a) A person who imports taxable goods into Nigeria shall render to the Board returns on all the taxable goods imported by him into Nigeria.

4. A taxable person shall, on rendering a return under subsection (1) of section 12 of this Decree.

a) If the output tax exceeds the input tax, remit the excess to the Board, or

b) If the input tax exceeds the output tax, be entitled to a refund of the excess tax from the Board on production of such documents as the Board may, from time to time require.

c) An importer of taxable goods shall, before clearing those goods, pay to the Board the tax due on those goods.

d) The Nigerian Customs Service shall, before releasing taxable goods to its importer, demand the Value Added Tax Compliance Certificate issued by the Board on those goods.

5. Where a taxable person fails to render returns or renders an incomplete or inaccurate return, the Board shall assess, to the best of its judgment, the amount of tax due on the taxable goods and services purchased or supplied by the taxable person.

6. If a taxable person does not remit the tax within the time specified in section 13 of this Decree, a sum equal to five per centum per annum (plus interest at the commercial rate) of the amount of tax remittable shall be added to the tax and the provisions of this Decree relating to collection and recovery of unremitted tax, penalty and interest shall apply.

a) The Board shall notify the taxable person or his agent of the tax due together with the penalty and interest and if payment is not made within thirty days from date of such notification, the Board may proceed to enforce payment as provided in section 16 of this Decree.

7. Any tax, penalty or interest that remains unpaid after the period specified for payment may be recovered by the Board through proceedings in the Federal High Court.

PART FOUR

VALUE ADDED TAX TECHNICAL COMMITTEE

1. There is hereby established a committee to be known as the Value Added Tax Technical Committee (in this Decree referred to as 'the Technical Committee') which shall comprise: -

a) A Chairman who shall be the Chairman of the Federal Board of Inland Revenue;

b) All Directors in the Federal Inland Revenue Service.

c) A Director in the Nigerian Customs Services, and

d) Three representatives of the State Government who shall be members of the Joint Tax Board.

FUNCTIONS

1. The functions of the Technical Committee shall be to: -

a) Consider all the tax matters that require professional and technical expertise and make recommendations to the Board;

b) Advice the Board on the duties specified in section 7 of this Decree and

c) Attend to such other matters as the Board may, from time to time give refer to it.

2. Subject such directions as the Board may, from time to time give the Technical Committee determine its quorum and otherwise regular in is own procedure.

2. The Federal Inland Revenue Services may post to the Technical Committee such staff as the Technical Committee may require for the discharge of its functions.

PART FIVE

OFFENCES AND PENALTIES

1. A person who: -

   a) With intent to deceive, produces, furnishes or sends for this Decree or otherwise makes use for that purpose a document which is false in any material particular;

   b) In furnishing an information to the Board, makes a statement value he knows to be false in a material particular or recklessly making statement which is false in any material particular; 'Motel means premises on which accommodation, flats service, apartments, bench cottages holiday cottages, game lodges are provided but excludes the following that is: -

   c) Premises run by a charitable or religious organization registered under the relevant law for charitable or religious purposes;

   d) Premises operated by a medical institution approved by the Secretary for the time being responsible for health for the use of the staff of that institution;

   e) Premises whose supply is under a lease or license of not less than one month, unless by prior arrangement, the occupier may without penalty terminate that lease or license on less than one month's notice;

2. 'Output Tax' has the meaning assigned to it in section 11 of this Decree;

3. 'Owner' means in respect of any goods, aircraft, vessel, vehicle, plant or any other goods, a person, other than an officer acting officially, who holds out himself to be the owner, manufacturer, agent or the person in possession of a beneficially interested in or having control of or power of disposition over the goods, aircraft, vessel, plant or other goods;

Chapter 15

BANKRUPTCY AND LIQUIDATION

BANKRUPTCY

1. The law relating to Bankruptcy Act 1979

2. A person who cannot meet his liabilities as they fall due is said to be insolvent.

3. Acts of Bankruptcy.

   a) A debtor who fails to meet the requirement of a bankruptcy notice served on him within 14 days.

   b) A debtor whose goods are seized under a process of law and the goods have either been sold or held by the Bailiff for twenty-one days.

   c) If a debtor files in the court a declaration of his inability to pay his debts or presents a Bankruptcy petition against himself.

CONDITIONS A CREDITOR MUST FULFIL BEFORE A PETITION CAN BE HONOURED

UK (Companies Act 1986, Insolvency Rules) – A creditor can petition to wind up a company if they are owed **£750 or more** and the debt is undisputed.

Australia (Corporations Act 2001) – The threshold is **AUD $4,000**.

U.S. (Bankruptcy Code) – For involuntary bankruptcy, a single creditor must be owed **$19,950** or more (as of 2025), and other conditions apply.

The exact amount depends on your country's insolvency legislation.

In **Nigeria**, under the **Companies and Allied Matters Act (CAMA) 2020**, a creditor can petition for a company's winding up (liquidation) if:

The company owes the creditor **₦200,000 or more** (Section 572 of CAMA 2020).

The creditor has **served a statutory demand** giving the company **at least 3 weeks** to pay, secure, or compound the debt.

The debt is **undisputed** and due.

If the company fails to comply within that period, it is deemed **unable to pay its debts**, and the creditor can proceed with a winding-up petition in court.

   a) The amount owed must not be less than N200,000.00 (Section 572 of CAMA 2020)
   b) The debt is a liquidated sum

   c) The Acts of Bankruptcy must have been committed within three months

   d) The debtor is ordinarily resident in Nigeria.

STATEMENT OF AFFAIRS

This is prepared by a debtor and submitted to the official receiver. It must be in the prescribed form and verified by an affidavit. It shows liability and Assets followed by a Deficiency Account.

The left-hand side = debit with liabilities

    a)   Unsecured creditors e.g. Bank overdraft

    b)   Secured creditors

    c)   Discounted Bills

    d)   Contingent liabilities e.g. uncalled capital

    e)   Preferential creditors e.g. Rates, Taxes PAYE, Wages

ASSETS

This is recorded on the right-hand side of the statement. this include:

    a)   Cash in Hand

    b)   Cash deposited

c) Stock

d) Plant and Machinery

e) Fixtures, fitting

f) Furniture, etc

ILLUSTRATION OF DEFICIENCY (OR SURPLUS) ACCOUNT

	$		$
Excess of Assets over liabilities	***	Excess of Liabilities over Asset	***
Net profit for the year	***	Net loss for the year	***
Estimated gains on realization	***	Drawings/Dividend paid	***
of the debtors Assets	***	Estimated losses on realization of assets	***
Any other income ***		Any bad debts ***	
Deficiency (if any) ***		other losses ***	
		Surplus (if any) ***	
		***	

Example 1

Bosse got into financial difficulties and was unable to meet his obligations. On 31 December, 2017, A receiver order was made against him when his financial affairs were as follows:

	$		$
Capital at 1 January , 2017	19,740	Freehold Building	15,000
Loss for the Year 3,200		Plant and Machinery	12,500
Drawings 4,500	7,700	Furniture and Fittings	5,600
	12,040	Motor Vehicles	6,100
Mortgage on Freehold		Stock	4,360
Buildings	12,000	Debtors	9,140
Bank overdraft (secure creditor)	24,750	Bills Receivable	2,400
Bills payable	7,500	Cash at Bank	1,100
		Cash at Hand	90
	6,290		56,290

The following additional information is given on the above financial affairs:

1. **Creditors comprised:**

Trade Creditors	12
PAYE deduction (2016) $700, 2017 $500)	1
Income tax (2016 $300, 2017 $450)	150
Rates (15 months to 31 December, 2017)	5050
Sundry creditors	19

Sundry Creditors includes six months' salary due to the accountant at rate of per month.

2. The Assets are estimated to be realised as follows:

GROSS Liability $	Liability	$	Expected to Rank $	Assets	$	Estimated to Produce $
25,380	Unsecured Creditors		25,380	Cash in Hand		90
12,000	Fully secured creditors	12,000		Cash at Bank		1,100
	Estimated value of security	14,500		Plant and Machinery		6,900
	Surplus to contra	2,500		Furniture and Fittings		3,400
5,500	Partly secured creditors	5,500		Motor Vehicles		2,600
	Estimated value of security	3900	1,600	Stock		3,450
1,400	Liabilities on					
	Bills receivable discounted		1,400	Debtors:		
1,370	Preferential creditors			Good		5,000
	Deducted contra	1,370		Doubtful	2,500	
				Bad	1,640	
					4,140	
				Estimated to produce		1,600
				Bills receivable		1,550
				Surplus from fully secured creditors		2,500
						28,190
				Less		
				Preferential creditors		1,370
						26,820
				Deficiency		1,560
45,650			28,380			28,380

DEFICIENCY ACCOUNTS			
Excess of Assets over liability at 1 Jan. 1987		Net loss for 2017	3,200
Business	19,740	Bad debts	2,540
Private (life policy)	3,900	Depreciation:	
Deficiency per statement	1,560	Stock	910
		Freehold Buildings	500
		Plant & Machinery	5,600
		Furniture &Fitting	2,200
		Motor Vehicles	3,500
		Bills receivable	850
		Drawings	4,500
		Loss on Bills discounted	1,400
	25,200		25,200

	Unsecured$	Preferential$
Creditors		
Trade Creditors	12,100	-
PAYE Deduction	700	500
Income Tax	300	450
Rates	30	120
Sundry Creditors		
Salary of accountant for four months		
Restricted to N300	-	300
Other (unsecured)	4,750	-
	17,880	1,370
	7,500	-
	25,380	1,370

Freehold Land and Buildings	14
Plant and Machinery	6,
Furniture and Fittings	3,
Motor Vehicles	2,
The stock is estimated to produce	3,

The debtor is made of:

	$		
Goods debts	5,000		
Doubtful debts	2,500	Estimated to produce	1,800
Bad debts	1,640	Estimated to produce	100

1. The bank overdraft was secured on the life policy of Bosede, the sure value of which is $3,900.

2. There was a contingent liability of $3,500 in respect of bills discounted this amount, $1,400 would not be honoured on maturity.

3. The bills receivable are expected to produce $1,550

4. You are required to prepare the Statement of Affairs and Deficiency Account presentation to a meeting of creditors.

Solution

BOSSE

STATEMENT OF AFFAIRS AS AT 31DECEMBER, 2017

Be prepared for the firm as well as individual partners

Example

On 31 March, 2010, a Receiving order in Bankruptcy was made against Peter and John trading in partnership as Peters. The Balance Sheet of the partnership on that date was as under:

	$		$
Capital		Freehold property	3,750
Peter	750	Plant-hire purchase	400
John	1,250	Others	1,750
Building Society (Secured)		Stock	6,895
On freehold property)	2,500	Debtors	11,820
Hire Purchase Installments	700	Cash	75
Creditors	13,490		
Bank overdrafts	6,000		
	24,690		24,690

With regard to the above Balance Sheet, the following additional information is relevant:

1. The assets were estimated to realize the following amounts: Freehold property $4,000; Stock $2,815; Plant under hire purchase $300; Other Plant $600: Debtors – good $6,390, doubtful ($1,800) estimated to realize $600: bad ($3,630), NIL.

2. Of the Creditors, $390 were preferential

3. The bank overdraft was secured by a second mortgage on the Freehold property and was further secured by the personal guarantees of Peter and John supported by the deposit of a Life Policy by Peter and all investments held by John.

You ascertain the following additional information concerning the personal estates of Peter and John.

1. They owned assets as follows; Furniture at cost – Peter $730, John $930; Investments at cost – Peter $800,. John $1,320, Cash at Bank John $3,100, Freehold residence at cost, Peter $3,180.

2. They owed Liabilities as follows: Bank overdraft –Peter $400, Creditors-Peter $3,700, John $650. Buildings Society Mortgage on Freehold residence-John $1,100.

3. Peter had an insurance policy on his life, the surrender value of which was $1,900.

4. Their assets were estimated to realize the following amounts: Furniture-Peter $500, John $800; Investments – Peter $1,000, John $1,200; Freehold residence John $3,000.

You are required to prepare as on 31 March, 2010 both as regards the joint estate and the separate estates of the partners in columnar form.

1. Statements of affairs

2. Deficiency Accounts

Solution

BANKRUPTCY OF PARTNERSHIP PETER AND JOHN

STATEMENT OF AFFAIRS AS AT 31 MARCH, 2010

	JOINT $	PETER $	JOHN $		JOINT $	PETER $	JOHN $
Unsecured creditors	13,100	14,100	650	Cash	75		3,100
Fully secured				Plant other	600		
Creditor	2,500	1,100		Stock	2,518		
Less Security	4,000	3,000		Furniture		500	800
Surplus	1,500	1,900		Investment		1,000	
Partly secured				Surplus from John	350		
					3,900	1,500	3,900
Creditors	6,700	6,000	6,000				
Less security	1,800	1,900	1,200	Debtors			
	4,900	4,100	4,800	Goods	6,390		
Preferential Creditors				Doubtful	1,800		
Deducted Colltra				Bad	3,630		
Surplus to joint Estate	390				5,430		
		350		Estimate to produce surplus from secured creditors	600		1,900
					10,890	1,500	5,800
				Less Preferential Creditors	390		
					10,500	1,500	5,800
				Deficiency	7,500	6,700	
	8,000	8,200	5,800		18,000	8,200	5,800

Note: Security for the partly secured creditors = 1,500 + 300 = 1,800

DEFICIENCY ACCOUNT

	JOINT $	PETER $	JOHN $		JOINT $	PETER $	JOHN $
Excess of assets				Losses Oni			
Over liabilities	2,000	80	8,050	Plant-H.P	100		
surplus from John	350			Other	1,090		
Surplus on Realization				Stock	4,080		
Freehold property	250			Bad debts	4,830		
Investments		200		furniture		230	150
Deficiency per							
Statement	7,500	6,700		Investments			120
				Freehold residence			180
				Liability on Bank			
				Guarantee		6,000	6,000
				Loss of capital In partnership		750	1,250
				Surplus per statement of affairs			350
	10,100	6,980	8,050		10,100	6,980	8,050

Excess of Assets over liabilities on 31 March, 2010					
Assets	**PETER $**	**JOHN$**			
Furniture	730	950			
Investments	800	1,320			
Capital in Partnership	750	1,250			
Cash at Bank		3,100			
Life policy	1,900				
Freehold residence		3,180			
	4,180	9,800			
Liabilities					
Bank overdraft 400					
Creditors 3,700		650			
Building Society					
Mortgage	4,100	1,100	1,750		
	80		8,050		

(1)   A and B are in Partnership and file petition in Bankruptcy from the following particulars, prepare the statements of Affairs and Deficiency Accounts of the Joint Estate and the separate estates of the partners.

BALANCE SHEET

	FIRM $	A $	B $		FIRM $	A $	B $
Mortgage Leasehold	3,000			Leasehold premises	6,000		
Bank overdraft	3,000			Plant	6,500		
Sundry Creditors	12,400	1,500	2,900	Furniture	400	1,000	1,200
Preferential Creditors	100			Stock	5,500	2,500	1,000
Capital A	3,000			Debtors	5,000		
Capital B	2,000			Investment (Cost)	-		
Surplus	-	5,000	13,000	Cash	100	3,000	2,000
	23,500	6,500	4,200	Capital A & B	23,500	6,500	4,200

The bank overdraft of the firm was secured by a second mortgage on the firm's premises, and by B's personal guarantee, supported by the B's investments as Collateral Security. The firm's are estimated to realize the following Lease $4,500, Plant $3,000; Furniture $150; Stock $3,100 Debtors – good $2,575; doubtful ($1,000) 50 percent: Bad ($1,425) nil. A's assets; furniture $600; Investments $2,000; B's assets; Furniture $800; Investments $300.

A and B shared profits and losses equally. In the year preceding the date of the receiving order the firm incurred a trading loss of $1,500 and the partners' drawings had been A $2,000, B $2,500 (including cost of a personal investment $500).

State the order of payments of liabilities by the Trustees in Bankruptcy and list some penalties against him when he retains more money hat requested?

The Accounts of a Trustee in Bankruptcy

The records to be kept:

1. A record of the Minutes of proceedings and resolutions passed at any meeting of Creditors or of the Committee of Inspection.

2. Estate (cash) account, a record of daily receipts and payments

3. A trading account, where he carried on the business of the debtor or company.

Advanced Financial Accounting

Penalty against Retention

If a trustee more than $500 without authority of the court, he:

1. Must pay interest on the amount so retained in excess at the rate of 20% per annum.
2. He will forfeit his renumeration.
3. May be removed from his office by the court.
4. Shall be liable to pay expenses occasioned by reason of his default.

The order of payments in Bankruptcy by the Trustee.

1. Costs and charges of the bankruptcy
2. Preferential debts
3. Unsecured creditors
4. Deferred creditors e.g. money lent to a husband by wife, money advanced to a firm and interest on debts.
5. Surplus, if any to the debtor.

LIQUIDATION

Winding up by the High court or compulsory winding up.

A Company may be wound up by the Court if:

1. The Company has by special resolution resolved that the company be wound up by the court.
2. Default is made in delivering the statutory meeting
3. The company does not commence its business within a year from its incorporation or suspends its business for a whole year.
4. The number of members is reduced beyond the authorized minimum
5. The company is unable to pay its debtors
6. The court is of the opinion that it is just and equitable that the company should be wound up.

GROUP ACCOUNTS

COLUMNAR APPROACH

1. Constitution of a group

A group of company consist of a holding (or parent company) and one or more subsidiary companies by the holding company.

Company S Limited is said to be a subsidiary of another company H Limited if, but only if:

1. H Limited holds more than half in nominal value of the equity share capital of S Limited.

2. H Limited is a member of S Limited and controls the composition of its Board of Directors, or

3. S Limited is a subsidiary of another company which itself, by virtue of (a) or (b) above is a subsidiary of H Limited. In this case, S Limited is said to be a sub-subsidiary of H Limited.

WHAT ARE GROUP ACCOUNTS

A group account is a conglomeration of individual accounts of separate companies in one organization through the preparation of consolidated accounts. A IAS 3- Consolidated Financial Statements defines consolidated accounts as: Statements which present the assets, liabilities, shareholders accounts, revenues and expenses of a parent company and its subsidiaries as those of a single enterprise.

A group account contains a package of:

1. A holding company balance sheet;

2. A consolidated Balance sheet

3. A consolidated profit and loss account

4. A consolidated statement of source and application of funds.

EXCLUSION OF SUBSIDIARY FROM GROUP ACCOUNTS

A subsidiary may be excluded from a group's consolidated accounts if, in the directors' judgment, its inclusion:

1. Is impracticable, or

2. Would be of no real value to members in view of the significant amounts involved, or

3. Would involve expenses or delay out of proportion to the value of members;

4. Would be misleading, or

5. Is undesirable because the business of the holding company and subsidiary are so different that they cannot reasonably be treated as a single undertaking.

A SIMPLE EXAMPLE

A Limited regularly sells goods to one of its subsidiary company B Limited. The Balance Sheets of the two companies on 31 December, 2016 are given below:

A LIMITED BALANCE SHEET AS AT 31 DECEMBER, 2016

	$	$	$
Fixed Assets		35,000	35,000
40,000 $1 shares in B Limited @ cost		40,000	40,000
		75,000	75,000
Current Assets			
Stock		16,000	
Debtors: B Limited	2,000		
Others	6,000	8,000	
Cash at Bank		1,000	
		10,600	
Current Liabilities			
Creditors		14,00	11,000
			86,000
Capital and Reserves			
70,000 $1 ordinary shares			70,000
Reserves			16,000
			86,000

B LIMITED BALANCE SHEET AS AT 31 DECEMBER, 2016

	$	$	$
Fixed Assets			45,000
Current Assets			
Stock		12,000	
Debtors		9,000	
		21,000	
Current Liabilities			
Bank overdraft		3,000	
Creditors: A Limited	2,000		
Others	2,000	4,000	
		7,000	14,000
			19,000
			59,000
Capital and Reserves			
40,000 $1 ordinary shares			40,000
Reserves			19,000
			59,000
Prepared the consolidated Balance Sheet of B Limited			

A LIMITED CONSOLIDATED BALANCE SHEET AS AT 31 DECEMBER, 2016			
	$	$	$
Fixed Assets			80,000
Current Assets:			
Stocks	28,000		
Debtors	15,000		
Cash at Bank	1,000		
		44,000	
	3,000		
	16,000		
		19,000	25,000
			105,000
Capital and Reserves:		70,000	
70,000 ordinary shares		35,000	
			105,000

Example 2

Owo Limited has owned 75% of the share capital of Fon Limited since the date of Fon Limited's incorporation. Their latest Balance Sheets are given below:

OWO LIMITED BALANCE SHEET

	$
Fixed Assets	50,000
30,000 $1 Ordinary Shares in Fon Ltd at cost	30,000
	80,000
Net current assets	25,000
	105,000
Capital and Reserves	
80,000 $1 Ordinary Shares	80,000
Reserves	25,000
	105,000

MO- LIMITED BALANCE SHEET

	$
Fixed Assets	35,000
Net current Assets	15,000
	50,000
Capital and Reserves	
40,000 $1 Ordinary Shares	40,000
Reserves	10,000
	50,000

Prepare the Consolidated Balance Sheet

Solution

	$
Minority share of share capital 25% of $40,000	10,000
Minority shares of reserves 25% of $10,000	2,500

OWO GROUP CONSOLIDATED BALANCE SHEET

	$
Fixed Assets	85,000
	40,000
	125,000
Finance by:	
Share Capital	80,000
Reserves N (25,000 + 75% of 10,000)	32,500
Shareholders' funds	112,500
Minority Interest	12,500
	125,000

HE COLUMNAR APPROACH TO CONSOLIDATION

Subsidiary	Cost of Control	Minority Interest	Consolidate Capital Reserve	Revenue Reserve
Column 1	Column 2	Column 3	Column 4	Column 5

TREATMENT OF DIVIDENDS

1. If the subsidiary has not yet accrued for the proposed dividend:

a) DR   Revenue Reserves

b) CR   Dividend Payable

2. If the holding company has not yet accrued for its share of the proposed dividend:

a) DR   Debtor's dividend receivable

b) CR   Revenue Reserves

Example:

Set out below are the draft Balance Sheets of Benin Limited and Azure Limited. Neither company has yet provided for any dividend, but you should now provide for:

1. The preference dividend of Azure Limited

2. The proposed ordinary dividend of 10% by Azure Limited

3. A proposed ordinary dividend of 20% by Jenin Limited

You are required to prepare the Consolidated Balance Sheet

JENIN LIMITED BALANCES SHEET

	$	$
Fixed Assets		36,000
Investment in Azure Limited		
15,000 $1 ordinary shares at cost	15,000	
3,000 $1 &% Preference shares at cost	3,000	18,000
		54,000
Current Assets	36,500	
Current Liabilities	(10,500)	26,000
	80,000	80,000
Capital and Reserves		50,000
Ordinary shares of $1.00 each		30,000
Revenue Reserves		80,000

AZURE LIMITED BALANCE SHEET

	$	$
Fixed Assets		20,000
Current Assets	25,850	
Current Liabilities	(9,500)	16,350
		36,350
		$
Capital and Reserves		20,000
Ordinary shares of $1.00 each		5,000
7% Preference shares of $1 each		25,000
Revenue Reserves		11,350
		36,350

Solution:

		Cost of control	Minority Interest	Revenue Reserves
Azure Limited		75% Ordinary 60% Preference	25% Ordinary 40% Preference	
	$	$	$	$
Ordinary shares	20,000	15,000	5,000	
Preference shares	5,000	3,000	2,000	
Revenue Reserves	9,000	-	2,250	6,750
Cost of Investment:				
Ordinary shares	15,000			
Preference shares	3,000	18,000		
Add Jenin Limited	-	-	9,250	
Reserves				21,710
				28,460
Workings				
			$	$

Dividends in Azure Limited			
DR Revenue Reserve		2,350	
CR Proposed Dividends:			
Preference shares 7% of 5,000			350
Ordinary shares 10% of 20,000			2,000
Akure Limited $11,350 = 9,000			
Benin Limited's share in dividends			
Preference shares 60%	210		
Ordinary 75%	1,500		
	1,710		
DR Debit Dividends receivable		1,710	
CR Revenue Reserves			1,710

Adjusted revenue in Jenin Limited

30,000 + 1,710 – 10,000 = $21,710

JENIN LIMITED CONSOLIDATED BALANCE SHEET

	$	$
Fixed Assets		56,000
Current Assets	62,350	
Current Liabilities: Sundry	(20,000)	
Proposed dividends	(10,000)	
Minority proposed dividend	(640)	31,710
		87,710
Capital & Reserves		50,000
Ordinary Shares of $1 each		28,460
Revenue Reserves		78,460
Minority Interest		9,250
		87,710

APPROACH TO CONSOLIDATED BALANCE SHEET
Step 1: Update the Draft Balance Sheets of both holding and subsidiary with any proposed dividend
Step 2: Agree inter-company current accounts with items in transit
Step 3: Cancel items common to both Balance Sheets
Step 4: Create minority interest column
Step 5: Create cost of control column

A COMPREHENSIVE EXAMPLE

Te draft Balance sheets of People Limited and Animal Limited on 30th June, 2014 were as follows:

PEOPLE LIMITED

	$	$
Fixed Assets	25,000	
10,000 ordinary shares in Animal Limited at cost	15,000	40,000
Current Assets		
Stock	1,500	
Debtors (including N2,000 dividends by Animal Ltd)	10,000	
Cash	1,000	
	12,500	
Current Liabilities: Caved to Animal Limited	40,000	
Trade Creditors	5,000	3,500
	9,000	43,500

Solution:

	$	Cost of control $	Minority Interest $	Consolidated Capital Revenue $	Revenue Reserve $
Animal Limited	$	**80% Ordinary**	**20% Ordinary**		
Ordinary shares	12,500	10,000	25,000		
Capital Reserves	2,500	2,000	500		
Revenue Reserves	11,500	2,400(80% of 3000)	2,300 (20% of 11500)		6,800 (1150-4700)
	14,400				
Cost of Investment	15,000				
Goodwill	600				
Add People's Ltd Reserves			-	6,000	15,000
			5,300	6,000	21,800

PEOPLE LIMITED

CONSOLIDATED BALANCE SHEET AS AT 30TH JUNE, 2014

	$	$
Goodwill arising on consolidation		600
Fixed Assets (23,000 +20,000)		45,000
Current Assets:		
Stocks (2,500 +4,000)	6,500	
Debtors (8,000 +3,500)	11,500	
Cash	1,000	19,000
Current Liabilities		
Trade Creditors (5,000 +3,500)	8,500	
Minority dividends (2,500 x 20%)	500	
	9,000	
Net current Assets		10,000
Total Assets less current liabilities		55,600
Capital and Reserves Ordinary shares of $1 Each	22,500	
Capital & Reserves	6,000	
Revenue Reserves	21,800	
	50,300	
	5,300	
Minority interest	55,600	

ACQUISITION OF SUBSIDIARIES

Distinguishing between profits earned before acquisition and profits earned after acquisition;

1. Pre-acquisition profits attributable to the group

   DR Consolidated Reserves

   CR Cost of Control

2. Minority interest not concerned with Pre-or post acquisition profit. So charge it in full.

Example

Hopeful PLC acquired 80% of the ordinary shares of Singer PLC on 1 April, 2015. On 31 December, 2014, Singer PLC's accounts showed a share premium account of $2,000 and Revenue Reserves of $7,500. The Balance Sheets of the two companies at 31 December, 2015 are set out below. Neither company has paid or proposed any dividends during the year.

You are required to prepare the consolidated Balance Sheet of Hopeful PLC as at 31st December, 2015.

HOPEFUL LIMITED BALANCE SHEET AS AT 31 DECEMBER, 2015

	$	$
Fixed		16,000
8,000 ordinary shares of 50c each in Singer PLC		25,000
		41,000
Net current Assets		32,500
		73,500
Capital and Reserves		50,000
Ordinary shares of $1 each	3,500	
Share premium account	20,000	23,500
Revenue reserves		73,500

CHAPTER SIXTEEN
IFRS 6,15/IAS 2,16 PETROLEUM

PART 1

INTRODUCTION

1. The petroleum industry occupies a very strategic position in the Nigerian economy as the nation's major provider of foreign income. Industry plays a major role in facilitating the economic development of the nation.

2. To date there is no authoritative pronouncement on accounting rules to be followed in the industry in spite of existing legislation. Since the oil companies operating within the industry come from different countries of the world, the industry has developed a wide diversity of accounting practices. There is, therefore, a need to develop an accounting standard to be used by all the companies within the industry in order to ensure the comparability of financial statements.

3. Activities of the industry can be divided into two broad categories: upstream and downstream. Upstream activities involve the acquisition of mineral interest in properties, exploration (including prospecting), development and production of crude and gas. Downstream activities involve transporting, refining and marketing of oil gas and derivatives.

4. This statement deals with accounting and reporting for upstream activities. It does not cover the downstream activities.

PART II

DEFINITION

The following terms are used in this statement with the meanings specified:

1. Abandonment is the process of giving up further exploration activities in a well or field in which oil or gas has not been found in commercial quantity. This does not include capped (plugged) wells. It can also relate to the giving up of production wells or field at the end of their productive lives.

2. Acquisition costs are costs of acquiring concession right in a lease area:

3. Amortization is used generically to mean the depreciation of tangible cost, depletion of mineral acquisition cost and intangible costs.

4. Appraisal well is a well drilled to ascertain the commercial potentials of a reservoir discovered from explanatory activities.

5. Barrel is a standard of measurement in the oil industry. One Barrel equals 42 U.S. Gallons (35 Imperial gallons) at standard conditions.

6. Bottom hole agreement refers to an agreement in which cash consideration or property is giving to another party for its use in drilling a well on a property in which the payor has no mineral right, in exchange for technical information from the drilling of the well.

7. Carried Interest is a working interest arrangement involving two or more parties in which a carrying or the assignee finances the exploration and development activities in consideration for a reward out of a future production (if any) and if necessary, from the carried party's or the assignor's share of future production. The assignor is typically the carried party, while the assignee is the carrying party. A Production Sharing Contract (PSC) is a type of carried interest arrangement.

8. Cashing Point is the point at which the drilling has reached its objective depth, in which determination can be made as to its productivity or otherwise.

9. Ceiling Test is a test to determine whether the recorded capitalised exploration, appraisal and development costs are recoverable from proved reserves.

10. Commercial Quantity is the quantity of oil or gas in a reservoir that can be produced economically at current prices existing technology. The petroleum Act 1969, however, defines commercial quantity as daily production of 10,000 barrels of crude oil.

11. Completion is the process of bringing an oil or gas into production. The process begins only after the well has reached the depth where oil or gas is thought to exist, and generally involves installation of casing pipes, perforation of the casing pipes, and acidizing and fracturing operations.

12. Concession is a right granted to a company by the Federal Government on behalf of the Federation to explore and produce oil and gas within a given area. In Nigeria, this involves the granting of oil exploration license, oil prospecting license or mining lease.

13. Conservation refers to the preservation or restoration of a drilling site to its state after drilling. It may also be related to economy and avoidance of waste during drilling.

14. Cost Pool is a cost Centre comprising a defined geographical area used under the full cost method of accounting as a basis for accumulating depreciable capitalised exploration, appraisal and development expenditure. Cost pools are usually not smaller in size than a country except were warranted by major differences in economic, fiscal or other factors in that country.

15. Development costs are additional capital costs incurred following a decision to develop a reservoir.

16. Discovery well is an exploratory (wildcat) well that finds a new deposit of oil or gas.

17. Discovery Value is the estimated value of oil and or gas at the date of discovery.

18. Dry Hole (also referred to as a duster to wet hole) is a well that either finds no oil or gas, or finds too little to make it commercially viable.

19. Dry Hole Agreement is similar to bottom hole agreement except that money or property contributions are made to another party only in event that the well reaches an agreed depth and is found to be non-productive.

20. Exploration and Appraisal Costs are costs incurred in the search for oil and gas deposits after obtaining a license but before a decision is taken to develop a reservoir.

21. Exploratory Project Area is an acreage usually larger than a field where initial finding efforts such as geological and geophysical surveys are undertaken.

22. Farm in refers to the transfer of all or part of an oil gas interest in consideration for an agreement by the transfer (frame) to meet certain oil exploration and development costs which would otherwise have been undertaken by the owner (farmer). See Farm Out.

23. Farm Out is a sharing of oil exploration and development activities and costs whereby a company with a concession, either because it has more potential oil acreage than it can handle or wishes to share risks, invites others to explore all or portions of the tract in return for a share of whatever oil is found. See Farm In.

24. Federal Government refers to the Federal Government of Nigeria.

25. Federation means the federal Governments, State Governments, the Federal Capital Territory and Local Governments.

26. Field is a given area or region, usually comprising a number of individual reservoirs in which oil and gas reserves exist.

27. Impairment is the possible diminution in the value of unproved properties of an exploration and production company arising from events or circumstances outside its control.

28. Joint Venture is a contractual arrangement whereby two or more parties undertake an economic activity which is subject to contractual agreed basis of sharing of control.

29. Oil Exploration License (OEL) is a license granted to a company under the Petroleum Act of 1969 to explore for petroleum and does not confer an exclusive right over the area of the license. This usually has a one-year term.

30. Oil Mining Lease (OML) means a license granted to a company under the Petroleum Act, 1969 for the purpose of winning petroleum or any assignment of such license. The term is usually between three and five years.

31. Oil Prospecting License (OPL) means a license granted to a company under the Petroleum Act, 1969 for the purpose of winning petroleum or any assignment of such license. The term is usually between three and five years.

32. Operator is the party that conducts the operations, under a joint venture. This may include the drilling of a well and or the production of oil from a tract or field under an agreed contract.

33. Pre-license Costs are incurred in the period prior to the acquisition of a legal right to explore for oil and gas in a particular location. Such costs include the acquisition of speculative seismic data and expenditure on the subsequent geological and geophysical analysis of these data.

34. Production Costs (operating or lifting costs) are the recurrent costs incurred in oil and gas production activities.

35. Property includes leases, reservations, royalty rights, and similar rights.

36. Proved Development Reserves represent oil and gas reserves that can be expected to be recovered from existing wells and facilities using existing technology.

37. Proved Reserves represent estimated quantity of oil and gas that can be recovered from unknown reservoirs using existing technology.

38. Proved Reserves represent estimated quantity of oil and gas that can be recovered from known reservoirs using existing technology.

39. Proved Undeveloped Reserves include all proved oil and gas that can be recovered from known reservoirs using existing technology.

40. Reservoir is a natural formation of porous and permeable spaces in the earth's crust containing accumulation of oil and gas. Each distinct reservoir is confined by impermeable rocks or barriers which help to trap oil and gas.

41. Stratigraphic Test Well is a well drilled to obtain information about the geological conditions of an exploration area.

42. Wildcat Well is any well drilled in unproven territory.

43. Work-over is a remedial operation required to restore oil flow from a well to its maximum production capacity or to enhance its production capacity following a decline in production

EXPLANATORY NOTES

DISTINCTIVE FEATURES OF UPSTREAM ACTIVITIES

1. The petroleum industry is capital intensive and the probability of not discovering oil in commercial quantity is high. As a part of the effort to reduce the risks inherent in oil and gas exploration, companies typically engage in arrangements such joint ventures, farmouts, carried interest, bottom hole and dry hole agreements and others.

2. The elapsed time between initial exploration, and bringing of such reserves into production, often run into several years, particularly in offshore locations. Consequently, the risk of loss of capital is high. The risk is affected by the nature of the location, availability of funds and government legislation.

3. The major economic assets of an oil company are its oil and gas reserves. These are usually not recorded sheets because several factors in the recovery cannot be readily quantified owing to uncertainties.

4. Recognition of gains and losses on disposals, retirements and surrenders of oil and gas assets are treated in a special manner due to these uncertainties.

ACTIVITIES PRIOR TO THEE START OF PRODUCTION

1. This can be subdivided into three separate phases: Mineral rights acquisition, exploration and drilling and development.

2. Mineral Rights Acquisition Phase covers:

   a) The period prior to the acquisition of a legal right to explore for petroleum in a particular location.

   b) Initial acquisition of a seismic data and the geological and geophysical evaluation of the relevant area:

   c) Obtaining oil prospecting license, oil lease or other concessions to explore for and exploit oil and gas in an area of interest.

3. The Expiration and Drilling Phase normally involves

   a) The conduct of a geological and geophysical surveys in order to identify most promising structures; and

   b) The drilling of exploration wells to establish the present or otherwise of petroleum in those structures.

4. If evaluation during drilling strongly indicates the presence of oil, tests may be carried out to determine the producibility of the well. Further wells known as appraisal wells maybe necessary to determine the extent of the reservoir and the flow rate of oil and gas.

5. Development Phase commences if the result of the appraisal and the evaluation mentioned above are positive. Usually, a single well may not be adequate to extract the oil in the reservoir in time and economically, thus more wells would be drilled and the boundaries of the reservoirs delineated. In addition to the drilling of more development wells, facilitated such as pipelines, separators treaters, Christmas trees and tank farms are usually installed for the treatment and storage of production.

CLASSIFICATION OF COSTS

Oil and gas producing activities involves cost which may be classified as:

1. Mineral Rights Acquisition Costs;

2. Exploration and drilling costs;

3. Development Cost;

4. Production Costs;

5. Support Equipment and Facilities Costs; and

6. General Costs

MINERAL RIGHT ACQUISITION COST

1. Mineral Rights Acquisition Costs are the costs of acquiring concession rights in a lease area. They include signature bonus (initial consideration paid by the lessee to the lessor), legal fees, local statutory and acquisition fees/levies reserves value fees etc. Acquisition costs may relate to prove or unproved properties.

2. Under the Nigerian Constitution, all mineral rights are vested in the Federation. This is in contrast with the practice in some other countries where individuals may hold mineral rights. Concessions are therefore issued by the Federal Government on behalf of the Federation in the form of oil prospecting licenses, oil exploration licenses and or oil mining leases normally in that sequence. These rights are assignable subject to the permission of the Federal Government.

3. Costs incurred to purchase, lease or otherwise acquire a property (whether proved or unproved) are initially capitalised when incurred, they include the costs of:

a)   Oil Prospecting License (OPL)

b)   Oil Exploration License (OEL)

c)   Oil Mining Lease (OML)

d)   Bonuses and option to Purchase or lease properties

e)   Minerals, when land, including mineral right is purchased; and

f)   Recording Fees, legal costs and other costs incurred in acquiring properties.

EXPLORATION AND DRILLING COSTS

1. Exploration and drilling involve:

a)   Identifying areas that may warrant evaluation; and

b)   Evaluating specific areas that are considered to have petroleum prospect, largely through drilling of exploratory wells.

2. Exploration costs may be incurred both before obtaining concessions (sometimes refer to in part as pre-license costs) and after acquiring concessions.

3. Principal types of exploration costs, which include depreciation and applicable operating costs of support equipment's and facilities and other costs of exploration activities are;

a) Cost of geological geophysical studies, rights of access to properties to conduct those studies, and salaries and other expenses of geologist, geophysical crews, and others conducting those studies;

b) Cost of carrying and retaining undeveloped properties, such as rentals, legal costs for title deeds, stamp duties and the maintenance of lease records.

c) Dry hole contributions and bottom hole contributions;

d) Cost of drilling and equipping explanatory wells; and

e) Other associated costs such as settlement of local communities compensation for economic loss, surface rights and road building.

4. Exploration Costs include appraisal costs which are costs incurred to determine the size and characteristics of a reservoir discovered, in order to assess its commercial potentials.

5. The costs of drilling exploratory wells are usually capitalised as part of the company's uncompleted wells, equipment and facilities (even though the well may not be completed as a production well). On the other hand, if the well is dry the treatment will depend on the accounting method adopted by the company.

6. An explanatory well may have found oil and gas reserves, but classification of those reserves as proved reserves cannot be made until drilling is completed.

7. On completion of drilling, classification of the reserves as proved reserves depends on whether a major capital expenditure can be justified, which in turn depends on whether additional appraisal wells confirm sufficient quantities or reserves. This situation arises principally with explanatory wells drilled in remote areas for which production would require construction of a network of pipelines and production facilities.

8. In such a case, the cost of drilling the explanatory well is usually carried as an asset provided sufficient quantity of reserve to justify its completion as a production well exists and the drilling of additional well has been firmly planned for the near future. Otherwise, the explanatory well is considered impaired and the explanatory well costs are written off if the company adopts a successful effort method of accounting.

9. It is not unusual for Oil Company to carry wells in progress for more than two years before a decision is taken to capitalize or expense costs of exploration or appraisal activities.

DEVELOPMENT COSTS

1. Development costs are incurred to obtain access to proved reserves and to provide facilities for extracting, gathering, treating and storing the oil and gas. These costs are incurred after a decision has been made to develop a field or reservoir and include the following:

a) Drilling, equipping and trusting development and production wells,

b) Production platforms, downhole and wellhead equipment, pipelines, production and initial treatment and storage facilities and utility and waste disposal system; and

2. Development costs are usually capitalised as part of the costs of a company's wells and related equipment and facilities. Thus, all costs incurred to drill and equip development wells and service wells are development costs and are capitalised whether the well is successful or unsuccessful. Costs of drilling those wells and costs of constructing equipment and facilities are usually included in the company's uncompleted wells, equipment, and facilities until drilling construction is completed.

PRODUCTION COSTS

1. Production involves lifting the oil and to the surface, gathering, treating field processing and storage. Production costs are usually determined to be all costs incurred from the maintenance of the wells and well heads to the storage facilities when the oil and gas are ready for export or delivery to a refinery.

2. Production costs are those costs incurred to operate and maintain a company's wells and related equipment and facilities, including depreciation, depletions and applicable operating costs of support equipment and facilities. Examples of production costs include:

   a) Costs of personnel engaged in the operation of wells and related equipment and facilities.

   b) Repairs and maintenance of production facilities

   c) Materials, supplies, fuel consumed and services utilized in such operation and

   d) Royalties

SUPPORT EQUIPMENT AND FACILITIES COSTS

1. Costs incurred on support equipment and facilities in oil and gas production activities such as vehicles repair shops, warehouses, supply points, camps and division, district of each offices, air craft and helicopters, safety and environmental facilities are usually accumulated and re-allocated to the classes of costs identified earlier as items (a) to (f) in paragraph 15, on some rational basis. For example, use of vehicles may be allocated on kilometer of power houses on the basis of wastage reading and so on.

GENERAL COSTS

1. Some costs incurred in a company's oil and gas producing activities do not always result in acquisition of an asset and therefore, are usually charged to expense. Example include geological and geophysical costs, the costs of carrying and retaining undeveloped properties and the costs of drilling those exploratory wells that do not result in proved reserves.

2. The costs of a company's well and related equipment and facilities and the costs of the related proved properties are usually amortised as the related oil and gas reserves are produced from the reserve. Depreciation, depletion and amortization of capitalised acquisition, exploration and

development cost also become part of the oil and gas produced along with production (lifting) costs identified above.

3. Oil companies incur substantial cost in providing amenities for the communities where they operate. Such costs which do not have future benefits to the company are usually expensed. Oil companies also incur costs on matters as corporate affairs and staff training and development.

OIL AND GAS ACCOUNTING METHOD

1. Methods and procedures followed by oil companies in accounting for exploration and development costs diverge significantly.

2. Two basic accounting methods in common use are the Full cost and the Successful Efforts Methods Both methods are widely followed and each of them has a valid conceptual justification. Companies using the Full Cost Method are referred to as Full Cost Companies while those using Successful Efforts Methods are referred to as Successful Efforts Companies.

3. A third method known as Reserve Recognition Accounting (RRA) allows an enterprise to recognize the value of proved oil and gas reserve as assets and changes in such reserve values as earnings in the financial statements. This method is however not in common use and is not recommended.

FULL COST METHOD

1. Under this method, all costs associated with acquisition, exploration and development activities are capitalised irrespective of whether or not the activities resulted in the discovery of reserves. Such costs are usually amortised against successful finds on gross revenue or unit of production basis. A ceiling test is required in order to determine whether the cost capitalised can be recovered from the proved reserves.

2. Proponents of the full cost method argue that the method recognizes that all acquisition, exploration and development activities are an integral part of and necessary for the ultimate production of reserves, and as such their cost should be viewed in total as successful activities will eventually absorb the unsuccessful.

3. It is further argued by proponents of this method that the intricate and the enormous capital outlay involved in the oil and gas business require that the search for oil and gas be looked at more globally rather than on well-by-well basis. Oil companies view the cost of oil and gas reserves discovered in terms of the overall exploratory effort and total cost incurred. Oil and gas reserves cannot be found without first incurring such costs. It is not contended that unsuccessful efforts add value to the already existing reserves but that without such cost oil may not likely be discovered. Such costs therefore enable tie valuable oil and gas to be discovered ultimately.

4. Furthermore, they fill that full cost accounting provides more meaningful financial statements. The Primary assets of an oil company are its underground oil and gas reserves but not the individual wells drilled in producing them.

5. Finally, it is argued that the amortization of the pooled costs over time produces more meaningful income statement through improved matching of cost with the related revenue. It also makes comparison more meaningful.

6. Opponents of the full cost method argue that it may result in a situation asset reported on the balance sheet may not be recoverable from the reserves. Accumulating losses in asset account amount to window dressing. The method is also more cumbersome to operate as it requires ceiling test and adjustment. It is further argued that the method flouts the prudence principle by deferring obvious losses.

SUCCESSFUL EFFORTS METHOD

1. Under the Successful Efforts Method, costs associated with successful well as capitalised while costs of unsuccessful acquisition and exploratory under the successful efforts methods and the basis of amortization of pooled costs is only of unit-of-production.

2. The proponents of successful efforts contend that:

a) It ensures that all assets are backed by adequate reserves. A dry or surrendered lease cannot possibly be an asset as it has no reserve backing and therefore is expensed.

b) It complies with the accounting principle of prudence which demands that known losses be immediately recognized in the accounts.

c) It is simple to operate as the need for periodic ceiling computation and adjustments is avoided.

d) Successful Efforts Method ensures that cost of inefficient exploration efforts are not hidden in assets as is the case with the Full Cost Method

e) It facilitates appraisal of the contributions of individual leases to total revenue or income.

3. Opponents of the Successful Efforts Method argue that, in the search for oil and gas, ail costs should be regarded as integral to the ultimate discovery of reserves. Attempting a cause-and-effect relationship between costs incurred and specific reserves is not relevant at all. It is further argued that huge write-offs may result in very low profit coupled with unattractive asset base, thus making it extremely difficult for such a company to raise external funds. The method also results in low stock market ratios which may affect the company's share price in the market.

FULL COST METHOD vs SUCCESSFUL EFFORT METHOD

1. Both successful efforts and full cost method use proved reserves to amortised acquisition costs. They differ however, in respect of amortization of well and related facilities. Whereas full cost companies usually use proved reserves for determining the unit of production, successful efforts companies used proved developed reserves. This difference arises because full cost companies usually include future development costs-in the cost subject to amortization.

2. Generally, small and new companies use full cost method until their asset bases have been substantially built up.

ASSESSMENT OF UNPROVED PROPERTIES

1. Unproved properties are usually assessed periodically to determine whether they have been impaired. A property would likely be impaired, for example if a dry hole has been drilled on it and the company has no firm plan to continue drilling. Also, the likelihood of partially or total impairment of a property increases as the expiration of the lease term approaches and drilling activities has not commenced on the property. If the result of the assessment indicates a loss is usually recognized by making a valuation revision.

2. Impairment of individual unproved properties whose acquisitions are relatively significant are usually assessed on a property-by-perry basis, and any losses; recognized by making a valuation provision.

3. When a company has a relatively large number of unproved properties whose acquisition cost are not individually significant, it is usually unpracticable to assess impairment on a property-by-property basis. In such situations, the amount of impairment to be recognized is determined by amortizing those either in the aggregate or by groups on the basis of:

   a) Information about such factors as the terms of the OPEML or OEL;

   b) The experience of the company in similar situation;

   c) The extent of the acreage leased;

   d) The average holding period of unproved properties.

   e) The relative proportion of such properties on which proved reserves has been found in the past.

4. If an unproved property on which impairment has been recorded on a group basis is surrendered or the right released, the net book value charged to expense.

5. When an unproved property on which impairment has been recorded on individual is surrendered or the rights released, the net book value charged to expense.

RECLASSIFICATION OF AN UNPROVED PROPERTY

1. A property may be reclassified from unproved property to prove property when proved reserve are discovered on or otherwise attributed to the properties. When a single concession covers a vast area, only the portion of the perry to which the proved reserve relate is usually reclassified from unproved to prove. For a property whose impairment has been assessed individually; the net book value (Acquisition cost minus impairment provision) is usually reclassified to prove properties whereas for properties amortised on a group basis the gross acquisition costs are usually reclassified.

DEPLETION OF ACQUISITION COST OF PROVED PROPERTIES

1. Capitalized acquisition costs of proved properties are usually depleted by the unit of production method so that each unit produce is assigned a pro-rate portion of the unamortized acquisition cost. Under the unit-of-production method depletion may be computed either on a property-by-property basis or on the basis of reservoir or field.

AMORTISATION AND DEPRECIATION OF CAPITALISED EXPLANATORY DRILLING AND DEVELOPMENT COST

1. Capitalized cost of exploratory wells that are found proved resents and capitalized development costs are usually amortized (depreciated) by the unit-of-production method so that each unit produce is assigned to a.pro-rata portion of the amortized cost. The unit costs are usually computed on the basis of the total estimated units of proved developed reserves in case of the successful efforts company and on the basis of proved reserves in the case of a full cost company.

2. If significant development costs (such as the cost of an offshore production platform) are incurred in connection with a planned group of development wells before all of the planned wells have been drilled, it usually necessary to exclude a portion of those development cost in determining the unit of production amortization rate until the additional development wells are drilled.

3. Similarly, the practice is to exclude in computing the amortization rate, those proved developed reserves that will be produced only after significant additions development costs are incurred, such as for improved recovery systems.

4. A full cost company usually includes estimated future development costs in computing its unit rate since its amortization is based on proved reserves. Conversely, future development cost may not be anticipated by a successful efforts company in computing the amortization rate since it uses proved developed reserves.

DEPRECIATION OF SUPPORT EQUIPMENT AND FACILITIES

1. Depreciation of support equipments and facilities used in oil and gas producing activities is usually allocated to exploration cost, development cost or reducing, cost appropriate.

REVISION OF ESTIMATED RESERVES

1. Unit of production depletion rates are revised whenever there is a revision of estimated proved reserves. Such a revision is usually carried oat annually computed on the basis of total estimated unit of proved developed reserves by successful efforts companies and proved reserves by full cost companies.

RESTORATION AND ABANDONMENT COSTS

1. Restoration and abandonment involve giving up further exploration activities of a well head or Field in which oil or gas has not been found in commercial quantity. It can also occur where the operators are of the view that oil or gas is exhausted and can no longer be profitably produced. On the other hand, restoration involves bringing the exploration site to its ecological state.

2. Subsequent to granting an Oil Prospecting License (OPL), an Oil Mining Lease (OML) is granted. An OML entities the lessee to enter a property, survey it locates a well site, perform drilling operations and removes any minerals found. The lessee is also given the right to perform all acts necessary and incidental to the operations.

3. However, on termination of each mining lease, the lessee shall. With the permission of the Federal Government, remove all related facilities. Regulation No. 35 of Petroleum (Drilling and Production) Regulations 1969 under petroleum, 1969 (No 51), stipulates that an abandonment program has to be approved or agreed to by the Head of Petroleum Inspectorate.

4. The actual restoration and abandonment costs in respect of each facility will become known once the facility ceases to produce and abandonment commence; therefore, it is important that the periodic charge for such costs less estimated acreage value are recognized In the accounts based on the best available estimates

   a) A charge against income on a systematic basis over the full production lives of the facilities concerned so that the accumulated provision will equal the cost of restoration and abandonment; or

   b) Recognizing the eventual liability at the outset, treating corresponding charge as a capital cost to be depreciated as deferred expenses to be amortized using the unit of production method.

ABANDONMENT OF UNPROVED ASSETS - SUCCESSFUL

EFFORTS METHOD

1. Where a company abandons an unproved property, the practice is to charge the relevant capitalized acquisition costs against the related provision for impairment to the extent that such a provision has been made. If the provision is inadequate, then a loss is usually recognized. Normally, there is no problem -in identifying the loss where the company has evaluated unproved property individually.

ABANDONMENT OF PROVED PROPERTIES - SUCCESSFUL EFFORTS METHOD

1. Generally, companies using this method do not recognize any gain or loss on the partial abandonment of proved properties-. Instead, the particular property being abandoned is usually deemed to be fully amortized and its cost charged to accumulated depreciation, depletion or amortization. When the entire property is abandoned then the company may recognize a gain or loss. Where there is a partial abandonment caused by any force majeure, the company usually recognizes a loss.

ABANDONMENT OF UNPROVED AND PROVES PROPERTIES -FULL COST METHOD

1. Abandonment of oil and gas properties are usually accounted for as adjustments of capitalized costs; that is, the costs of abandoned properties are charged to the full cost center and amortized arid no gains or losses are recognized. Where the abandonment is sufficiently significant to alter the amortization per urn; of reserves, a gain or loss is usually recognized.

DEFERRED TAXES

1. In the petroleum industry, deferred tax is very significant because of the huge investments associated with the industry. Among the major expenditure items that result in timing- differences are geological and geophysical costs, development costs, intangible drilling costs, depletion costs, abandonment costs, and accelerated depreciation by way of enhance capital allowances in tax-computation. The choice between successful efforts and full cost methods of accounting affects the resulting deferred tax.

2. Currently, most companies in the petroleum industry recognize deferred taxes by way of notes in their financial statements. Others provide Tor deferred taxes in their financial statements.

CONVEYANCES

1. A mineral conveyance is a transfer of any type of ownership interest in minerals from one entity so another, in the initial mineral conveyance. the lessor conveys to the lessee a mineral interest m the property, and the lessor retains a royalty interest such as when the Federal Government grants a concession to an oil company. The lessee may, in turn, transfer in another conveyance all or part of the mineral interest to a third party.

2. There are many reasons why owners, especially working interest owners, convey interests in mineral properties. These reasons include the desire to share the, risks of ownership and the cost of exploration and development with others, to obtain financing, to improve operating efficiency or conservation and to achieve lax benefits.

TYPES OF CONVEYANCES

A conveyance agreement may take any of the following forms;

- A sale:
- An exchange of non-monetary assets;
- A pooling of assets in a joint undertaking; or
- Some combination of the above.

Conveyance arrangement involving farmouts, carried, interest, utilization production payments fall within the above broad categories.

CARRIED INTEREST

1. Under this arrangement, the transferee (the carrying party) agrees to pay for a portion or all of the pre-production costs of another party (the carried party) for share of the working interest. The arrangement is usually adopted carried party is either unwilling to bear the risk of exploration or is fund directly the cost of exploration and development.

2. The transferee is usually reimbursed either in cash, out of the proceed of carried party's share of production, or by receiving a disproportion share of the production until the carried costs have been recovered. However, if the project is unsuccessful, the carrying party may not be able to part of the costs it has incurred on behalf of the carried party.

3. The accounting treatment given to carried interest arrangement usually on the terms of the agreement. Where the carrying party is to be reimbursed, cash the arrangement is essentially a contingent payable financing. On the other hand, in case of reimbursement by increased share production, the arrangement represents acquisition of additional reserves by the carrying party:

FARMOUT

1. This is a financing arrangement in which the concern holder (the farmer) transfer part of the oil and gas interest to another party (the farmer) in consideration for an agreement by the farmer to bear costs of exploration and development which would otherwise have been borne by the farmer. Farmouts are usually adopted where the concession under does not have the resources or does not intend to explore it in the near future.

2. Farmouts are usually considered to be a pooling of assess in a joint undertaking and as such no gain or loss is recognized. The caused costs previously incurred by the farmer become the cost of interest referred to as participation risks.

UNITIZATION

1. Unitization is a form of joint undertaking whereby cession holders pool their interest together to form a single unit in return for participating interest in the combined unit of reservoir. Among the reasons for undertaking unitization are to increase operational efficiency, achieve fax advises and minimize risks.

2. Unitization is governed by a unit operating agreement which usually includes the list of the parties and their fractional interests refer to as participation factors.

   The participation factor forms the basis for the equalization of individual investments, Joint costs distribution and the sharing production and or production proceeds. Since the original factors are determined using limited data about the reservoir, agreements usually provide for one or more redeterminations. Revision of participation factors may i.e. adjustment of the unit members' share of production and costs. Since redetermination adjustments are usually accounted for on a prospective basis rather than by way of prior period restatement.

PRODCUTION SHARING CONTRACTS

1. Exploration costs incurred on a concession which is subject to a production sharing contract are normally recovered out of production at will be made from the concession. The operator is normally paid in quantities of oil and not cash. The operator usually treats the costs incurred as direct exploration costs or as a loan, bearing in mind the terms of the contract and the possibility of repayment.

2. Where costs under a production sharing contract are treated as a loan, and before establishing commercial reserves, a provision. &' equivalent to exploration cost is usually made if the effort is determined to be unsuccessful under the successful effort's method or impaired under the full cost method. Where commercial reserves are found, the provisions against all costs incurred are reserved to income subject to the limit of the loan being recovered from the reserves. Future exploration costs in the contract area are usually carried as exploration costs id the costs will be recoverable from- a future production. The balance outstanding at the end of each year is usually written down to the outstanding balance of recoverable costs at the time.

3. Where costs under a production sharing contract are treated as concession costs, the costs incurred are usually accounted for in. accordance with the company's accounting policy-using either the successful efforts or the full cost method Capitalized exploration and development costs are basis subject to impairment and ceiling tests, in line with the established accounting policy.

4. In accounting for production sharing contract, reference is made to the agreement, and the operator and the non-operator usually record their share assets, liabilities, costs and revenues, in accordance with the terms of the agreement and their respective accounting policies.

GENERAL PRINCIPLES FOR ACCOUNTING FOR CONVEYANCES

There are several important issues in respect of accounting for conveyance. transactions, among which are

1. Determination of gains or loss, if any of the parties is involved;

2. Determination of when revenue and expenses are to be recognized

3. Determination of the exact costs involved;

4. Determination of how to reflect the relevant informal' lion in financial state of the parties concerned.

5. Sometimes, oil companies in order to secure the supply of oil or gas make available to operators in consideration for a right to purchase oil or gas discovery is made. In such a situation, conveyance; is in. essence, a borrower repayable in cash or its equivalent. Thus, one party to the transaction is as a borrower while the other is a lender, especially where cash refund is expected if the oil or gas; covered is insufficient to offset the cash advance received.

6. When a convert is consummated with a view of retaining the assets in the production of gas oil, gains or losses are usually not recognized in the accounts of the parties concerned for example:

a) A transfer of assets used in oil and gas production activities exchanges for other assets also used in oil and gas producing activities; and

b) A pooling of assets in a joint venture situation for the purpose of finding development or producing oil and gas from a joint concession.

7. However, the parties involved generally recognized losses but not gains in conveyance in circumstances such as: -

a) The disposal of part or the interest or if there are doubts concerning the recoverability of the remaining interests in the concession; and

b) The disposal of part of the interest, since the seller remains obligated to drill or to operate the property if both activities arc expected to result in future loss.

CONVEYANCE VOER SUCCESSFUL EFFORTS METHOD

1. Successful efforts companies may recognize gains and losses on other types of conveyances in it with generally accepted accounting principles. In determining the appropriate accounting treatment for a company using the successful efforts method, the factors to be considered include whether:

a) The properties classified as proved or unproved;

b) Impairment an unproved property is being recorded on an individual

c) basis or on a basis of a geological group: and

d) Only partial- entire interest is conveyed

2. The general practice recognition of gains are as follows:

a) If the entire interest in an unproved property, for which impairment is recorded on individual basis is sold, gain or loss is recognized to the extent of the difference between the proceeds and the net book value.

b) If entire interest in an unproved property, for which impairment is recorded on group basis is sold, no gain or loss is recognized unless the proceeds except the original cost of the lease.

c) If a portion of interest in unproved property for winch individual impairment is record is sold, and the proceeds exceeds the total carrying value of the property, the excess of proceeds over net book value is recognized as a gain.

d) If a portion of interest in unproved property for which group impairment is recorded is sold, the excess of proceeds the total cost of the property, the excess of process over the net book value of the group is recognized as a gain.

e) If the entire interest in a proved property on which amortization is recorded is sold, as the proceeds exceeds the total cost of the property, the excess of proceed over the net book value of the group is recognized as gain or loss the difference between the proceeds is recognized as a gain or loss.

f) If a portion of an interest in a proved property on which amortization is individually camped is sold the difference between the proceeds and a proportion share of each cost and the amortization provision (book values) is recognized as gain or loss.

g) If an unproved property on which impairment has been recorded on an individual basis surrendered or the rights released, the book value of the property is charged to expenses.

h) If an unproved property on which impairment has been recorded on a group basis is surrendered or the rights released, the book value of the property is charging the accumulated impairment account and no loss is recognized.

CONYEYANCES UNBE FULL-COST METHOD.

1. Under full cost method, mineral-property conveyances, whether or not the properties are currently amortized, do not result in recognition of gain or loss, in per words, under full cost, disposal proceeds are credited to fixed assets and no gain or loss is recorded. Therefore, the sale is usually recognized in lower depletion charges in the future.

2. If the conveyance could significantly alter the relationship between capitalised costs at proved reserves of oil and gas attributable to the costs center, hen gain or loss may be recognized in the income statement.

3. A significant alteration would not ordinarily be expected to occur for conveyances involving less than 5% of the reserves qualities in the cost center or when the unit-of production amortization rate is altered by less than 25%. A cost value attributable to a significant conveyance may be calculated by multiplying the current depletion rate by the amount of reserves sold.

JOINT VENTURES

1. In the oil industry, a joint venture or unit operation of an oil and gas oil is the cooperative effort of two or more mineral owners, usually called joint venture partners. The partners accomplish, through their combined efforts and knowledge, the maximum amount of recovery from a common concession.

2. Joint venture operation may be referred to as the practice of consolidating under a single operational responsibility, the separate concessions whereby each concession holder receives the amount of production from the entire pool that is attributable to his separate ownership.

3. This relationship is usually governed by a written operating agreement which gives the joint venture partners joint control. Under the agreement, one of the parties is appointed the operator and an accounting procedure adopted.

4. In Nigeria, joint ventures arose historically from participation of the Federal Government in the existing concession held by major oil producing companies. By this arrangement, the Federal through the Federal Government acquires up to sixty percent working interest in the concessions held by those companies. Subsequently, cash calls are made on die joint venture partners to

contribute their shares of such costs as acquisition, exploration and drilling development and production in the agreed participating interest. Similarly, the production from their joint venture is shared proportionately.

5. Joint ventures evolve in various forms such as the conventional joint ventures production sharing and service contracts. The need for joint ventures may arise from any of the following: Minimization of risks, operational efficiency, sharing of huge capital outlay and political consideration.

6. A joint venture may be long-term as in the case of conventional venture agreements and production sharing or short-term as in the case of unitization.

ACCOUNTING TREATMENT OF JOINT VENTURES

There are three ways the transactions of a joint venture could be recorded. These are:

1. Separate set of books for the joint venture

Under this, the operator maintains a separate set of books dedicated solely to recording the transactions relating to the venture.

2. Common set of books for the joint venture and the operator.

Under this approach, the operator maintains common set of books in which it maintains both the joint venture and its exclusive transactions.

3. Memorandum entries

This method is similar to (a) but with one difference. While under (a) the joint venture account is part of the double entry system, under (c) it is merely a memorandum entry. This method is rare in practice.

4. Returns are usually rendered by the operator to the joint venture partners a enable them prepare their own financial statements. These returns show how cash calls received have been expended.

ACCOUNTING FOR CRUDE OIL AND OVERLEFTS AND UNDERLIFTS

1. The joint venture arrangements under which most exploration operations are conducted give rise to special accounting issues in reporting turnover and crude oil stock by upstream companies; Oil producing under joint venture arrangements are shared according to agreed nomination and schedules. However, tanker loads usually do not equate to the joint exact entitlements at the date of each lifting. Therefore, at any reporting date each partner would have over lifted or under lifted its proportionate share of total production.

2. A company may choose to account for its interest in oil production on the basis of the quantities physically received and delivered (lifting basis) or on the basis of entitlements (entitlements basis). The method adopted would impart differently on the reported stock and sales/turnover. Generally, large companies report stocks and sales simply on lifting basis as the impact of overlifts or underlifts are considered immaterial to their financial statements. On the other hand, smaller companies generally report on the basis of entitlements, and usually adjust reported turnover and stock for their

net overlifts or underlifts positions. The overlifts or underlifts are recorded as creditors and debtors, respectively, or as part of stock. Turnover would, therefore reflect the value of a company's share of production during an accounting period.

3. In practice, one of the following methods is used to account for underlies and overlifts:

a) Underlies and overlifts are included as stock at the lower of cost or market value.

b) Revenue is adjusted to exclude overlifts and to include underlifts at the lower of cost or market value.

FUNCTIONAL CURRENCY

1. An oil company in Nigeria must, by virtue of the provisions of the Companies and Allied Matters Decree 19909, prepare its statutory accounts in Naira. However, because most of their expenses and income are incurred and earned in U.S. Dollars, most oil companies have always used U.S. Dollar as their functional currency for accounting purposes and they are also now required to do so for the purpose of petroleum profit tax. These dollar accounts are translated into Naira accounts for statutory purposes in accordance with the provisions of IAS-7 Statements of Accounting Standard on Foreign Currency Conversion and Translation.

PART V
ACCOUNTING STANDARD

ACCOUNTING FOR PETROLEUM

The Accounting Standard comprises paragraphs -102-138 of this Statement.

The standard should be read in the context of all other parts of this statement and the preface to the Statements of Accounting Standards published by NASB

ACCOUNTING POLICY

1. All companies engaged in oil and gas exploration, development, and production activities shall state in their financial statements the policy for accounting for cost incurred and the manner of disposing of capitalised costs in respect of such activities. In addition, the policy on accounting for restoration and abandonment costs and the total restoration and abandonment costs should be disclosed in their financial statements, even if already included in the cost of safes.

2. A company may use either the full cost method of the successful efforts method. The method used should be consistently applied and disclosed.

CLASSIFICATION OF COSTS

Oil and gas producing activities involve special types of costs which should be classified as follows:

1. Mineral rights acquisition costs;

2. Exploration and. drilling costs;

3. Development costs

4. Production costs;

5. Support equipment and facilities costs; and

6. General costs.

FULL COST METHOD

INITIAL TREATMENT OF COSTS

1. Costs incurred on mineral rights acquisition, exploration, appraisal at development activities should be capitalised.

AMORTIZATION OF CAPITALISED COSTS

90. All capitalized costs incurred in a cost center should be depreciated on the unit of production basis using proved reserves. The determination of the capitalist I costs should be on a countrywide basis.

CEILING TEST

1. Ceiling tests should be conducted at least annually at balance sheet date, while country-wide basis. Such tests should use discounted values for revenues costs, estimated future taxes, and estimated future development costs.

2. The price used for the test should be that ruling at the balance sheet date, while the reserve used should be proved reserves. Where the accounts are prepared it. U.S. Dollars, the discount rate to be used for estimating, future cash flow shall be ten percent. Where accounts are prepared in Naira. CBN rediscount rate should be used.

3. If the net discounted revenue is lower that the capitalised costs, the differs should be written off.

SUCCESS EFFORTS METHOD

INITIAL TREATMENT OF COSTS

1. Costs incurred acquisition of mineral rights and other exploration activities not specifically corrected to an identifiable structure should be expensed in the period they are incurred.

2. All costs incurred on mineral rights acquisition, exploration appraisal and development activities should be capitalised initially on the basis of wells, field or exploration centers, pending determination. Such costs should be written off when it is determined that the well is dry.

RETENTION PERIOD PENDING DETERMINATION

1. If further appraisal of concession is placed, cost of exploration and appraisal activities may be carried forward pending determination of proved reserves in commercial quantities for a period of:

   a) Not more than 3 years following completion of drilling in an offshore area where major development costs may need to be incurred, or

   b) For a maximum of 2 years in an onshore area.

AMORTISATION OF CAPITALISED COSTS

1. Mineral rights acquisition costs which have not been allocated should be amortized over the remaining life of the license. Net book value of un0depreciated mineral rights acquisition costs should be reviewed annually for impairment on well-by-well. Any impairment discovered should be written off.

2. Amortization of exploration and drilling costs incurred within each well, field or property, should be on a unit-of-production basis using proved developed reserves.

DEFERRED TAX

1. Deferred tax provision should be made in the accounts in accordance with IAS 12-Accounting for Deferred Taxes.

COST OF PROVIDING AMENITIES FOR COMMUNITIES

1. Cost of providing amenities for communities in areas of operation should be written off as incurred.

CONVEYANCES

Recognition of gains or losses under conveyances should be as follows:

1. If the entire interest in an unproved property, for which impairment recorded on an individual basis is sold, gain or loss is recognized to the extent of the difference between tie proceeds and the net book value,

2. If entire interest in an unproved property, for which impairment is recorded on a group basis is sold, no gain or loss is recognized unless the proceeds exceeds the original cost of the lease.

3. If a portion of interest in unproved property for which impairment is recorded is sold, and the proceeds exceeds the period carrying value of the property, the excess of proceeds over net book value is recognized as a gain.

4. If portion of interest in unproved property for which group impairment is recorded is sold and the proceeds exceeds the total cost of the property the excess of proceeds over the net book value of the group is recognized as a gain.

5. If the entire interest in a proved property on which amortization individually computed is sold, the difference between the property and the net book value is recognized as a gain or toss.

6. If a portion of an interest in a proved property on which is individually computed is sold, the difference between the property and a proportionate share of each cost and the amortization (book value) is recognized as gain or loss.

7. If an unproved property on which impairment has an individual basis is surrendered or the rights released, the book value of the property is charged to expenses.

8. If an unproved property on which impairment has been recorded group basis is surrendered or the rights released, the book value property is charged to the accumulated impairment account and no loss is recognized.

CARRIED INTERESTS

1. The carrying party should record the total cost incurred in respect of the carried interest as capital expenditure. Disclosure should be made of the carrying arrangements, including the amount of carried expenditure to date.

2. The carrying party should record recoveries made out of production from the carried interest as follows:

   a) If the full cost method is adopted, the entire amount should be credited to the appropriate cost center. If the successful efforts method is adopted, the recovery of carried costs should be credited to the relevant fixed asset account. When recoveries exceed the carried costs, the surplus should be recognized as income on an appropriate basis. This action should only be taken when full recovery of all carried costs is reasonably certain.

   b) The expenditure borne by carrying party should not be recorded in the carried party's book, nor production from the carried interest on the extent that it is used by the carrying party to recover costs.

3. The carried party should record all expenditure and production after payout.

4. Where reimbursement is in cash, the following practice should be followed.

   a) Neither the carried party nor the carrying party should accrue any contingent repayment of the financing until the outcome of the specified event, i.e. discovery of reserves, commencement of production, or declaration of reserves in commercial quantity can be determined:

   b) In a carried interest arrangement involving exploration cost, the carrying party should capitalize or expense the costs borne on behalf of the carried party by its normal accounting practice. If the carrying party should record a debtor and should credit the accounts, whether capital or revenue, in which the costs have been charged.

c) In a carried interest arrangement involving development costs, where the carrying party is assumed to be fully reimbursed, the reimbursable costs incurred should be classified as a debtor and provided for to the extent that recovery is reasonably assured:

d) If the amount to be reimbursed by the carried party includes interest or a premium, these additional costs should be accounted for by both parties under the accounting policy for fixed assets and interest expense or income;

e) Following the occurrence of the specified event, the carried party should record any sums repayable directly in cash within creditors and fixed interest expense or income;

f) Once production commences, the carried party will be reimbursed the carrying party out of the proceeds of its share of production, and the debtor and creditor balance should be eliminated.

5. Exploration and drilling costs of the carried party should be amortized using the reserves and production estimates of the carried interest after payout.

FARMOUTS AND SIMILAR ARRANGEMENTS

1. The farmer should not record any expenditure made on its behalf by the farmer. Any capitalized costs previously incurred by the farmer in relation to the whole interest should be redesignated as relating to the partial interest retained.

2. Where cash reimbursement of past costs takes place, the farmer should credit any proceeds to the accounts, whether capital or expenses, in which such costs were originally recorded.

3. The farmer should record all of its expenditure relating to the arrangement, both respect of its own interest and that retained by the farmer as and when the costs are incurred.

UNITIZATION AND DETERMINATION

1. No gain or loss should be recognized on a unitization arrangement except where cash received exceeds costs.

2. Where there is a redetermination of interest, the resulting adjustment of the unit members' shares of production and costs should be accounted for on a productive basis rather than by way of prior period restatement.

JOINT VENTURE

1. The operator of a joint venture should maintain a separate set of books dedicated solely to recording the transactions relating to the venture.

2. Each partner should account for its proportionate share of the costs, production, assets, and liabilities of the joint venture in line with its accounting policy.

OVERLIFTS AND UNDERLIFTS

1. One of the following methods should be used to account for under lifts and overlifts:

   a) Both under lifts and overlifts should be accrued for. Under lifts should be included as stock at the lower of cost or market value while overlifts should be valued at year-end spot price.

   b) Invoiced sales should be adjusted to exclude overlifts at year end spot price and to include under lifts at the lower of cost or net realizable value.

RESTORATION AND ABANDONMENT

1. Companies should make provision for restoration and abandonment costs less estimated salvage values based on the best available estimate by:

   a) A charge against income on a systematic basis over the full productive lives of the facilities concerned so that the accumulated provision will cover the cost of restoration and abandonment; or

   b) Recognition of eventual liability at the outset, the corresponding debit should be treated as a capital cost to be depreciated or as deferred expenses to be amortized using the unit-of-production basis.

2. Restoration and abandonment costs should be deducted in arriving at estimated future net revenues for ceiling test calculation.

FUNCTIONALITY CURRENCY

1. The dollar accounts of an oil company should be translated to Naira by the provisions of IAS 7- Statement of Accounting Standard of Foreign Currency Conversions and Translations.

DISCLOSURE

The oil industry is peculiar in the sense that a large proportion of its assets (reserves) is off-balance-sheet. Furthermore, the diversity of treatment between full cost and successful efforts demands at some efforts be made at harmonization to enhance comparability. As such, the following disclosures are required:

   a) Total proved developed and undeveloped reserves, for oil and condensations expressed in barrels, and for gas expressed in cubic feet. The disclosure should show movements in reserves during the year under such headings as:

   i. Revision of previous estimates;

   ii. Purchase of reserves in place;

   iii. New discoveries;

   iv. Sales of reserves in place; and

v. Production

In addition, each of the joint venture partners should be disclosed for the current year and the preceding four years.

b) Costs relating to oil and gas exploration for the current year setting out proved and unproved properties, accumulated depreciation depletion and amortization and share of net capitalised costs of joints ventures, distinguishing between offshore and onshore.

c) Capitalised costs relating to oil and gas producing activities.

d) Details of concession (OEL, OPL and OML), showing the original and the unexpired terms of the concessions.

e) The amount of depreciation, depletion and amortization and the average rates used;

f) Results of operations from producing activities showing revenues (both third party and intra), production costs, exploration costs, depreciation and amortization and income taxes.

g) Standardized measure of oil and gas (SMOG), using 10% discount rate where the account are prepared in U.S. Dollars and central Bank of Nigeria rediscount rate as at the balance sheet date, where the accounts are prepared in Naira.

h) Significant non-producing development costs such as offshore production platform, which have been excluded from the amortization base in determining the unit of production amortization.

i) Total cash calls made on the partners for the year and the amount of such cash calls received, indicating clearly the U.S. Dollar and Naira components.

j) Deferred taxes

k) Costs of providing amenities for communities in areas of operation of company;

l) Summarized comparative balance sheet and income statements for five years, including the current years,

m) The prices used for purposes of the ceiling test and the prices at the measurement date and, if the use of price at the measurement date would have resulted in a write-off, the amount so written off,

n) The total estimated liability of the company for restoration and abandonment costs calculated at current year-end prices

FARMOUT

1. If the consideration for the farmout includes an arrangement for the farmer to bear subsequent costs which would otherwise fall to the retained interest for the farmer, the farmer should disclose the amount of such expenditure incurred by the farmer in aggregate during the accounting period to provide an indication on the consideration received from the farmouts.

CONSTRUCTION IN PROGRESS

1. Where there are in progress items, these should be disclosed separately

FUNCTIONAL CURRENCY

1. Where an oil company uses functional currency other than the Naira in keeping its books, it should disclose the currency and the basis of transaction in its accounting policies.

GROUP ACCOUNTS

1. Where group accounts including downstream activities are prepared in the turnover from the exploration and production activities exceed 10% the group turnover the above disclosure requirement will apply.

PART V

NOTES ON LEGAL REQUIREMENTS

The requirements of this standard are complimentary to any accounts and disclosure requirements of Companies and Allied Matters Decree 19 and other relevant laws and regulations.

EFFECTIVE DATE

This Standard becomes operative for financial statements covering periods beginning on or after January 1, 1994.

CHAPTER SEVENTEEN
OIL AND GAS ACCOUNTING

Accounting in the Oil Industry can only be understood when the following terms are known:

1. Exploration and Production Costs

2. Methods of recognizing Revenue and Cost

3. Auditing and Appraisal of Oil and Gas Reserves

4. Refineries and Petrochemicals Accounting

5. Accounting for Refinery Operations

6. Accounting for Petrochemical Operations

7. Accounting Standards of Petroleum Accounting

8. Examples and Accounting Entries

EXPLORATIION AND PRODUCTION COSTS

Oil exploration to the discovery of the hydrocarbons in commercial quantities Some wells may have Oil while some may not. Three conflicting views to accounts for unsuccessful exploration are:

1. The Full Cost Approach

2. The Successful Efforts Approach

3. Reserve Recognition Accounting

Under Full Cost Accounting all exploration costs are capitalised subject to a recoverable test in operations that are both successful or not.

This supports the accrual concept as capitalizing nonproductive expenditure on the grounds that it is an integral part of the cost of finding and producing Oil and Gas.

Successful Efforts Accounting. This approach capitalizes only the costs of wells that find oil and gas and writes off the failures. That means that, exploration and development costs are carried forward in the Balance Sheet for areas where the value of the Reserves discovered the cost incurred.

Under Reserve Recognition Accounting, Revenue is recognized when the Reserves are discovered rather than when the oil is sold. Consequently, exploration and development costs are not carried forward instead the oil reserves discovered are valued and the unexploited Balance Sheet from time to time.

CEILING TEST

Ceiling Test is a valuation procedure to determine whether the stated value of a company is oil and gas assets are in excess of their recoverable amount.

DEPRECIATION, DEPLETION AND AMORTISATION

Depreciation of costs are based on the volume of oil and gas removed in the current year as a percentage of what id left in the ground. Hence the Estimated useful life of a pool is dependent upon the value in the ground, rate of extraction and amount of expenditure put into developing the pool.

METHODS FOR DEPLETION

1. Tangible Vs Intangible

    Separate calculations are made for tangible and intangible costs. Tangible would be depreciated over their estimated useful lives

2. Unit of Production

    Costs are depleted based on the Naira value of the reserves in the ground rather than the volume.

3. Reserve Depletion

    Costs are depleted based on the value of the reserves in the ground rather than the volume. This method reduces the depletion charge in the periods of rising prices when compared to the unit of production.

    If the successful efforts approach is used, it calculates depletion charge on a well-to-well basis while Full Cost Method uses very large costs centers.

COVEYANCES

A conveyance is the transfer of any type of ownership interest in concession from one entity to another. Conveyances of property interests can be calculated as follows: A sale, a borrowing an exchange of non-monetary assets, or a pooling of assets in joint undertaking.

Conveyance contracts can be quite complex and raises accounting problems of

1. Determination of gains or loss.
2. Timing of revenue and expenses recognition,
3. Measurement of costs and presentation in financial statements.

OTHER DEFINITION OF TERMS

JOINT INTEREST OPERATIONS

Joint ventures Account for the investments in a joint Venture using the Proportionate Consolidation Method. Under this method, each joint venture records its own protrata share of assets, liabilities, revenue and expenses from returns and statements rendered monthly by the operator.

AUDITING AND APPRAISAL OF OIL AND GAS RESERVES

The stages in auditing and appraising Oil and Gas Reserves can be broken into the following major sequences:

Planning the audit, Assessing risks and potentials errors or mis-statements, developing the Audit plan, performing the audit and conclusion.

THE DIFFERENT RESERVES ARE:

1. Oil and Gas reserves

   Oil and Gas reserves classified according to the degree of confidence in estimates of the quantities of oil and gas in reserves.

2. Proved Reserves

   Proved reserves can be classified as developed or undeveloped according to whether or not. They can be expected to be recovered through existing well with existing equipment and operating methods.

3. Probable Reserves

   These are the reserves which are not yet proved but are estimated to have better that 50 percent chance of being technically and economically productible

4. Possible Reserves

   This are reserves estimated to have significant but less than 50 percent chance of being technically and economically productible.

AUDITING PROCESS IN THE INDUSTRY

1. Understanding the accounting process oil and gas reserves

   This involves the gathering of information relating to the company's accounting system.

2. Understanding the Control Environment

   It is necessary for the Auditor to understand the nature of controls available to ensure accuracy and reliability of reserve data.

3. Confirming the Auditor's Understanding

This involves the use of work through the accounting manual, performance and observation.

4. Assessing Risks of Potential error or misstatement level

It is important to visualize the perverse nature of the effort of errors and misstatement in reserves as it would affect of the financial statements. Reserves estimates are useful in management Base for depletion calculations, base of computing information about country's resources and basis for determining cost ceiling.

5. Developing the Audit Plan

The Auditor must rely on controls that made the risk and perform a basic level of substantive tests or perform focused substantive tests, some test are:

a)   He must develop an audit plan to test controls that mitigate risks

b)   He must plant tests to confirm the reliability of the system of controls.

6. Performing the Audit

Two level test that are relevant to the audit of oil and gas reserves:

a)   The focused substantive tests;

b)   The basic level of substantive tests

7. The Auditor's involvement with the Audit and Appraisal of Oil and Gas Reserves

This involves the information of the base of valuation.

Some peculiar problems in oil and gas.

a)   Uncertainty in search of oil;

b)   Lack of uniform accounting policies

c)   Oil exploration – what to capitalize not

d)   Well workover – capitalize initial during costs;

e)   Well development –Accumulate cost work in progress account;

f)   Use of contractors;

g)   Budget approval;

h)   Depletion, Depreciation and Amortization

i)   Production costs;

j)   Material Control;

k)   Crude Oil;

l)   Crude Oil Stock;

m) Use of Specialists;

n) Reserve Estimate;

o) Crude Oil Production;

p) Royalty;

q) Petroleum profit tax based on fiscal value of oil;

r) Memorandum of understanding.

REFINERIES AND PETROCHEMICAL ACCOUNTING

Oil refining started in 1950 when Mr. Samuel Kier commission a chemistry purify him oil uses as 'Cure all' medicine of its foul smell, when the offensive odour did not vanish, Kier noticed that the refined oil burnt with bright light so he started selling it for domestic illumination.

UNDERSTANDING OIL REFINING

Oil is not a rot, a compound, but a mixture of several hydrocarbon compounds, this means that the various hydrocarbons mixed together to form crude oil still retain their individual characteristics.

Oil is refined by heating the use of continuous crude distillation process and products are removed at various position in the Tower.

Flashing is the procedure for boiling straight run residue at lower than atmosphere pressure so it boils at lower temperature and maximizes gasoline yield.

ACCOUNTIGN OPERATIONS:

1. Appropriate crude oil must be available. The balancing can only be attained by 'trading' with or exchanging with other companies

2. Transfer pricing e.g. market-based pricing, cost-based pricing and negotiated pricing.

3. Crude Inventory Control – cover quantity, quality and steady/ready availability.

SINGER PLC

BALANCE SHEET AS AT 31 DECEMBER, 2015

	$	$
Fixed Assets		15,000
Net Current Assets		11,500
		26,500
Capital and Reserves		
10,000 ordinary shares of 50c each		5,000
Share premium account	2,000	
Revenue Reserves	19,500	21,500
		26,500
Capital & Reserves		
10,000 ordinary shares of 50c each		5,000
Share premium account	2,000	
Revenue Reserves	19,500	21,500
		26,500

Solution:

Singer PLC post acquisition profit is $12,000 (19,500-7,500)

$

Coy's pre-acquisition profit

Balance as at 31 December, 2014   7,500

Profit for three months to 31 March, 2015   3,000

Pre-acquisition Revenue Reserves   10,000

The Balance of $2,000 on share premium account is all pre-acquisition

Treatment of Singer PLC Reserves on consolidation i.e. $2,000 Reserves

	$	$
Minority Interest Total reserve 20%	400	3,900
Cost of control –Group		
Share of pre-acquisition elements		
80% of $2,000	1,600	
80% of $10,500	8,400	

Consolidated Reserve – Group share of post

Acquisition 80% of 49,000 (12,000-3,000)   7,200

                                            2,000   19,500

Consolidated workings:

SINGER PLC

	$	Cost of Control $	Minority Interest $	Share Premium $	Revenue Reserve $
Ordinary shares	5,000	80% ordinary	20% Ordinary		
Share premium	2,000	4,000	1,000		
Share Premium	2,000	1,600	400		
Revenue Reserves	19,500	8,400 8/10			
		8/10 x 10,500	3,900		7,200
		1			
		14,000			
Cost of investments in Singer		(25,000)			
Singer Goodwill		(11,000)			
			5,300		
Add Hopeful PLC's Reserves				3,500	20,000
				3,500	27,200

HOPEFUL PLC

CONSOLIDATED BALANCE SHEET AS AT 31 DECEMBER, 2015

	$	$
Goodwill arising from consolidation		11,000
Fixed Assets		31,000
Net current Assets		44,000
		86,000
Capital and Reserves		
Ordinary shares at $1 each		50,000
Reserves	3,500	30,700
Revenue Reserves	27,200	80,700
		5,300
Minority Interest		86,000

DIVIDENDS AND PRE-ACQUISITION PROFITS

Heaven Limited acquired 16,000 of 20,000 $1 ordinary shares of Saviour Limited on 1 January, 2015 for $50,000. Savior Limited's Balance Sheet at 31 December 2014 showed a proposed ordinary dividends of $8,000 and referred reserves of $24,000. The Balance Sheets of the two companies at 31 December, 2015 are given below:-

HEAVEN LIMITED

BALANCE SHEET AS AT 31 DECEMBER, 2015

	$
Fixed Assets	70,000
Investment in Saviour Limited at cost	43,600
Less amounts written down	113,600
	54,000
Net Current Assets	167,600
Capital and Reserves	
Ordinary Shares of $1 each	100,000
Retained Reserves	67,600
	167,600

SAVIOUR LIMITED BALANCE SHEET AS AT 31 DECEMBER, 2015	
	$
Fixed Assets	29,000
Net Current Assets	25,000
	54,000
Capital and Reserves	20,000
Ordinary Shares of $1 each	34,000
Retained Reserves	54,00

You are required to prepare the consolidated Balance Sheet of Heaven Limited at 30 December, 2015.

Solution:

INVESTMENT IN SAVIOUR LIMITED

	$		$
Bank-purchase of	16,000	Bank-dividend received from	
$1 ordinary shares	50,000	pre-acquisition profits	6,400

		Balance c/d	43,600
	50,000		50,000

HEAVEN LIMITED

CONSOLIDATION BALANCE SHEET AS AT 31 DECEMBER, 2015

	$
Goodwill arising on consolidation	8,400
Fixed Assets	99,000
Net Current Assets	79,000
	186,400
Capital and Reserves	100,000
Ordinary Shares of $1 each	75,600
Retained Reserves	175,600
	10,800
Minority Interest	186,400

Example on Dividends and Pre-acquisition profit A Limited and B Limited each make up their accounts to 31 December. A Limited buys 40,000 of 50,000 $1 ordinary shares of B Limited for $87,500 on 1 October, 2011. B Limited's revenue is reserves (after deducting proposed dividends) stood at $25,000 on 31 December, 2010. B Limited's profits after tax for the year to 31 December,2011 were $10,000. In January 2012 B Limited declared a first and final dividend for 2011 of $5,000. At 31 December, 2011. A Limited reserves stood at $55,000, this does not include any adjustment for dividends receivable from S Limited.

You are required to prepare ledger Accounts for the Revenue Reserves, Minority Interest and Cost of Controls as at 31 December, 2011.

Solution:

LEDGER ACCOUNTS

	$	Cost of Control 80% Ordinary$	Minority Interest 20% Ordinary $	Revenue Reserves $
Share capital	50,000	40,000	10,000	
Revenue Reserve	30,000	23,000	6,000	1,000
		63,000		
Cost of Investment in B Limited	87,500			
Pre-acquisition	3,000	90,000		
Goodwill	(27,500)		16,000	
Dividend Receivable out				1,000
Of post Acquisition Profit				55,000
Add A Limited Reserves				57,000

Example of Revaluation of Assets

Field Limited acquire 75% of the Ordinary Shares of Tessy Limited on 1 September, 2008. At the date the fair values of Tessy Limited's fixed assets was $46,000 greater than their net book value, and the balance of Retained Profits was $42,000. The Balance Sheet s of both companies at 31 August, 2009 are given below. Tessy Limited has not incorporated any revaluation in its books of account.

FIDEL LIMITED BALANCE SHEET AS AT 31 AUGUST, 2009.

	$
Fixed Assets	126,000
Investment in Tessy Limited at cost	102,000
	228,000
Net Current Assets	124,000
	352,000
Capital and Reserves	160,000
Ordinary Shares of $1 each	192,000
Retained Profits	352,000

Date	No. of Shares bought in the purchase $	Cost $	Reserves of Simbe Ltd at the date of purchase $
1 February, 2010	5,000	8,000	20,000
1 November ,2010	12,500	21,000	30,000
1 April, 2011	10,000	20,000	20,000

Calculate the pre-acquisition profits of the Bisi Group I Simbe Limited when Simbe Limited eventually became a subsidiary on 1April, 2011.

Solution-Assumptions

1. Ignore share purchase which keep the buying company's share of equity below 20%

2. When the purchase of shares first takes a company's holding above 20% and up to 50%.

3. For future purchases up to the time when control is eventually acquired, take step by step method should be applied.

Step	Date	% of share bought	% of holding
1	1 February, 2010	10%	10% - ignore
2	1 November, 2010	25%	35%-holding in Simbe Ltd now exceeds 20%
3.	1 April, 2011	20%	55% Simbe Ltd now a subsidiary

Using an Assumption (b)

Pre-acquisition profits:

	$
35% of reserves at 1 November, 2010 (35% of 30,000)	10,500
Plus 20% of Reserves at 1 April, 2011 (20% of 40,000)	8,000
	18,500

The minority interest at 1 April, 2011 is 45% of 40,000 – 18,000

Post-acquisition profits are (40-18,500) – 18,000 = $3,500

INTER COMPANY PROFITS

Treatments:

1) To remove only the group's shares of the profit loading

2) To remove the whole profit loading, charging the minority with their proportion.

3) To remove the whole of the profit without charging the minority

MULTI-COMPANY STRUCTURES

The major problem on this type of consolidation is to identify the minority interest share of the reserves of the subsidiaries using any of these methods:-

1) The two stages method or

2) The single stage method

It is advisable to use the single-stage method in an examination as it saves time.

Example

The Draft Balance Sheets of kare Limited, kere Limited and kole Limited on 30 June, 2012 were as follows:-

	kare Limited $	kere Limited $	kole Limited $
Fixed Assets	52,500	62,500	90,000
Investment at cost			
40,000 shares in kere Ltd	70,000	-	-
30,000 shares in kole Ltd	-	55,000	-
Current Assets	30,000	35,000	30,000
Creditors	(15,000)	(17,500)	(12,500)
	137,500	135,000	107,500
Capital and Reserves			
Ordinary Shares of $1 each	40,000	50,000	50,000
Reserves	97,500	85,000	57,500
	137,500	135,000	107,500

kare Limited acquired its shares in kere Limited when the reserves of kere Limited stood at $35,000, and kere Limited acquired its shares in kole Limited when the Reserves of kole Limited stood at $25,000

Prepare the Draft Consolidated Balance Sheet of kere Limited

Solution:

The Group Structures

kare Limited 8%

kere Limited minor interest (direct 200) 60%

kole Limited Minority Interest (direct) 40%

Minority interest (indirect) 12%

Advanced Financial Accounting

Of the post acquisition reserves of $153, 100, $97,500 is in the books of Kere 80% x (85-35) = $40,00 in the books of Kere Limited

48% x (57,500 – 25,000, $25,600 in the books of Kole Limited

KARE LIMITED CONSOLIDATED BALANCE SHEET AT 30 JUNE, 2012

	$	$
Goodwill arising on consolidation	10,000	
Fixed Assets	205,000	215,000
Current Assets	95,000	
Current Liabilities –Creditor	45,000	50,000
		265,000
		$
Capital and Reserves		40,000
Ordinary Shares of $1 each paid		153,100
Reserves		193,100
		71,900
		265,000

Using Single Method

Cost of control kare Limited Direct 80% Ordinary	Minority kare Limited Indirect 80% Indirect 80% Indirect kole Limited	Consolidated Reserves

kole Limited	$	$	$	$	$
Ordinary shares	50,000		24,000	26,000	
Reserves	57,500		12,000	29,900	15,600 (Balancing)
kole Ltd					
Ordinary Shares	50,000	40,000	-	10,000	
Reserves	85,000	28,000	-	17,000	40,000 (Balancing)
		68,000	36,000		
Cost of Investments					
kole Limited	55,000		(44,000)	(11,000)	
kere Limited		70,000			
Goodwill		(2,000)	(8,000)		
				1,900	
					79,500
					153,100

270

Consolidation using the two-stage method involved

1) Stage 1 – Consolidation kere Limited with kole Limited

2) Stage 2 – Consolidation of kare Limited with kere Limited group

Stage 1

Consolidation of kole Limited and kere Limited

	$	Cost of Control kere Limited in kole Ltd	kare Limited in kere Ltd	Minority Interest	Consolidated Reserves
Stage 1	$	60% Direct in kole $	80% Direct in kere	40% Direct in kole 20% in kere $	$
kole Limited					
Ord. Shares	50,000	30,000		20,000	
Reserves	57,500	15,000		23,000	19,500 (Balancing)
		45,000			
Cost of Investment in kole Limited		(55,000)			
Goodwill		(10,000)			
Share in Goodwill in kole Limited		10,000	(10,000)	(20,000)	
Add kere Limited Reserves					85,0000
					104,500

Stage 2

Cost of Control

	kere Limited in kole Ltd	kare Limited in kere Ltd	Minority Interest	Consolidation Reserves
Stage 1	$ 60% Direct in kole $	80% Direct in kere $	40% Direct in kole 20% in kere $	$
kere Limited Group				
Ord. Shares	50,000	40,000	10,000	
Reserves	104,500	28,000	20,000	55,000 (Balancing)
Cost of Investments	60,000	60,000		
In kere Limited	(70,000)	(70,000)		
Goodwill		(10,000)		
			71,900	
				97,500
				153,100

Solution –Two Stage Method

KARE LIMITED CONSOLIDATED BALANCE SHEET AT 30 JUNE, 2012

(Two Stage Method)

	$	$
Goodwill arising on consolidation		10,000
Fixed Assets		205,000
Current Assets		50,000
Creditors		265,000
Capital and Reserves		40,000
Ordinary shares of $1 each fully paid		153,100
Reserves		193,100
Minority Interest		71,900
		265,000

	$	Jenin Limited $	$	Azure Limited $	$	Ebugu Limited $	$
Fixed Assets			180,000		120,000	120,000	
Investments in Subsidiaries at cost							
Shares in Azure Ltd	180,000						
Shares in Ebugu Ltd	50,000	230,000	84,000	84,000			
			4,000	204,000			120,000
	80,000		100,000		80,0000		
Current Assets							
Current Liabilities							
Proposed Dividends	60,000		40,000		20,000		
Other Creditors	40,000	(20,000)	40,000	20,000	30,000		30,000
		390,000		224,000			150,000
Capital and Reserves							
Ordinary shares of $1 allotted & fully paid		200,000		100,000			100,000
Shares Premium Account		100,000		40,000			-
Profit and Loss Reserves		90,000		64,000			50,000
		390,000		204,000			150,000
Long term Liabilities – 12% Loan Stock		-		20,000			-
		390,000		224,000			150,000

Example

The draft Balance Sheets of Jenin Limited, Azure Limited and Ebugu Limited as at 31st May 2015 are as follows:

1) Jenin Limited acquired 60% of the shares in Azure Limited on 1 January, 2013 when the balance on that company's profit and Loss Reserves was $16,000 (credit) and there was no Share Premium Account.

2) Jenin Limited acquired 20% of the shares of Ebugu Limited and Azure Limited acquired 60% of the shares of Ebugu Limited on 1 January, 2014 when that company's Profit and Loss Reserves stood at N30,000.

3) There has been no payments of dividends by either Azure Limited or Ebugu Limited since they become subsidiaries.

4) The proposed dividends have not yet been recorded in the books of the shareholding companies as dividends receivable.

Prepare the Consolidated Balance Sheet of Jenin Limited as at 31st May, 2015 using the Stage 1.

Solution:

1) The direct minority interest in Azure Limited is 40%

2) The direct minority interest in Ebugu Limited is 20%

3) The indirect minority interest in Ebugu Limited is (40% of 60%) 24%

4) The total minority interest in Ebugu Limited is 44%

The group share of Azure Limited is 60% and of Ebugu Limited is (00-44)% = 56%

Dividends Receivable	$	$
In Azure Limited's books		
DR Dividends receivable	120,000	
CR Profit and Loss Receives		120,000

Being 60% of Ebugu Limited's proposed dividends in Jenin Limited books

DR Dividends Receivable	28,000	
CR Profit and Loss Reserves		28,000

Being 20% of Ebugu Limited's proposed dividends plus 60% of Azure Limited proposed dividends.

Cost of Control

Ebugu Limited	Azure Limited	Minority Interest	Consolidated
20% Direct	40% Direct in A		P & L
36% indirect	20% direct in E		Reserves
56%	24% indirect in E		
	44%		

	$	$		$	$	$
Ebugu Limited						
Ord. shares	100,000	56,000		44,000		12,200
Profit & Loss Reserves	50,000	16,800		22,000		Balance
Akure Limited						
Ordinary Shares	100,000		60,000	40,000		
Share Premium						
All post acquisition	40,000			16,000 (4x40) 1	24,000	
P & L Reserves	64,000					
Add; Dividends	12,000		9,600	30,400 (4 x 76) 10		36,000
	76,000	72,800	69,000			
Cost of Investments:						
In Ebugu Limited						
Direct		50,000				
Indirect		50,400 (6 x 84) 10				
Azure Limited			(180,000)	(33,600) (4 x 84) 10		
Goodwill		27,600	110,400			
			118,800		100,000	90,000
Jenin Limited Reserve						28,000
Dividends from Ebugu & Azure					124,000	165,200

JENIN LIMITED CONSOLIDATED BALANCE SHEET

	$	$
Goodwill arising on consolidation		138,000
Fixed Assets		420,000
Current Assets	260,000	
Current Liabilities		
Minority proposed Dividends	20,000	
Proposed Dividends	60,000	
Other Creditors	110,000	
	190,000	
Net Current Assets		70,000
		682,000

TESSY LIMITED BALANCE SHEET AS AT 31 AUUST, 2019		
	$	$
Fixed Assets		56,000
Net Current Assets		66,000
		122,000
Capital and Reserves		40,000
Ordinary Shares of $1 each		82,000
Retained Profits		122,000

If Tessy Limited had revalued its Fixed Assets at 1st September, 2018, an addition of $60,000 would have added to the depreciation charged in the Profit and Loss Account for 2018/19.

You are required to prepare Fidel Limited Consolidated Balance Sheet as at 31 August,2019.

Solution:

FIDEL LIMITED BALANCE SHEET AS AT 31 AUGUST, 2019

	$
Goodwill arising on consolidation	6,000
Fixed Assets $126 +96	222,000
Net Current Assets	190,000
	418,000
Capital and Reserves	160,000
Ordinary Shares of $1 each	160,000
Retained Profits	217,500
	377,500
Minority Interest	40,500
	418,000

Note:

The consolidated Balance Sheet of Tessy Limited's Fixed Assets will appear at there revalued amount (56 + 46 = 6) = $9600

PIECEMEAL ACQUISITION

Under this, the recommended procedure that the pre-acquisition reserves and profits should be established each purchase of shares.

Example

Bisi Limited acquired shares in Simbe Limited which has issued and fully paid up share capital of 50,000 $1 ordinary share on three separate dates.

THE CONSOLIDATED PROFIT AND LOSS

There are two major methods in the preparation of the consolidation schedule of Profit and loss Account. These are:

1) Past Year Method

2) The whole Year Method

Example

Father Limited acquired 60% of the of Son Limited on 1 April, 2015. The Profit and Loss Account of the two companies for the year ended 31 December 2015 are set out below:

	$	$
Turnover		
Cost of Sales	340,00	160,000
Gross Profit	130,000	72,000
Administration etc. cost	210,000	88,000
Profit before Tax	86,000	24,000
Taxation	124,000	64,000
	46,000	16,000
Dividends (paid 31 Dec.)	78,000	48,000
Retained Profit for the year	24,000	12,000
Retained Profit b/f	54,000	36,000
	162,000	80,000
	216,000	116,000

Father Limited has not yet accounted for the dividend recurred from Son Limited Prepare the Consolidated Schedule using the Past Year Method. Using the past acquisition proportions.

FATHER LIMITED CONSOLIDATION SCHEDULE FOR THE YEAR ENDED 31 DECEMBER, 2015			
	Group $	Father Ltd $	Son $
Turnover	460,000	240,000	12,000
Profit before tax	172,000	124,000	4,000
Taxation	(58,000)	(46,000)	(1,200)
Profit after taxation	114,000	78,000	3,600
Minority interest (40% of 36,00)	(14,400)	-	(1,400)
	99,600	78,000	2,000
Adjustment for Inter-compound Dividends: 60% of (9/12 x 12,000)	-	5,400	(500)
Group Profit for the year	99,600	83,400	1,000
Dividends (father Ltd only)	(24,000)	(24,000)	1,000
Retained Profits for the year	75,600	59,000	1,000
Retained Profit b/f	162,000	162,000	1,000
	237,600	221,400	1,000

Note all the Son`s Ltd profit brought forward are pre-acquisition.

FATHER LIMITED CONSOLIDATED PROFIT AND LOSS ACCOUNT FOR THE YEAR ENDED 31 DECEMBER, 2015

	$
Turnover	460,000
Profit before taxation	
Taxation	172,000
Profit after taxation	(58,000)
Minority Interest	114,000
Group profit for the financial year	14,400
(of which $83,400 is dealt with the acts of Fathers Ltd)	99,600
Dividends	24,000
Retained profit for the financial year	75,600
Retained profit b/f	162,000
Retained profits c/f	237,600

The Whole Year Method

FATHER LIMITED CONSOLIDATED SCHEDULE FOR THE YEAR ENDED 31 DECEMBER, 2015

	$	$	$
Turnover	500,000	340,000	160,000
Profit before taxation	188,000	124,000	64,000
Taxation	62,000	46,000	16,000
Minority Interest (40% of 48)	126,000	78,000	48,000
	19,200	-	19,200
	106,800	-	28,800
Pre-acquisition projects (3/12 x 60% of 48,000)	7,200		7,200
	99,600	78,000	21,000
Adjustment for inter-company dividends			
(60% of 9/12 x 12,000)	-	5,400	(5,400)
Gross profit for the year	99,600	83,400	16,200
Dividends Father Ltd only	(24,000)	(24,000)	-
Retained profits for the year	75,600	59,400	16,200
Retained profit b/f	162,000	162,000	-
	237,600	221,400	16,200

FATHER LIMITED CONSOLIDATED PROFIT AND LOSS ACCOUNT FOR THE YEAR ENDED 31ST DECEMBER, 2015

	$
Turnover	460,000
Profit before taxation	
Taxation	172,000
Profit after Taxation	(58,000)
Minority Interest	114,000
	14,400
Gross profit for the financial year (of which $83,400 is on with the acts of Father Ltd)	99,600
Dividends	24,000
Retained Profits for the financial year	75,600
Retained profit b/f	162,000
Retained profits c/f	237,600

1) The Full Cost Approach

2) The Successful Efforts Approach

3) Reserve Recognition Accounting

Under Full Cost Accounting all exploration costs are capitalised subject to a recoverable test in operations that are both successful or not.

This supports the accrual concept as capitalizing non productive expenditure on the grounds that it is an integral part of the cost of finding and producing Oil and Gas.

Successful Efforts Accounting. This approach capitalizes only the costs of wells that find oil and gas and writes off the failures. That means that, exploration and development costs are carried forward in the Balance Sheet for areas where the value of the Reserves discovered the cost incurred.

Under Reserve Recognition Accounting, Revenue is recognized when the Reserves are discovered rather than when the oil is sold. Consequently, exploration and development costs are not carried forward instead, the oil reserves discovered are valued and the unexploited Balance Sheet is periodically audited.

CEILING TEST

The Ceiling Test is a valuation procedure used to determine whether the stated value of a company's oil and gas assets exceeds their recoverable amount.

DEPRECIATION, DEPLETION AND AMORTISATION
Depreciation of costs are based on the volume of oil and gas removed in the current year as a percentage of what id left in the ground. Hence the Estimated useful life of a pool is dependent upon the value in the ground, rate of extraction and amount of expenditure put into developing the pool.

METHODS FOR DEPLETION

1) Tangible Vs Intangible

Separate calculations are made for tangible and intangible costs. Tangible would be depreciated over their estimated useful lives

2) Unit of Production

Costs are depleted based on the Naira (Local Value) value of the reserves in the ground rather than the volume.

3) Reserve Depletion

Costs are depleted based on the value of the reserves in the ground rather than the volume. This method reduces the depletion charge in the periods of rising prices when compared to the unit of production.

If the successful efforts approach is used, it calculates depletion charge on a well-to-well basis while Full Cost Method uses very large costs centers.

COVEYANCES

A conveyance is the transfer of any type of ownership interest in concession from one entity to another. Conveyances of property interests can be calculated as follows: A sales, a borrowing an exchange of non-monetary assets, or a pooling of assets in joint undertaking.

Conveyance contracts can be quite complex and raises accounting problems of

1. Determination of gains or loss.

2. Timing of revenue and expenses recognition,

3. Measurement of costs and presentation in financial statements.

OTHER DEFINITION OF TERMS

JOINT INTEREST OPERATIONS

Joint ventures Account for the investments in a joint Venture using the Proportionate Consolidation Method. Under this method, each joint venture records its own share of assets, liabilities, revenue and expenses from returns and statements rendered monthly by the operator.

AUDITING AND APPRAISAL OF OIL AND GAS RESERVES

The stages in auditing and appraising Oil and Gas Reserves can be broken into the following major sequences:

Planning the audit, Assessing risks and potentials errors or mis-statements, developing the Audit plan, performing the audit and conclusion.

THE DIFFERENT RESERVES ARE:

1. Oil and Gas reserves

   Oil and Gas reserves classified according to the degree of confidence in estimates of the quantities of oil and gas in reserves.

2. Proved Reserves

   Proved reserves can be classified as developed or undeveloped according to whether or not. They can be expected to be recovered through existing well with existing equipment and operating methods.

3. Probable Reserves

   These are the reserves which are not yet proved but are estimated to have better that 50 percent chance of being technically and economically producible

4. Possible Reserves

This are reserves estimated to have significant but less than 50 percent chance of being technically and economically producible.

AUDITING PROCESS IN THE INDUSTRY

1. Understanding the accounting process oil and gas reserves

This involves the gathering of information relating to the company's accounting system.

2. Understanding the Control Environment

It is necessary for the Auditor to understand the nature of controls available to ensure accuracy and reliability of reserve data.

3. Confirming the Auditor's Understanding

This involves the use of work through the accounting manual, performance and observation.

4. Assessing Risks of Potential error or misstatement level

It is important to visualize the perverse nature of the effort of errors and misstatement in reserves as it would affect Of the financial statements. Reserves estimates are useful in management Base for depletion calculations, base of computing information about country's resources and basis for determining cost ceiling.

5. Developing the Audit Plan

The Auditor must rely on controls that made the risk and perform a basic level of substantive tests or perform focused substantive tests, some test are:

a) He must develop an audit plan to test controls that mitigate risks

b) He must plant tests to confirm the reliability of the system of controls.

6. Performing the Audit

Two level test that are relevant to the audit of oil and gas reserves:

a) The focused substantive tests;

b) The basic level of substantive tests

7. The Auditor's involvement with the Audit and Appraisal of Oil and Gas Reserves

This involves the information of the base of valuation.

Some peculiar problems in oil and gas

a) Uncertainty in search of oil;

b) Lack of uniform accounting policies

c) Oil exploration – what to capitalize not

d)   Well workover – capitalize initial during costs;

e)   Well development –Accumulate cost work in progress account;

f)   Use of contractors;

g)   Budget approval;

h)   Depletion, Depreciation and Amortization

i)   Production costs;

j)   Material Control;

k)   Crude Oil;

l)   Crude Oil Stock;

m)   Use of Specialists;

n)   Reserve Estimate;

o)   Crude Oil Production;

p)   Royalty;

q)   Petroleum profit tax based on fiscal value of oil;

r)   Memorandum of understanding.

QUESTIONS/ANSWERS

1. What is the definition of accounting according to AICPA?

Solution: The AICPA defines accounting as "the art of recording, classifying, and summarizing in a significant manner and in terms of money, transactions and events which are, in part at least, of a financial character, and interpreting the results thereof."

2. What is the difference between bookkeeping and accounting?

Solution: Bookkeeping involves the actual recording of financial transactions, while accounting extends to analyzing, interpreting, and summarizing those records for decision-making.

3. Name three users of accounting information and why they need it.

Solution:

i.   Managers – For planning and controlling business operations.

ii.   Shareholders – To assess profitability and dividends.

iii.   Banks – To evaluate loan repayment capacity.

4. What are the three main elements of a Balance Sheet?

Solution: Assets, Liabilities, and Owner's Equity (Capital).

5. What is the accounting equation?

Solution:

Capital = Assets – Liabilities

or

Assets = Liabilities + Owner's Equity

6. Differentiate between fixed assets and current assets.

Solution:

i.   Fixed assets are long-term (e.g., machinery, buildings) used for business operations.

ii.   Current assets are short-term (e.g., cash, inventory) expected to be converted into cash within a year.

7. What is the Going Concern Concept?

Solution: It assumes that a business will continue operating indefinitely unless there is evidence to the contrary.

8. How does the Prudence Concept affect financial reporting?

Solution: It requires accountants to record expenses and liabilities as soon as possible but only recognize revenues when they are certain, avoiding overstatement of profits.

9. What is the Matching Concept?

Solution: Expenses should be recorded in the same period as the revenues they help generate.

10. If a company has assets worth $50,000 and liabilities of $20,000, what is the owner's equity?

Solution:

Capital = Assets – Liabilities = $50,000 – $20,000 = $30,000

11. What is the difference between Accrual Basis and Cash Basis accounting?

Solution:

i. Accrual Basis records revenues/expenses when earned/incurred, regardless of cash flow.

ii. Cash Basis records only when cash is received/paid.

12. Why is the Historical Cost Concept important?

Solution: It ensures that assets are recorded at their original purchase price, providing reliability and verifiability in financial statements.

13. Classify the following as assets or liabilities:

i. Motor vehicles (Asset)

ii. Bank overdraft (Liability)

iii. Debtors (Asset)

iv. Loan from a bank (Liability)

14. What is the purpose of a Profit and Loss Account?

Solution: It summarizes revenues, expenses, and profits/losses over a specific period.

15. What is the Consistency Concept?

Solution A company should use the same accounting methods year after year for comparability.

16. If a business has $15,000 in cash, $10,000 in debtors, and $8,000 in creditors, what is its working capital?

Solution:

Working Capital = Current Assets – Current Liabilities

= ($15,000 + $10,000) – $8,000 = $17,000

17. What is Materiality in accounting?

Solution: It refers to the significance of financial information—whether its omission/misstatement could influence decisions.

18. How does the Realization Concept determine revenue recognition?

Solution: Revenue is recognized when goods/services are delivered, not necessarily when cash is received.

19. What is the difference between tangible and intangible assets?

Solution:

i. Tangible assets have physical form (e.g., machinery).

ii. Intangible assets lack physical form (e.g., patents, goodwill).

20. Why is the Entity Concept important?

Solution: It ensures that business transactions are separate from the owner's personal finances, providing clarity in financial reporting.

21. What are the key components of "historical cost" for stock valuation?

Solution:

Historical cost includes:

i. Cost of purchase (initial price + duties, taxes, freight).

ii. Incidental costs (e.g., transportation to location).

iii. Cost of conversion (direct labor + attributable production overheads).

Trade discounts/rebates are deducted from the purchase cost.

22. Explain the "lower of cost or net realizable value" rule with an example.

Solution:

i. Rule: Stocks must be valued at the lower of their historical cost or net realizable value (NRV = estimated selling price – completion/marketing costs).

ii. Example: If a product costs $10,000 to produce but its NRV is $8,000 due to market decline, it is valued at $8,000, and the $2,000 loss is charged to income.

23. Compare FIFO and LIFO stock valuation methods. Why does SAS 4 prohibit LIFO?

Solution:

i. FIFO (First-In, First-Out): Assumes oldest stock is sold first. Reflects current market prices in closing stock.

ii. LIFO (Last-In, First-Out): Assumes newest stock is sold first. Can understate closing stock value during inflation.

Prohibition: LIFO distorts profit and balance sheet values, violating the "matching principle" and historical cost convention (SAS 4, para 46).

24. How should mineral rights acquisition costs be amortized according to the standard?

Solution:

Unallocated mineral rights acquisition costs must be amortized over the remaining life of the license.

The net book value should be reviewed annually for impairment (well-by-well basis). Any impairment discovered is written off immediately.

25.   What is the key principle for recognizing deferred taxes in oil and gas accounting?

Solution:

Deferred tax provisions must comply with SAS 12 (Accounting for Deferred Taxes).

This ensures taxes attributable to temporary differences

(e.g., between book and tax depreciation) are accounted for in the period they arise.

26.   What constitutes an "act of bankruptcy" under the Bankruptcy Act 1979?

Solution:

A debtor commits an act of bankruptcy if they:

Fail to comply with a bankruptcy notice within 14 days.

Have goods seized and held/sold by a bailiff for 21+ days.

File a court declaration of inability to pay debts or petition for their own bankruptcy.

27.   What are the criteria for classifying a lease as a finance lease?

A lease qualifies as a finance lease if it meets two main conditions:

The lease is non-cancellable.

Additionally, one of the following must apply:

The lease term covers substantially 80% or more of the useful life of the asset.

The net present value of the lease payments at the inception, using the minimum lease payments and the implicit interest rate, is equal to or greater than the fair value of the leased asset.

The lease has a purchase option that is likely to be exercised.

28.   What is the difference between direct finance leases and sales-type leases?

The primary difference between a direct finance lease and a sales-type lease is the manufacturer's or dealer's profit or loss from the sale to the lessee. In a direct finance lease, the lessor typically receives payments over time for providing the right to use the asset, whereas, in a sales-type lease, the lessor recognizes the sale of the asset to the lessee at the inception of the lease, which includes any profit or loss made on the sale of the asset.

29.   How are initial direct costs handled in lease agreements?

Initial direct costs incurred by a lessor in negotiating and executing a lease agreement are treated based on the type of lease. These costs may either be written off immediately or amortized over the lease term. In the case of a sales-type lease, the costs are often charged to the cost of sales and not amortized over the life of the lease.

REFERENCES

Agboroh, F. O. (ACA). Principles and Techniques in Accounting Practice (Referenced for definitions of accounting).

American Accounting Association (1966). A Statement of Basic Accounting Theory. Sarasota, FL: AAA.

(Definition of accounting and its purpose for decision-making.)

American Institute of Certified Public Accountants (AICPA) (1966). Accounting Terminology Bulletin No. 1.

(Definition of accounting as an art of recording and summarizing transactions.)

Pacioli, L. (1494). Summa de Arithmetica, Geometria, Proportioni et Proportionalità. Venice: Paganinus de Paganinis.

(Foundation text on double-entry bookkeeping.)

Hicks, J. R. (1946). Value and Capital: An Inquiry into Some Fundamental Principles of Economic Theory. Oxford: Clarendon Press.

(Referenced for the economic concept of income and capital maintenance.)

Fisher, I. (1906). The Nature of Capital and Income. New York: Macmillan.

(Cited for the economic interpretation of income as consumption.)

Institute of Chartered Accountants of Nigeria (ICAN). Professional Examination Questions and Suggested Solutions. Various years.

(Cited for past exam questions and accounting policy discussion.)

Nigerian Accounting Standards Board (NASB). (Various Years). Statements of Accounting Standards (IAS).

(Referenced throughout for accounting standards in Nigeria, including IAS 1 and IAS 2.)

International Accounting Standards Committee (IASC). International Accounting Standards (IAS).

(Referenced for international comparison and influence on IAS.)

Sandilands Committee. (1975). Report of the Inflation Accounting Committee. London: HMSO.

(Referenced for the definition of accounting profit under inflation conditions.)